UNIVERSITY OF NORTH CAROLINA AT CHAPEL HILL
DEPARTMENT OF ROMANCE LANGUAGES

NORTH CAROLINA STUDIES
IN THE ROMANCE LANGUAGES AND LITERATURES

*Founder:* URBAN TIGNER HOLMES
*Editor:* FRANK A. DOMÍNGUEZ

*Distributed by:*

UNIVERSITY OF NORTH CAROLINA PRESS

CHAPEL HILL
North Carolina 27515-2288
U.S.A.

NORTH CAROLINA STUDIES IN THE
ROMANCE LANGUAGES AND LITERATURES
Number 281

QUESTIONING RACINIAN TRAGEDY

# QUESTIONING RACINIAN TRAGEDY

BY
JOHN CAMPBELL

CHAPEL HILL

NORTH CAROLINA STUDIES IN THE ROMANCE
LANGUAGES AND LITERATURES
U.N.C. DEPARTMENT OF ROMANCE LANGUAGES

2005

**Library of Congress Cataloging-in-Publication Data**

Campbell, John, 1947 Feb. 18-
  Questioning Racinian tragedy / by John Campbell.
  p. cm. – (North Carolina studies in the Romance languages and literatures ; no. 281).
  Includes bibliographical references.
  ISBN 0-8078-9285-8 (pbk.)
  1. Racine, Jean, 1639-1699–Criticism and interpretation. 2. Tragedy. I. Title. II. Series.

PQ1905.C35 2005
842'.4–dc22                                                                                          2004061664




Cover design: Heidi Perov

© 2005. Department of Romance Languages. The University of North Carolina at Chapel Hill.

ISBN 0-8078-9285-8




DEPÓSITO LEGAL: V. 1.596 - 2005

ARTES GRÁFICAS SOLER, S. L. - LA OLIVERETA, 28 - 46018 VALENCIA

# CONTENTS

|  | Page |
|---|---|
| ACKNOWLEDGMENTS ............................... | 9 |
| PREFATORY NOTE: REFERENCES AND ABBREVIATIONS ........... | 11 |
| INTRODUCTION: "RACINIAN TRAGEDY" ..................... | 13 |
| 1. FROM THE PARTICULAR TO THE PARTICULAR: PLOTS AND TIME . | 37 |
| 'The life and soul of tragedy' ........................... | 38 |
| Creating a time-machine: *Bérénice* ...................... | 45 |
| *Play or poetry?* ................................... | 45 |
| *A plot at work* ................................... | 49 |
| *A sense of time* ................................... | 56 |
| Plot as suspension: *Mithridate* ........................ | 65 |
| *Suspense and suspension* ............................ | 65 |
| *A flight in time* .................................. | 71 |
| The uses of time: *Athalie* ............................ | 78 |
| *The Unity of Time* ................................ | 78 |
| *The dimensions of time* ............................ | 82 |
| 2. EXCEPTIONS AND EXPECTATIONS: "RACINE" AND *BAJAZET* ..... | 85 |
| *A problem play* ................................... | 87 |
| *Credibility and coherence* .......................... | 91 |
| *Strange roles* .................................... | 106 |
| *A "Racinian" language?* ............................ | 109 |
| *Expectations* ..................................... | 115 |
| 3. "PESSIMISM" AND "THE RACINIAN TRAGIC VISION" ........... | 118 |
| "Pessimism" and "tragic vision" ....................... | 120 |
| *Britannicus*: proof positive of "pessimism"? ............... | 126 |
| *A moral dimension?* ............................... | 128 |

Tragedy between "optimism" and "pessimism": *Iphigénie* ..... 133
   *The tragic plot* ..... 135
   *A family drama?* ..... 140
   *And the Gods?* ..... 143
   *A happy end?* ..... 145

## 4. THE GOD QUESTION ..... 151

Jansenist tragedy? ..... 151
Using the evidence: *Andromaque* ..... 156
   *The Jansenism of "Racine": a case in favor* ..... 157
   *The Jansenism of "Racine": a case against* ..... 163
   *Imitation and pleasure* ..... 172
God at Work? *Athalie* ..... 176
   *The implications of plot* ..... 180
   *Identities and tragedy* ..... 186
   *What recognition?* ..... 191
   *Despair?* ..... 194
   *A sense of God?* ..... 198

## 5. THE PROBLEM WITH *PHÈDRE* ..... 205

   *An ordinary play?* ..... 207
   Phèdre and *Phèdre* ..... 211
   *Plot, after all* ..... 215
   *What truth?* ..... 218
   *Fatalism, dependency, responsibility* ..... 222
   *The Gods* ..... 233
   *The problem of evil* ..... 238
   *Final clarity?* ..... 241
   *Uncertainties* ..... 243

## CONCLUSION ..... 245

## BIBLIOGRAPHY ..... 254

## ACKNOWLEDGMENTS

SOME of the material of this book draws on revised elements from the following studies published over the past decade and a half: "The God of *Athalie*." *French Studies* 43 (1989): 385-404; "The exposition of *Athalie*." *Seventeenth-Century French Studies* 12 (1990): 149-57; "The Unity of Time in *Athalie*." *Modern Language Review* 86 (1991): 573-79; "Playing for time in *Bérénice*." *Nottingham French Studies* 32 (1993): 23-28; "*Bérénice*: the plotting of a tragedy." *Seventeenth-Century French Studies* 15 (1993): 145-55; "Tragedy and time in Racine's *Mithridate*." *Modern Language Review* 92 (1997): 590-98; "Racine and the Augustinian inheritance: the case of *Andromaque*." *French Studies* 53 (1999): 279-92; "*Bajazet* and Racinian tragedy: Expectations and Difference." Richard-Laurent Barnett, ed. *Les Epreuves du Labyrinthe. Essais de Poétique et d'Herméneutique raciniennes. Hommage tricentenaire.* Special Issue, *Dalhousie French Studies*, 49 (1999): 103-118; "Racine's *Iphigénie*: a 'happy tragedy'?" Claire Carlin and Katherine Wine, eds. *Theatrum mundi. Studies in Honor of Ronald W. Tobin*. Charlottesville: Rockwood Press, 2003: 214-21. I thank the editors and publishers for their permission to draw from this material, and to transform it.

I should like to express my gratitude to the Carnegie Trust for the Universities of Scotland, for supporting this publication, and for their very great efficiency and courtesy. I wish to record my thanks to the Arts and Humanities Research Board of Great Britain and to the Arts Faculty of the University of Glasgow for having funded two terms of study leave, to the British Academy for having provided financial assistance for study in Paris, to the staff in those libraries in which I have worked, and in particular, to the staff of Glasgow University Library. I should also like to express my gratitude to the University of North Carolina Press, for the care and attention they have given to this project at every stage, and in particular Paul Rogers, that ever-reliable and friendly source of editorial help and advice. In this context I also wish to thank the publishers' readers, who offered positive suggestions and proposed much-needed corrections to the manuscript. It goes without saying that for the errors of whatever variety that remain, the author is alone responsible.

As the bibliography indicates, I owe a debt to countless other scholars. To some that debt is massive, especially perhaps those with whose conclusions I take issue in this book: a prime example is the ever courteous Jean Rohou, without whose challenging ideas and well-documented research this book would not have existed in its present form. Many colleagues have given intellectual stimulation, moral encouragement, and friendship. In this context, while it is always invidious to choose, and thus to exclude, it would be unfair not to mention Harry Barnwell, Mathilde Bombart, Gilles Declercq, Jean Emelina, Georges Forestier, John Lyons, and Guillaume Peureux. In particular, I should like to express my deepest gratitude to three colleagues. First, to Angus Kennedy and Nadia Margolis, for their unstinting counsel, support, and friendship: Nadia read the book's Introduction in an early draft, and her advice was, as always, lucid and persuasive. I should also like to thank Ronald Tobin as warmly as decorum permits. Without his astute advice and constant encouragement, this project would not have come to fruition in its present form. In addition, without counting the cost to himself in his own busy academic life, he carefully scrutinized the completed manuscript, helping its hapless author not just to remove some egregious errors but also to strengthen the overall focus. In our Republic of Letters he truly is *le Chevalier sans peur et sans reproche*.

And finally, I should like to thank my children Pierre and Marion for their support, and my wife Elisabeth for being at my side in all weathers: *en Ecosse ce n'est pas peu dire*.

# PREFATORY NOTE

### REFERENCES

THIS book, by its very nature, refers to a large number of critical works. To avoid hundreds of footnotes in each chapter, parenthetical notes have been used, with apologies for the interruption that this represents. The parenthetical notes refer to the bibliography, where full references are given. Each parenthetical note contains a page-number, preceded where necessary by the name of the author and work referred to. The work in question is referred to in abbreviated form, whether of the title of a book (e.g. Lyons, *Kingdom*), or of an article, where one or more identifying words are used (e.g. "Iphigénie" 43). References to Racine's plays are from the Pléiade edition by Georges Forestier.

### ABBREVIATIONS

Two particular abbreviations should be noted:
a) For the works of Racine.
– Reference to comments by the editor(s) of complete works is given using the name of the editor (where necessary) followed by Ed. and the page-number. For example, "as claimed by Jean Rohou (Ed. 1141)."
– Reference to comments by the editor(s) of an individual play is given by Ed. followed by the name of that play. For example: "as claimed by Philip Butler (Ed. *Britannicus* 45)."

b) For the works of Voltaire.

– References to the different editions of the *Œuvres complètes* are to the different editors, Moland and Besterman, followed by volume and page number. For example: Moland 65: 961.

TRANSLATIONS INTO ENGLISH

Unless otherwise indicated in the bibliography, translations from the French are mine.

# INTRODUCTION: "RACINIAN TRAGEDY"

SOME years before Roland Barthes wrote his famous book on Racine, he had sought, appropriately enough in *Mythologies*, to dispel the notion that "Racine" had any kind of neutral, objective meaning to which all could assent: "Pure 'Racine', the zero degree of Racine, simply does not exist. [...] Racine is always something other than Racine" (98). It is therefore paradoxical that this explorer of modern myths should have helped, with his *homme racinien*, to give renewed vigor to another enduring myth: that of "Racine" as a coherent set of attributes that together contain and explain a single entity called *le tragique racinien* or "Racinian tragedy" (the English expression being an imperfect rendering of the more abstract French phrase). This book seeks to ask some questions about the meaning of such terms.

The critical output of the past decades is prodigious. It has done much to stimulate and inform me. But it has also generated a growing, chafing sense of doubt. That doubt is the fuel of this book. The questions it asks have been prompted by a perceived gap between "Racinian tragedy," the apparently uniform object whose identity is asserted or implied by much of this modern criticism, and my own attempts, in scattered studies over the years, to come to terms with specific issues in individual tragedies. The time therefore seemed ripe to match this "Racinian" identity with my own changing, uncertain experience of plays that were written to come to life on the stage. This has also meant undertaking a global review of recent criticism, through an examination, or often a re-examination, of significant issues in different plays.

The design of this book, therefore, is less to propose a particular theory than to ask questions about different theories that have been proposed. Its approach is openly skeptical. As will be seen, that skepticism concerns ideas such as identity, structure, coherence, and vision. The questions asked focus on certain fundamental critical presuppositions that together constitute the identity of the modern "Racine." In other words, is there a single body of work with enough unvarying characteristics for "Racinian" to mean more than just "of, by, or relating to Racine"? With what justification may critics speak, in any evaluative way, of a "Racinian tragedy" abstracted from a variety of different plays which each poses its own problems of interpretation? Does any one critical paradigm, propounded to explain this "Racinian tragedy" even permit a convincing interpretation of the complexities inherent in any one particular play? And do the various tragedies, considered together, constitute a body of work methodologically and ideologically cohesive enough to demonstrate any set of clearly identifiable structuring patterns?

These are abstract, complex, and controversial issues. While a term such as "Racinian tragedy" clearly implies the existence of a certain number of common features that confer identity and coherence, there is no clear agreement as to what these identifiers are. This seems only natural. After all, if in our critical works we offer what in essence means "This is how Racinian tragedy works," are we doing anything more, or less, than presenting our own tastes and interests in a rhetoric designed to convince? As Raymond Picard pointed out some time ago, all critics offer the *real* Racine, that is, *their* Racine, based on the plays or parts of plays they themselves find significant (*Parthénon* 5).

It is this conflict between the particular and the general that explains the method chosen in this book. Many prefer to remain at the level of general ideas that they can identify across the range of Racine's tragedies considered as a closed set. My own doubts as to the validity of these general ideas has led me to choose a different way of proceeding. This book will therefore attempt to "question Racinian tragedy" in an oblique manner, by scrutinizing the particular on which the general is based. By exploring some important questions in Racine's major tragedies, I seek to show that each of the different plays chosen is constructed in a different way, poses different problems, and that each has distinctive features not easily identified by recourse to the general descriptors most commonly used. It seems a reasonable premise that the examination of individual questions in individual plays permits a progressive assessment of the evidence for something so often taken for granted, or even explicitly stated: the existence of an identifiable set of structures that can map out "Racine," or the presence of features that, from one tragedy to the next, are commonly accepted as symptomatic of "Racinian tragedy."

This deliberately pragmatic approach is thus the very opposite of any attempt to "cover," still less to "explain," all the tragedies of Jean Racine. Not all his plays receive attention here; that attention has not been evenly distributed; and only a small number of issues have been addressed. For example, there is no examination of Racine's first two plays, *La Thébaïde* and *Alexandre le Grand*, nor of the late biblical drama *Esther*. This is not primarily a question of those limits placed on any critical endeavor by time, space, and the reader's patience. Nor does the fact that these plays do not get their day in this particular court in any way imply that they lack interest, originality, or dramatic and poetic qualities. However, since the aim of this book is to question the coherence of a supposed entity called "Racinian tragedy," it would be battering at an open door to call witnesses often considered by advocates of such a notion to be unreliable representatives of it. Eugène Vinaver, for example, considered that Racine only "became himself" with *Andromaque* (*Entretiens* 20). And for Jean Rohou, Racine's vocabulary is not sufficiently "Racinian" in *La Thébaïde*, his style is that of a beginner in *Alexandre le Grand*, while with *Esther* he wrote less a tragedy than a religious poem (Ed. 864, 871, 1089). In the light of comments such as these, I have preferred to focus on those plays whose testimony is traditionally solicited by those who advocate, pre-suppose, or imply an essential unity in what has become known as "Racine." The pages that follow concentrate either on problems that have not always received the critical attention their importance deserves, or, conversely, on issues that have been the subject of much discussion, and no great critical resolution.

This introduction will look briefly at the notion called "Racine," that structure erected in the centuries following the playwright's death on a foundation he himself had chosen. The first chapter will then seek to question the idea that some overarching or underpinning "Racinian tragic vision" can easily be identified in Racine's tragedies. It does so through an examination of the quite distinct plotting strategies in *Bérénice*, *Mithridate*, and *Athalie*. It asks whether the tragic effect in these plays arises from some general *angst* about the human condition that permeates "Racinian tragedy" viewed as a whole entity, or whether it depends on the different ways in which different plots work to create emotion. The second chapter probes the consistency of norms and qualities commonly supposed to be "Racinian," be that in plot, characterization, or language, and this through an examination of one problem play, *Bajazet*. In other words, does this tragedy present "exceptions" to a norm, or to common expectations of what that "Racinian" norm should be? The third and fourth chapters use the examples of *Britannicus*, *Iphigénie*, *Andromaque*, and *Athalie* to ask questions about certain qualities commonly seen as constituting the very basis of the "Racinian tragic vision": examples are "pessimism," "Jansenism," and different avatars of determinism. Is a bleak view of the human condition in general, and of human freedom in particular, a fundamental constituent of "Racinian tragedy," and a necessary reflection of the equally bleak metaphysic of the age in which it was composed? The final chapter deals with *Phèdre*, the work so frequently viewed as expressing the essence of "Racine" more completely and profoundly than the other tragedies, and yet paradoxically itself seen as "exceptional." It considers the advantages of viewing *Phèdre* first and foremost as a play, as a tragic action driven by a plot in which characters other than Phèdre have determining roles. It also assesses the evidence that might seem to support those theses about "Racinian tragedy" of which this one play has become the emblem.

As such, this work will have to respond to two immediate reactions. The first is instinctive and appealing. "What? Another book on Racine?" Those outside the Academy might gaze with wonder on the continuing cascade of publications, and even those inside might ask plaintively if there is anything left to say. "Racine has been served up to nearly every known sauce," warned Roy Knight, in his introduction to a *Modern Judgments* of the playwright compiled ... thirty-five years ago (17). Since then many new sauces have been prepared. This abundance led Georges Forestier, in his "Approche bibliographique" of 1996, to speak of the "quasi-exponential growth" in publications devoted to Racine over the preceding thirty years (217). By the tercentenary year of 1999, "Racine" seemed to have been prepared in every way critical gastronomes could invent or possibly appreciate. "Racine is impossible to translate, and probably to perform," claimed Guy Dumur (60). The temptation must be to add "writing a balanced critical study" to these impossibilities. That has not stopped many making the attempt: small wonder some palates are jaded. "Everything has already been said: we have arrived too late," sighed La Bruyère (85), a phrase repeated by Paul Ginestier at the beginning of his own extended study of Racine's tragedies. Here the only plea that can be entered in mitigation is that one or two useful things have been actually been written since La Bruyère made this observation three centuries ago about the attempt to write anything on anything, in the book he himself was writing. For an author, seemingly, hell is other authors.

The second reaction to an enterprise such as this is equally understandable and, in the context of the present book, equally paradoxical. It springs from the expectation that any new critical venture should be grounded in a theory or system, or provide one particular angle of interpretation, that will to a large extent account for an entity called "Racinian tragedy." The failure to proceed in this manner may be judged severely, as here, by Odette de Mourgues:

> One basic necessity remains for the critic; that of putting forward a coherent and complete interpretation of a work. This is what the critical studies I have mentioned fail to do. This is hardly surprising: dismembering Racinian tragedy, they tend to focus on one aspect while ignoring the others, and can therefore in no way account for that perfection and relevance of structure which are the hallmark of any masterpiece and which even the most superficial reader of Racine can feel to be present in the dramatist's works. (166)

On the contrary, one might object, there has been no shortage of attempts to find the Holy Grail of the "coherent and complete." The problem is that each new coherent and complete mapping of "Racine" sees itself as more coherent and complete than previous attempts at the job. Implicit each time, and sometimes quite explicit, is the idea that the subject has become so overlaid with conventional interpretations that radical action is necessary. "We have to do a sandblasting job on Racine," went up the cry from Michel

Butor, in 1973 (29). Ironically, this was a mere ten years after Roland Barthes, like Malraux simultaneously with the monuments of Paris, had done a vigorous sandblasting job on a "Racine" seen as a venerable monument. Another alluring metaphor is that of the dissecting room. The critic will cut the work down to the bone, expose the vital organs, show it as it *really* is. "My aim," declared Peter Nurse without false modesty, "is to provide an anatomy of Racinian tragedy" ("Tragique racinien" 197). As one might expect, however, each different dissection tends to focus on a different anatomy lesson. The body is never cut up in the same way, for the same purpose. For students of real human anatomy, prepared to undertake thousands of dissections, "completeness" may be an attainable reality. It hardly seems to be a critical one.

Why then should anyone seek to write yet another book, but without leaning on a new theory which alone, for many, guarantees the appropriate degree of academic rigor and a pleasingly rounded outcome? After all, many critics have developed persuasive, well-argued theories of "Racinian tragedy," based on their own experience of the text, in works that one invariably reads with profit, and often with pleasure. Why then expose oneself to the familiar arrow, that not to proceed on these lines is—*horresco referens*—to be "subjective" and "impressionistic"? Gilles Revaz, for example, exposes with great clarity the reasons why what he calls "non-literary theories" cannot suitably be applied to literary texts, because in the end the text is calibrated to fit the theory. Strangely enough, however, he does not accept that the same calibration can take place with "literary" theories:

> My conviction remains that literary criticism needs a theory to support it. Without that, criticism would be back in the realms of personal taste, and while such criticism might be inspired, it has no general application and no pedagogical relevance. (175)

This is a distinction of a sort common in the latter decades of the century just past. On the one hand, there is the quasi-scientific investigation, with its own methodology and language. On the other, there is everything else: criticism rooted in "personal taste," that perhaps even goes so far as to use ordinary words. Such criticism is thus merely "subjective" or "impressionistic," and in consequence has no scientific validity or "pedagogical pertinence."

The distinction is sweeping, and deserves some qualification. In what is now called "Theory," there are many different possible theories, which can be mutually exclusive. It seems perfectly normal to adopt any one of them that is felt to shed new light. It even seems reasonable to use the hermetic critical idiom that might accompany it, if the particular critic feels that this is the best way to articulate a current of thought too strong for the tired wiring of conventional vocabulary. And it can undoubtedly be exciting to apply a particular theory to a work of the creative imagination. All of this can only be enriching. Equally, however, there seems no reason why any critics should feel, in so doing, that they are the monopoly generators of intellectual light, or that the particular vocabulary they use in some way gives a more objective basis to the critical quest. Difficulty and novelty are not in themselves a guarantee of intellectual rigor, nor is adherence to a particular system of thought. And there is always the risk, as Montaigne remarked, having quoted Lucretius on the same subject, that "difficulty is a coin that the learned conjure with, so as not to reveal the vanity of their studies" (*Essays* 566; *Essais* 1: 564). A theory is a hypothesis with good public relations. Only argument and evidence can take it from the realm of the purely "subjective," and this to the extent that it convinces others.

This book will attempt to convince by argument, and to argue from evidence. If that is "impressionism," so be it. The underlying methodological premise, or prejudice, is that it is a "pedagogically relevant" activity simply to ask questions, and, by so doing, to help to address them. It is for this reason that the term "questioning" figures in the title given to this present work. That title is, as titles tend to be, unsatisfactory. "Questioning Racinian tragedy" could more accurately be formulated with a mouthful such as "questioning the general identity of what is called 'Racinian tragedy' through an examination of some aspects of some questions in some of Racine's tragedies." The title retained still points to a series of issues that, in the light of recent critical debates, remain controversial and unresolved. If the pages that follow attempt to convince by appealing to evidence, that will always be with the knowledge that others will look at the same evidence in radically different ways. For some, the evidence is simply what is self-evident: "Let the self-evident have its say," exclaims Maurice Delcroix ("Phèdre" 36). But, self-evidently, not everyone views the evidence in the same way. There seems room to doubt that literary criticism, whatever its cravings, can achieve the objective certainties aspired to by experimental science. It is salutary to remember that university departments of literature are the recent progeny of schools of rhetoric. Are different theories, methods, and approaches not different forms of rhetoric? Are literary critics, great and small, not all engaged in attempts to persuade?

This persuasive activity has often been based on the idea of a "Racine" that is a coherent whole. From the very beginning there has been a tendency, desire, or temptation to see the tragedies of Racine, at least from *Andromaque* to *Phèdre* if not to *Athalie*, as something smooth, finished, and even uniform. La Bruyère viewed Racine as "regular, sustained, always the same everywhere" (104), as did another contemporary, Longepierre, making what he saw as a favorable comparison with Corneille: "There is more uniformity in Mr. Racine [...]. He is like a great and beautiful river whose peaceful and majestic waters keep flowing smoothly on" (Granet 1: 55-56). In the following century Louis-Sébastien Mercier found all this smoothness and conformity very boring: "there is a very monotonous color to this great poet, and his characters almost always look the same" (43), while La Harpe managed to deliver a favorable verdict on "Racine" while using the same evidence: "He was always found identical to himself, because he was always perfect" (*Éloge de Racine* 79). As Gilles Siouffi has pointed out (434), in 1767 the grammarian D'Olivet was expressing astonishment that Racine's style should have kept its freshness and "changeless purity" a hundred years after *Andromaque*. Very early on, in other words, "Racine" was much more than the plays of Racine: it was a myth of perfection.

"A new Racine was born," comments André Blanc (492), on the identity given to the playwright by sustained comparisons with Corneille at the beginning of the eighteenth century. That century indeed played a crucial role in the establishment of the iconic literary identities of the *Grand Siècle*. For example, when the English epithet "classic" was first used in its literary sense, as Roy Knight pointed out (*Modern Judgments* 9), it was in the eighteenth century, and was applied first to Racine. For this reason Emmanuel Bury (*Classicisme* 5) avers that the 1660-85 period, which tends to be seen as "classical," and judged accordingly, never saw itself or defined itself as such. It was in the eighteenth century, perhaps, that "Racine" and "Corneille" tended to become representations of a certain number of fixed qualities and norms. How much of this comes down to Voltaire's own tastes, and to the vigor with which he championed what he saw as good taste itself?

> But it would be to wish to insult the memory of Corneille to dwell at length on all the blemishes of a work where blemishes are almost all there is. [...] so let us acknowledge that he was a great man who was too often at variance with himself. (Moland 55: 961)

The term *racinien* is first recorded in French in 1772. It was at the same period that Voltaire was using Racine as a champion of French civilization, and therefore of good taste, in attempting to resist the assaults of Shakespeare.[1]

The perceived unity of style and convention in "Racine" thus goes back a long way. "Racine is always beautiful," proclaimed Diderot (15: 37). This apparently homogeneous aesthetic has also often been viewed as expressing some deeper unity of purpose and theme, or as being the dress for a single, explicable world-vision. In the middle years of the last century, the thesis of a coherent whole, in which might be uncovered a series of patterns or organic laws, was proposed most vigorously by those three famous expositors of the *racinien*, Lucien Goldmann, Charles Mauron, and Roland Barthes. This led to a no less spirited counter-offensive led by Raymond Picard, and produced a last charge from René Pommier in 1988. Taking sides in this conflict also meant making a statement in terms of academic politics, in which the forces of enlightenment, using Barthes as a banner, played at storming the Bastille in Picard's supposedly reactionary Sorbonne. As the years went by this confusing battlefield began more to resemble the Waterloo of Fabrice del Dongo: much rushing-about, but some confusion as to where the real battle was taking place or what the opposing forces were. The controversies of that time are well documented: the so-called *nouvelle critique*, like the *nouveau roman*, might now seem to belong to history.[2] This is, however, not quite the case. The fact that Jean

---

[1] On these questions see Bayley, "Let's dump Classicism"; M. Bury, "Racine et Shakespeare"; Caldicott, "Non-Classical"; Campbell, "La part du classique"; Lyons, "What do we mean?".

[2] For varying accounts, see for example A. Blanc 593-622; Bonzon; Goldzink, "Que sont nos amours devenues?"; F. Reiss; Revaz; Schröder, "Situation des études raciniennes"; Supple, "Pommier versus Barthes."

Rohou, in the year 2000, felt the need to denounce the Barthes approach, in an appendix to his *Avez-vous lu Racine?*, shows that his target is still perceived to wield influence. Paradoxically, the outpouring of critical works by Rohou in recent years on the subject of "Racine" is itself the most eloquent testimony to the abiding persuasive power of mid-twentieth-century structuralism.

Whatever the variety of approaches, the critical foundation remains: that of "Racinian tragedy" as a coherent whole. In the seminal works of Lucien Goldmann, Charles Mauron, and Roland Barthes, in those of their principal inheritor, Jean Rohou, as in the many others by different critics proposing related hypotheses, a basic premise is that of Racinian tragedy as a closed set, a single unit of human experience, *le tragique racinien*. This premise admitted, the organizing principles of "Racine" can thus more easily be related to permanent features of the human psyche, and/or to salient features of the biographical, historical, and cultural context. One might select orphanhood, for example, or Jansenism, or absolutism, or the rise of the middle classes, or any mix of any such features. A mid-century example is Guy de Chambrure's description of this procedure, in the title of his study, as "Operation Survival" for the study of "Racine." It was in this general context that Goldmann, half a century ago in his "Structure de la tragédie racinienne," depicted Racine as "someone whose mental structures were determined by Jansenism" (258), with the implication that "Racine" was a self-contained world that could be mapped out, if only critics used the right instruments. He portrayed himself here as standing at a critical crossroads, with only one possible road to take: "We are now at a watershed [...] characterized by the notion of structure, and by the fact that the researcher can no longer look at any aspect of human reality as an isolated element set beside other such elements" (251).

The new millennium began as the old had finished, with Rohou yet again seeking to uncover what he calls the "the fundamental anthropological structure" of Racinian tragedy (*Avez-vous lu Racine?* 315). In this now-familiar anatomy lesson he follows a path that Goldmann saw as trailblazing, but which perhaps has its roots in nineteenth-century Positivism, if not in neoplatonic theories of Pure Forms, and which surfaced in a variety of different critical approaches before and after the salad days of High Structuralism. This orientation doubtless has parallels in many other fields, for example, in the Durkheimian vision behind so much twentieth-century ethnography: under the critical eye the artifact is transformed into an ethnographical object, and the individual characteristics of the artifact matter less than what the object "represents." Even Henri Brémond, in 1930, while concentrating on the essentially poetic quality of Racine's tragedies, saw the different plays as being "successive fragments of a single musical score" (54), while almost three decades later René Jasinski, reading the same works in a radically different manner, similarly maintained that in the tragedies there is an overarching tragedy "which encompasses them and transcends them" (2: 556). It thus seems fair to suggest that the notion of an essential unity of "Racinian tragedy" has dominated critical interpretations in the past decades. The thesis of this book is that it continues to do so.

Interpretation of *le tragique racinien* necessarily implicates *le tragique*, that child of nineteenth-century German philosophy. This fact is sometimes overlooked. Moreover, Nietzsche's *Birth of Tragedy* makes only makes cursory references to French seventeenth-century theater. And Hegel's *On Tragedy*, which makes more than a hundred references to Shakespeare, only makes two (disparaging) ones to Racine.[3] It is this anachronistic ambiguity that leads Alain Couprie to preface his *Lire la tragédie* with the warning that "if we wish to understand tragedy, let us begin by forgetting the tragic" (xiii). This *tragique* does not describe what *happens* in a tragedy (for example, an error producing reversal and disproportionate consequences), but a world of essences captured in terms such as "vision," "structure," and "model." Thus Jean Rohou: "tragic alienation consists in being riven by something essential that is lacking: characters are carried away by their aching desire to fill this void, and are conscious that this cannot be achieved" (Ed. 885).

Roland Barthes, for whom "All Racinian conflicts follow a single model," quite logically therefore, in his *Sur Racine*, uncovered the *homme racinien* as the perfect expression of this *vision tragique*. The tragedies of Racine become a "Racine" that can be defined by certain unvarying structuring forces, and can even be condensed into a moment of psychic epiphany: "The whole of Racine is con-

---

[3] On Hegel's bias against post-Renaissance theatre, see Gellrich, p. 92. On "le tragique," see Biet, "De l'épique au dramatique" 131-35; Escola 35; Riffaud 129; Truchet, *Tragédie classique* 175.

tained in that paradoxical moment when the child discovers that his father is bad and yet still wishes to remain his child" (48). This approach–together with Barthes's tendency in this book to deliver peremptory judgments such as "Conflict is fundamental in Racine" (34), as though conflict was not equally fundamental in almost any drama one cared to name–enabled Raymond Picard to score an undoubted debating hit, by pointing to two other words that recur in his adversary's book: "*Always, never*: the critic delivers his truths like a prophet: they are absolute, universal, definitive" (*Nouvelle critique* 35). Rohou, perhaps underestimating Barthes's desire to provoke thought and debate, denounces his "totalitarian assertions that crumble when confronted with the text" (*Avez-vous* lu *Racine?* 388). He is himself always careful to provide chapter and verse to support his own hypotheses. That said, he remains an inheritor of fifties' structuralism, and deserves attention as the most articulate contemporary representative of a half-century of paradigm making. Apart from the intrinsic interest of what he writes, his works offer a synthesis of a whole movement, and for both these reasons will often be quoted in these pages. Rohou sees the tragedies in terms of certain organizing principles, of which the *homme racinien*, fixed for eternity, is the expression and the culmination. Developing a notion first explored by Ronald Tobin ("Incomplétude"), he asserts that "the *homme racinien*, in spite of his lucidity, can only blindly follow a passion that expresses the anguish of his incompleteness" (Ed. 880).

There is, however, a paradoxical problem at the heart of such apparently comprehensive paradigms, laws, models, and visions: their Procrustean nature. As Gaston Bachelard remarked in relation to scientific determinism, such criticism cannot exist "without a conscious choice to exclude phenomena viewed as disruptive or insignificant" (104). In the case of Racine's actual works, no single theory or structure has yet been found that fits the bed constructed for a body called "Racine," unless, that is, the tragedies are made to fit, and bits are lopped off here and there when necessary. Thus Lucien Goldmann speaks of "those tragedies of Racine that are strictly speaking tragedies," in other words, those tragedies that replicate the structure previously defined as "Racinian" ("Structure" 25). Unfortunately, as Pierre Zoberman amongst others has pointed out (211), different critics have different lists of Racine's "authentic tragedies," constructed from different criteria. The following viewpoints, in different ways, sum up the problem well:

> The theories at present in the field offer us a choice of determining factors, from childhood memories or traumata, conscious or unconscious, to a Weltanschauung, several philosophical concepts, a religious conflict determined by an economic and political set-up, and a selection of archetypal symbols; so it is impossible to point to any universally acceptable results after all the efforts that have been made so far. (Knight, *Modern Judgments* 14)

> Attempts to systematize the metaphysical elements in Racinian tragedy run into formidable problems, involving the sacrifice of much of his theatre. Goldmann's analysis based on the triple relationship–god, humanity, and the world–produces only three and a half "authentic" tragedies, leaving the remainder untragic. The three tragedies are *Britannicus*, *Bérénice*, and *Phèdre*, while Andromaque's "innocent stratagème" makes her only half-tragic. (Maskell 219)

> It is actually hard to believe, and even understand, as Goldmann would have us do, that Racine's plays could function as a seismograph, faithfully recording the evolution of the relationship between the Jansenists and the authorities. [...] It is all as beautifully worked out as *The Phenomenology of Mind*, but, alas, it is too beautiful for this mortal world. (Goldzink, "Que sont nos amours devenues?" 25)

It may be thought that things have now moved on from attempts to map out "Racine" like the human genome. Certainly in 1996 Christian Delmas felt able to say that the totalizing ideologies inspired by Freud and Marx were on the wane ("Stratégie" 115). This must remain a matter of interpretation. But the Goldmann approach continues to be influential, and Freud has not been dismissed like some naughty child caught out of the nursery. More importantly, at least from the point of view of this book, the idea of a coherent whole called "Racinian tragedy" continues to provide the implicit framework for many interpretations. Even Christopher Braider, in his recent well-documented analysis of "Racine" as a cross between historical personage, corpus of writings, and critical artifact, still seems to suggest that this artifact is one body. While he says on the one hand that "'Racine' is the name for what we make of him in the process of construing his work" (358), he constantly uses the term "Racinian" to suggest that this work has an essential homogeneity, as in the following:

> There is something almost autistic about Racinian tragedy, a magnificent if at times monstrous solipsism comparable to nothing so much as the hermetic self-involvement of its leading characters. Racinian "love" is fundamentally self-directed, a psychomoral pathology rather than an erotic relation whose paradigmatic symptom is the poet's predilection for the intransitive form of the relevant verb. (326)

Another indication that "Racine" is alive and well is that Procrustes is still being called out to get him into shape. Patrick Dandrey, for example, excludes certain plays from the "tragic vision" he constructs (17). Jean Rohou for his part can write a book entitled *Avez-vous lu Racine?*, whose very title suggests that most readers tend to overlook important points. And yet in this same work he asserts that certain aspects of Racine's plays, and certain moments in them, need to be left to one side in order to validate his hypothesis that the *tragique racinien* is the expression of an Augustinian vision of the world, and of a childhood in which that vision became the subconscious template of the playwright's creative consciousness (298). Four plays in particular–*La Thébaïde*, *Bérénice*, *Iphigénie*, and *Esther*–are not considered "Augustinian" enough ("Pour une étude" 4: 14). As Jean Emelina remarks, in his review of Rohou's book: "Where does that leave the fundamental 'hypothesis' of his 'tragic vision'? Are we to believe that Racine was only 'Augustinian' on an intermittent basis?" (353).

While notions of a single *tragique racinien*, explicable in terms of certain underlying mental structures, are commonly associated with varying forms of twentieth-century Structuralism, the idea of "Racine" as a fixed set of definable attributes has never been far off, as evidenced by La Bruyère's famous remark that Corneille depicts human beings as they should be, and Racine as they are (104). Charles Péguy declared confidently that "every Racinian tragedy, or rather, Racinian tragedy, has an arithmetical pattern" (170). This supposition of an underlying "Racinian" pattern leaves little room for significant differences between characters, plots, and performances. Thus Jean Starobinski, for example, felt able to state that "the Racinian gaze is a restless question plunged into the soul of others" (257). And it is not just Lucien Goldmann, Charles Mauron, Roland Barthes, and their inheritors who have sought to display the "essential Racine" they had revealed. Here, for example, is

Thierry Maulnier, a voice from the thirties, in support of his theory that Racine's theater is one of primal, pagan violence, telling his readers how it is about women in "Racine":

> From the fact that Racine seeks out, beneath the masks and rigors of a civilization whose hallmark is severity, human instinct at its most primitive, it follows that his favorite characters are women. Racine chooses women: he chooses, in other words, those creatures in whom delicacy and nuance are the most exquisite as well as being the most superficial, those creatures that civilization has the most refined, and the least developed, those in whom the barbaric traditions of the human species have been best preserved, in whom the flesh most commands the spirit, in whom frenzy of feeling takes the most uncompromising and demanding forms [...]. (*Racine* 196)

And so on.

The evolving "Racine" that has confronted succeeding generations has to some extent emanated from one privileged source: the image presented by the playwright himself as the one he wished later generations to retain. Alain Viala has pointed out that, already in 1676 by bringing out an edition of his works, Racine followed what turned out to be a successful strategy for directing critical attention in a certain way: "In so doing, he is suggesting that his tragedies are a complete whole, that each must be read as part of some Racinian 'great text'" (*Racine* 172). In particular, the taste for generalizations and overarching theories has always found support in the final edition Racine prepared of his plays, just before his death, when he was reconciled with Port-Royal, and was warning his son of the dangers of the theater. This edition seems a natural choice. It incorporates all the different changes made by the playwright since the first performances, and until recently it was the only one readily available. But it is not a neutral choice. To accept that this final edition is "Racine" is also to accept, as Georges Forestier has stressed, an image of Racine's work as a single unit, an image constructed *a posteriori* and for posterity:

> This choice having been made, and by the force of circumstances, Racine's readers have been led to overlook one essential fact: that we have readily complied with the image that Racine wished us to have of him for all eternity, at a moment when he

had stopped writing plays. What this amounts to us is that we have accepted his own interpretation of his works. (Ed. xiii)

In other words, with this final and finalized edition the "Racinian" is born, perhaps Racine's most discreet creative act. In Forestier's phrase, "Racine is the inventor of his own critical myth" (Ed. xv).

The choice of this final edition has consequences for the interpretation of particular elements of Racine's work. A clear example, from *Andromaque*, is the substitution, in this 1697 edition, of *destin* for *transport* in Oreste's "Je me livre en aveugle au destin qui m'entraîne": how much more noble to be swept away by fate than by passion. More generally, this choice of edition tends necessarily to reinforce the idea of the tragedies as a coherent whole, as expressed in the title of Jean Rohou's article, "A single work in eleven stages," a reprise of Péguy's idea that every year Racine composed what was "perpetually the same tragedy" (170). In this perspective, each play's identity is thus determined by its place within the complete structure, as Christian Surber points out, approvingly: "To have given priority to the final edition of 1697, through the textual closure that this postulates, tends to transform a group of plays into the successive episodes of a single tragedy" (235). This choice of the final edition certainly makes it easier to treat "Racine" as a single work, of which the tragedies are considered to be the only significant chapters. As Georges Molinié explains, "the object called *Racine* constitutes a text, a discourse composed of words linked together to make sentences, and set out in lines of poetry" (272). This "Racine" is perfect laboratory material for the literary theorist. Since the object is complete, and inert, it can objectively be examined, dissected, and "explained." In Claudia Brodsky's words, "Racine's tragedies appear closed, comprehensive rather than ineffable, entirely legible in that they are entirely articulated, or paradigmatic" (164).

The existence of a closed set, in which the plays may be considered from the perspective of a final outcome, has also made it easier to view Racine's tragedies as evolving in accordance with a determinable pattern, and towards an end that gives meaning to the whole. "Every artist," declared Bernard Weinberg, "as he works towards the perfection of his art, must consider each completed piece as an apprentice piece for the next" (vii). A flavor of this approach may be gained in Jean Rohou's notes on *Athalie*, a play he views as a significant terminus for an orphan whose work is determined by an Augustinian vision of the Fall, the Father, and human concupiscence:

> The course of Racinian tragedy, begun in *La Thébaïde* with the suicidal violence resulting from the suicide of a physical father, ends when the salutary violence of the Heavenly Father destroys rebellious passion. In this tragedy, the forces of conscience, which have been gaining in strength from *Bérénice* to *Phèdre*, triumph over human urges, which are dominant in *La Thébaïde*, *Andromaque*, *Britannicus*, and *Bajazet*, and in this tragedy comes the solution to the problem of the *homme racinien* [...]. (Ed. 1137)

This last phrase seems to sum up a half-century of a certain type of highly influential criticism: first create your *homme racinien*, and then uncover the solution to a problem you yourself have constructed.

Coming into this closed world of the "Racinian," Georges Forestier's new Pléiade edition of 1999 marked a significant change of emphasis, and has perhaps opened a new century of criticism. For the first time in one volume, this edition allowed ready access to each of Racine's plays in the form in which they first appeared. It was as if, say, the shockwaves from the transformation in performances of Baroque music, in the second half of the twentieth century, through the adoption of period instruments and greater attention to the original scoring, had at last reached the emblematic author of the *Grand Siècle*.[4] Forestier's immense erudition, harnessed to his piercing judgment, intellectual stamina, and sheer common sense, reveal the monolithic *Œuvre* called "Racine" for what it always has been: a series of individual works composed for different reasons, and according to different criteria, to satisfy different public expectations at different times. "There is no evolution in Racine's plays, from *Andromaque* onwards: there is only a series of experiments, each as different from the others as possible" (Ed. xxxviii). The difference is all. Suddenly theories based on the closed set, and an evolutionary outlook, seem less securely based, and more attention can be paid to other voices:

---

[4] On this, see also Forestier, "Editer Racine" and Hawcroft, "Reading Racine." For a case against this approach, see Giraud, "Lire Racine, vraiment?" (which contains the Pléiade editor's response).

> Mauron implies that Racine, in *Britannicus*, falls back on the same dramatic structure he had already used in *Andromaque*. But in reality it is Mauron himself who, in order to explain *Andromaque*, uses a structure he has uncovered–or at least that he imagines he has been able to uncover–in his interpretation of *Britannicus*. [...] For while Racine had not yet written *Britannicus* when he was writing *Andromaque*, Mauron already knew all about *Britannicus* when he was studying *Andromaque*. (Pommier, *Britannicus* 14-15)

> What Racine's early plays teach us is that there is no way we can speak of a linear progression: the tragedies that follow are not directed at some particular goal or demonstration [...]. In each play Racine tries something that, while being specific to the tragic genre, has its own particular identity. (Biet, "Le mythe" xv)

Words such as these, considered in the new perspective opened by the Forestier edition, go some way to explaining the motivation behind this present work. Not only is there another way to proceed than to see Racine's plays as necessarily manifesting some grand design. The validity of such a coherent whole can be challenged, at least implicitly, by the scrutiny of particular issues in particular plays, each of which can be seen to pose different problems. This is not to divide up "Racine" into a series of autonomous republics: it would be self-evidently absurd to propose that no links exist between plays, written by the same author, that broadly adhere to an accepted set of dramatic conventions. There is, however, a fundamental distinction to be made between seeing such links and, on the other hand, maintaining that the separate plays derive their identity from an ideal centralized state. Even Jean Rohou, for example, continually points to differences between the plays, while always returning to an essential "Racine," that mix of biography, history, theology, sociology, and psychology that produces the "Racinian vision." But for Rohou, in his *Avez-vous lu Racine?*, the fact that this "vision" does not manifest itself clearly in every tragic drama by Racine does not impair the concept of a "Racinian tragedy" that, at some unexplained fundamental level, expresses and legitimizes this vision. This "Racine" remains stable whatever the variants, "Racine modified by the vision, themes, and issues proper to each play" (114). Even the notion of an essential "Racine," however, might not be so neat if the focus were to shift to individual plays, each written to be performed or read for particular audiences in particular social and literary contexts, as the following critics suggest:

> To say that apart from the first play, and the last two, love is at the heart of Racine's tragedies is saying something that is true, but it is not saying very much: it is not always the same love, nor is it "at the heart of the play" in the same way. (Viala, "Racine galant" 43)

> One point is too often overlooked: the evenness and coherence we find in Racine should not lead us to smooth over the differences between the tragedies. [...] His plays were always successful because he paid close attention to his audience and to changes in taste. (Declercq, "Racine" 128)

> Racinian "tragedy" does not exist: there are tragedies. They have a family likeness that comes from the standardization of norms to be found in neo-classical cultural products; you can see it in most other such products of the age. (Emelina, *Racine infiniment* 194)

With this idea of the primacy of the individual play come two others, which are of capital importance. The first concerns the delicate relationship between Racine the person and "Racine," that curiously circular relationship formed from the *homme* neatly constructed to reflect the *œuvre* neatly deconstructed to reflect the *homme*. This idea is perhaps linked to a notion that, as Ralph Albanese has shown (*Molière* 38), has been influential since the mid-nineteenth century: that by examining every detail of writers' lives, including the political, social, and cultural environment in which they lived, readers can accede to the reality of their work.

Reality? Who or what then is *le vrai Racine*? René Jasinski's book of that name was immediately pilloried by those who, like Jean Pommier, could say authoritatively that this *vrai Racine* could not be the *real* Racine ("Un nouveau Racine" 528). André Blanc's recent "Vers le vrai Racine" is only slightly more tentative (585-92). And Jean Rohou feels even now able to declare, with some confidence, that "it was his life at Port-Royal that instilled in Racine the intense need to conform and to please" ("Racine à Port-Royal" 408). It is still worth reading Paul Delbouille's skeptical assessment, over forty years ago, of attempts to make deductions from the biographical data available. And it must be asked whether the amount and reliability of historical data available have been much transformed since Maurice Descotes made the following gentle suggestion at the same period:

> The uncertainty concerning Racine's education and development is too great for us to be able to determine with any degree of assurance what non-religious or non-literary images nourished the dramatist's childhood and adolescence. ("Menaces sur l'État" 91)

Different biographers have created different images of the interaction between Jean Racine the man and Racine the playwright. The most notable, partial, and influential was certainly the picture painted by his son Louis, through which the dramatist became, as Georges Forestier expressed in his article of that name, "Le Véritable saint Racine." It has been possible, and even easy, to construct a splendidly coherent image of the struggling orphan conditioned by Port-Royal, whose creative life would be spent mining the subconscious for an absent/cruel Father/God. However, if a different biography produces a different portrait of the artist as a young man, will this give a different image of the work? In the circumstances, it seems wiser to take the lead from Raymond Picard's conclusion to his *Carrière de Jean Racine*, that little of importance about the *œuvre* could be concluded from the *homme*:

> For the historian, the identity of Racine is completely bound up with the events of his career; but the human being who created or experienced them, and suffered the consequences within himself, in other words the human being who lived out this career, has disappeared forever. Bringing him back to life could well be a purely arbitrary venture, in that no secret letter or no text of a genuinely personal nature has survived. Rarely has a writer been so absolutely reduced to what he has written. (266)

In his own edition Georges Forestier followed Picard's lead with a demonstration, of compelling erudition, that "biography"–or rather, any hypothesis based on a selection of the scattered facts now available–is less important, for understanding a play by Racine, than the sources and conventions exploited by a playwright who was not writing about some tortured pre-Romantic self:

> Nothing is more foreign to the art of the Seventeenth Century than Flaubert's "Madame Bovary is me." Hermione, Bérénice, Roxane, or Phèdre are not "Racine," or one of the hidden facets of Racine that his work might in some way reveal: their source is Ovid and his *Heroides*; and beyond that they come from Virgil, and the Dido of his *Aeneid*; and beyond that again, they come from the whole elegiac tradition in Greek and Latin literature. (li-lii)

The idea of going back to the individual work, and its various intertextualities, is also present in Volker Schröder's recent study of *Britannicus*, which is not an attempt to close discussion on "Racine," but to open minds to the complexity of what is involved by close examination of a single play.

This point ties in with a second and related one, which is the importance of examining the construction of each play, the subject of which in each case involves a different strategy for arriving at a given ending. An excellent example of this approach is again the Forestier edition. Following on from his pioneering *Essai de génétique* on Corneille's theater, the editor's detailed commentary on each play places the playwright's plot-construction resolutely center stage. This explains the emphasis he constantly gives to the word *travail*, the work undertaken by Racine to transform sources, subject, and conventions, in the working-out of a plot that in each play has its own unique character. In its own way this approach is a tribute to Harry Barnwell, who in his *Tragic Drama of Corneille and Racine* devoted a full chapter to plot. Following these excellent examples, this book will also concentrate on plot. This is not only because of the central place it occupied in the making of a tragedy, for Racine as for Aristotle. It is also because there is often a conflict between the way each tragedy is put together and general ideas of how a "Racinian tragedy" should be. In any assessment of the validity of those general ideas for a particular play, the individual plot invariably provides the most persuasive testimony.

This is not to underplay the value of a single one of the critical positions that have been adopted in order to shed some light on the tragedies of Racine. The fact that no general Racine bibliography is available to scholars cannot hide the sheer number of well-researched and well-argued points of view that are on offer.[5] Each

---

[5] For a sharp, informative, and highly readable synthesis of the latest critical

of the multiple hundreds of studies that have appeared in the past decades contributes its own distinctive piece to what is a fascinating mosaic. In other words, Racine's tragedies defy attempts to contain them within a single perspective. There is room for someone, following the lead of William James, to write a *Varieties of Racine Experience*.

It is in this context that the present work has been written. Its starting-point is a degree of skepticism, often tempered by respect and admiration, towards overarching systems of explanation for a body of individual works that often for convenience alone are given the name "Racinian tragedy." It will at every stage compare what is asserted or argued by critics and what is suggested by close textual analysis of individual plays treated as separate entities. In particular, it will look closely at interpretations of different questions, in different plays, that flow from a general understanding of "Racine" that sometimes seems at variance with what this textual analysis reveals. Different questions, thus, in different plays. For in judging any attempt to constitute a set of global identifiers that together might serve to identify and indeed constitute the *tragique racinien*, "difference" is obviously crucial. In other words, this work seeks primarily to ask, explore, contest, and only then to propose.

In this light, two final points are worth keeping in mind. The first is the sheer difficulty of writing anything that is at the same time fresh, coherent, and well documented on the tragedies of Jean Racine. Some decades ago William Stewart expressed well what the would-be critic might reasonably feel when approaching this difficult and often treacherous terrain:

> When I come to these plays, which constitute one of the summits of tragic drama, I realize that I am walking into a minefield, with the contradictory interpretations and violent reactions provoked by complex characters and ambiguous situations. ("Le Tragique et le Sacré" 277)

A second point concerns the focus represented by the title, *Questioning Racinian Tragedy*. This might well be found either too tentative, or else too assertive, for a work that, by its very nature, tackles

---

approaches to each play, see Tobin, *Jean Racine Revisited*. On the bibliographical front, note Delcroix, "Critique racinienne"; Forestier, "Approche bibliographique"; Roubine, *Lectures*.

different questions in different plays. Faced with similar problems, Jacques Scherer chose the word *cérémonie*, but even then in the formulation *Racine et/ou la cérémonie*. Scherer is not just a prince among critics. For all those of us who have felt the pull of Racine's tragedies, but who have hesitated, doubted, and changed in their reactions to the different plays, and continue so to do, Scherer's work is a kindly beacon, and this beam of humanity illuminates the critical sky:

> I do not know any task in the world of literary criticism that is more difficult that to give an account of the plays of Racine. For a long time I was in the dark, casting around for something, but I could not bring myself to be as intrepid as the critics who came before me. In the end the idea of "ceremony" came out of the blue. I will not try to hide how fragile this idea is, but it may perhaps have provided an acceptable framework for my analysis of Racine's quite original contribution as a dramatist. (222)

With this caveat in mind, it is time to question some aspects of "Racinian tragedy," by looking at some tragedies by Racine.

CHAPTER 1

FROM THE PARTICULAR TO THE PARTICULAR:
PLOTS AND TIME

As mentioned in the Introduction, the phrase "Racinian tragedy" often means something more than just "the tragedies of Racine." It can imply some structural unity, tragic vision, or determining pattern, a degree of uniformity or conformity great enough to give the impression that the plays are parts of a whole, chapters of a book, and can only be explained as such. Overarching formulae such as *vision tragique racinienne* suggest that there is a common "Racinian" identity that is more significant than any particular feature of any particular play, and that the particular can always be explained in terms of this general identity. For example, Jean Rohou claims in his *Avez-vous lu Racine?* that the Forestier edition takes the wrong path in concentrating on how the plays are constructed "without taking an interest in the tragic vision on which they are based" (185). This chapter will take the first empirical step in the assessment of this critical commonplace, by examining in some detail how some individual plays work as dramatic mechanisms. It will attempt to show that it is not primarily some underlying or overriding "Racinian tragic vision" that lies at the heart of the emotions and thus of the interest that each play generates, but the way in which each is put together for a particular end. This means looking closely at some different ways in which Racine constructs his plots and, as part of that plotting, at how he adjusts the time dimension in which the tragic action is placed.

To place the plot center stage might be deemed a provocation. It is certainly more acceptable to give the main role to language, despite David Maskell's cogent refutation of this idea. Nothing is more common than the common notion, expressed for example by George Steiner, that in a tragedy by Racine "all that happens, happens inside language" (96), and that, consequently, as Christian Surber asserts, "everything is in his language" (8). Why then the plot? Simply because, though often overlooked, it is the engine driving forward the tragic action, the main way in which the tragic emotions are aroused. This chapter will consider three such engines of tragedy, in *Bérénice*, *Mithridate*, and *Athalie*. These plays have not been chosen because they are "typical": for a start, as this book will continually strive to show, a single "type" is difficult to identify. On the contrary, questions specific to each play are raised by the particular way in which each is constructed. Rather than any simple body called "Racinian tragedy," there is a series of different plays acting in different ways to achieve different effects, and in each case raising different questions.

"The life and soul of tragedy"

A necessary preliminary is to establish the importance of the plot for any consideration of Racine's tragedies. For Aristotle, famously, in chapter 6 of his *Poetics*, "tragedy is the imitation of an action." Much ink has been spilt glossing this phrase. One essential point, however, is that those who are watching or reading a play are not listening passively to speeches: they are caught up in an action, something that moves, transitive and intransitive. This point is emphasized by D'Aubignac's much-quoted "Speaking is acting":

> This poem is called a *Drama*, in other words an *Action*, and not a *Story*. Those who perform are called *Actors*, and not *Orators*. Even those who are present are called *Spectators*, or *Lookers-on*, and not *Listeners*. And the place used for these Performances is called a *Theater*, not an *Auditorium*, that is, it is a Place where one looks at what is happening, and not where one listens to what is being said. (407)

In other words, an audience at the theater (or, more commonly with a Racine play, a reader following the dramatic action with the mind's eye) wants to see what happens. The plot is the way in which things are made to happen, the machine that drives the play forward. It is thus the principal way in which an audience is caught up in the dramatic action. For any interpretation of the plays, therefore, it must reasonably be as important a factor as where Racine went to school.

Aristotle insisted strongly on the primacy of the plot. It is a view that has more than a tenuous connection with Racine's own practice as a dramatist. The importance of the *Poetics* for seventeenth-century dramatic theory and practice hardly needs restating here. Racine's interest in this text is also well documented: his translation of some extracts has been collated by Eugène Vinaver under the title *Principes de la Tragédie*. That does not of course mean that the playwright slavishly followed any one of the philosopher's precepts. But it does tend to make Aristotle a privileged witness, at the very least, one worth listening to because Racine, at the very least, listened to him too. And to read the *Poetics* is to realize how crucial for Aristotle the plot was: "We maintain, therefore, that the first essential, the life and soul, so to speak, of Tragedy is the Plot" (ch. 6). In some contexts the term translated here as "plot," *muthos*, can also mean the tragic subject. (It was often rendered in French as "la Fable," a doubly confusing term in that it could also, like *muthos* itself, refer to those traditional stories now called "myth.") However, in this particular context Aristotle defines the word unambiguously as "a combination of incidents."

This begs an obvious question. How can something so dry, mechanical, and apparently subordinate, be possibly described as "the life and soul of tragedy"? Aristotle's response is to explain what the dramatist is setting out to do. For the philosopher, the dramatist is not a historian who records, but a craftsman who makes fictions: "the poet's function is to describe, not the thing that has happened, but a kind of thing that might happen" (ch. 9). If tragedy is the imitation of an action, that imitation is a conscious artifact. In other words, its effect depends primarily on the way it is put together:

> One may string together a series of characteristic speeches of the utmost finish as regards Diction or Thought, and yet fail to produce the true tragic effect; but one will have much better success with a tragedy which, however inferior in these respects, has a Plot, a combination of incidents in it. (ch. 6)

Heinsius, that most faithful seventeenth-century commentator of Aristotle, lays particular stress on what he called this need to "order the events of a play in a coherent way." Taking up Aristotle's metaphor of "life and soul," he declares that the plot is as distinctive a mark of tragedy as reason is of the human being: "The Plot is more than just the main component of Tragedy; it is almost the whole of Tragedy" (143).

Not everyone is convinced of the plot's importance. Edwin Williams, speaking of *Athalie*, suggests that Racine, like a Greek tragedian, "could expect his audience to be reasonably familiar with the plot and its sequel" (37). For Georges May, quite simply, if the subject was known, so was the plot (144), while Eugène Vinaver asserts, perhaps surprisingly in that edition of Racine's *Principes de la Tragédie* drawn from Aristotle (43), that the French dramatist never expressed any admiration for the way Greek tragedians constructed their plays. These assertions have been countered with hard evidence, for example by Harry Barnwell (*The Tragic Drama* 93-132) and, more recently, by Susanna Phillippo. This chapter will argue, similarly, that the distinction between subject and plot is an important one to make. Since the subjects of tragedy generally came from a common stock, and often recurred, the audience would normally be familiar with them, and thus their outcome. The construction of a plot therefore meant reaching that outcome in a way that held the audience's attention. It did so principally by leaving open different possibilities, creating expectations, and overthrowing them. In his *Essay on Taste*, Montesquieu describes this fundamental dramatic mechanism:

> When we are watching a play our curiosity is aroused because we are shown some things while other things are hidden from us. We keep being surprised, because we think that what is hidden will happen in one way when it will actually happen in another. In other words, we make false predictions on the basis of what we have already seen. (3: 270)

In his first Preface to *Alexandre le Grand*, Racine stresses that what matters is the making of the play, its logical construction, how it works. "Works" here means how it works on an audience, to "keep it involved in the dramatic action, perhaps despite itself." If we as an audience know the subject of the tragedy, we already know the outcome (though an exception might be made for *Bajazet*). What we want to know, as Georges Forestier explains, is how Racine is going to get us there:

> [...] a tragedy by Racine comes across as a genuine "action," that is, as a chain of cause and effect, a space in which characters have choices to make. For even if, in reality, it is not a question of choice, since this action must lead inexorably to a pre-existing denouement, the illusion must be created that this denouement flows from the decisions, mistakes, and passions of the characters. (Ed. 1531)

This insistence on the centrality of the plot is easy to understand, and should dispel the notion that in Racine "it is less the plot than the passions that move audiences" (Norman 254). It will annoy many who hold that "the tragic" is something more noble, more philosophical, than anything than might issue from a purely artificial mechanism. This is especially so in that few descend into the engine-room. But it was Boileau, hardly a philistine, who in his *Art Poétique* III advised budding dramatists that if they wanted to involve him in their play, they had to "invent mechanisms" that would do so. If it is the emotions created that confer on the play its tragic quality, then it is primarily the mechanism of the plot that creates these emotions.

For Racine's generation, the "tragic" thus implied not that kind of metaphysical "tragic vision" that nineteenth-century German philosophy has bequeathed to the modern world, but a certain quality of emotion. That emotion is at the heart of the tragic experience. In John Lyons's words, "almost all contemporary theorists consider tragedy a failure if it permits the viewer to stand back and to consider the tragic events in rational terms" (*Kingdom of Disorder* 45). Nor does Racine ever suggest, as asserted by Georges May (156), that his purpose was to keep his audience in a state of certainty and emotional equanimity. Susanna Phillippo remarks that one of the main features of Euripides that interested Racine was "the Greek tragedian's skill in emotive engagement of an audience at the level of pathos" (137). This interests surfaces, for example, in his Preface to *Iphigénie*. Here Racine uses a term Aristotle employed in connection with Euripides, *tragikotatos*, but goes much further than Aristotle in explaining it, a point well brought out by Claire Nancy (34). He translates it as "extremely tragic," meaning that Euripides "knew in the most wonderful way how to arouse pity and terror, which is the real effect tragedy should have." The paradoxical pleasure of tragedy is thus inseparable from the emotion it arouses, and that emotion is itself inseparably bound up with the working of the play. As the following extracts show, while different commentators in different ages have expressed this idea in different ways, they all stress its central importance:

> A tragedy leads you on, right up to the catastrophe, by means of tears, uncertainty, hope, fear, surprise, and horror. (La Bruyère 102)

> I do not understand how fear and pity can purge us, as Aristotle says. But I well understand how fear and pity can trouble our souls for two hours, in the most natural manner, and how this can give pleasure of a very noble and delicate kind, one that can only fully be experienced by cultivated minds. (Voltaire, Moland 55: 1031)

> In the particular case of tragic poetry we may speak of an *emotive hedonism*: the *primary pleasure* appropriate to tragedy is that which accompanies the excitation of an emotional response [...]. The main task of the tragedies, therefore, is to portray events to which a response of this kind is appropriate, and to do so in such a way that the emotive quality of those events is brought out and the response evoked in the most effective and satisfying way. (Heath 35)

> All the theoretical writings of our two greatest tragic dramatists demonstrate that they were concerned primarily with what they felt was at the very heart of tragedy: the arousal of emotion. (Forestier, *Passions tragiques* 197)

The importance given to the plot has evident implications for notions of some overall "Racinian tragic vision" through which "Racine" might be "explained." It is undoubtedly easier to see the different plays as presenting such a "vision" if differences between the plots are neglected, at the expense of concentration on subject and character. But just as the subjects of the plays are generally well known beforehand, so different roles are familiar: monarch, father, lover, rival, victim, and so on. The impression of familiarity and congruence is only increased by Racine's adherence to certain dramatic and poetic conventions, and by his use of a limited and thus ever-recurring vocabulary. Pattern, harmony, and a certain uniformity, or conformity to a model, are easily found. A quite different picture emerges, however, if it is accepted that, in Bénédicte Louvat's words, "what counts for Racine, as for the dramatists of the age, is the ordering of events in the play" (*Poétique* 56). If what Aristotle calls the "combination of incidents" is necessarily particular to each play, it follows that each different play will seek to move an audience, and hold its interest, in a manner proper to that particular combination.

One significant way in which this difference is expressed is in Racine's handling of time. The transformation of "real" time into dramatic time is, in Eugène Vinaver's formulation, a moment of magical change (*Entretiens* 57). Alain Chartier has even suggested that time is the central, hidden character in tragedy (qtd. in Elthes 33). It is thus surprising to realize how little has been written about time in drama, at least in proportion to its importance. One reason is perhaps that the whole subject of time in general is one of riddling complexity, as can be gauged from St Augustine's famous meditation in chapter 9 of the *Confessions*, so finely analyzed by Paul Ricœur in *Temps et Récit*: "*how* can time be, if the past is no more, if the future is still to be, and if the present is not always present?" (1: 23).[1] Though burdened with less ontological anxiety, the role played by time in a dramatic action has a parallel complexity. That has not prevented many generalizations about "Racinian" time. Lucien Goldmann, for example, asserts that time is a dimension of existence that tragedy suppresses. As evidence for what is a large claim, he quotes the following lines: "Et si je vous parlais pour la dernière fois!" (*Britannicus*, 1554), "Et je vais lui parler pour la dernière fois" (*Bérénice*, 490), "Soleil, je te viens voir pour la dernière fois" (*Phèdre*, 172). For Goldmann these lines well up from a Jansenist vision in which the world, and thus its time, are refused: "time in Racine's tragedies is an instant, one that coincides with conversion to the tragic universe" ("Structure" 258). One can see a correlation here between this atemporality and the self-contained, inert body of a *tragique racinien* that can be laid out for critical dis-

---

[1] On seventeenth-century conceptions of time, see Racevskis, 122; T. Reiss 262; Yandell 24-29.

section, so that its anatomy may be described once and for all with clinical rigor.

There is, however, another way of looking at the evidence. That is to see the many temporal references in Racine's tragedies as emphasizing the importance of this whole dimension. Not for nothing, as John Lyons points out in his "Dramaturgie du temps," did the pundit Chapelain call the tragic dramatist a "master of time" (129). As Jacques Scherer reminds us, the way in which playwrights handle time is inseparable from their conduct of the tragic plot. It is thus intimately associated with the ever uneasy balance maintained between the freedom of characters and the implacably mounting restraints within which this freedom is exercised:

> In tragedy, freedom of this kind is closely linked to the time dimension of tragedy. The tragic action is rich in possibilities, but only lasts for a short time; and during that time characters, whether already in the grip of an emotion or in the process of being overwhelmed by one, have to give in to it or not. Everything in tragedy is so carefully timed that, quite literally, once the moment comes and goes, it never comes back. ("Liberté du personnage" 266)

In her *Time in Greek Tragedy*, Jacqueline de Romilly provides a more philosophical statement of the centrality of time to tragic drama:

> Time shows through change, and in that respect it is obvious that tragedy deals with time. Its subject matter is always one great event, which overthrows all that existed before: it means death, destruction, reversal of fortune; its strength rests on a contrast between before and after; and the deeper the contrast, the more tragic the event. [...]
> Tragedy is not only connected with the consciousness of time in so far as it reproduces a continuous series of events, carried by the very rhythm of time; it is also connected with this consciousness in another and wider matter. For it suggests a perpetual reflection about the relation between this series of events and the past or the future; it discusses and mediates about intricate causes and responsibilities. Therefore it always presents us with a more or less conscious philosophy of time. (5, 11)

Time must therefore form an important part of any attempt to consider what "Racinian tragedy" might mean in different plays, not least because this has not often been done. It is for this reason that the workings of plot and time will be examined in three sample plays, in an attempt to place in a different perspective subjects that have attracted considerable discussion. The focus will be on the relationship between plot, tragedy, and elegy in *Bérénice*, between plot and tragedy in *Mithridate*, and between past, present, and future in *Athalie*. In each of these plays Racine conducts his plots differently, and each different plot is expressed in a different experience of time. In other words, each of these different experiences has its own individual coherence as a single dramatic artifact created on a particular occasion.

## Creating a time-machine: *Bérénice*

### Play or poetry?

From the beginning the term "elegy" has stuck to *Bérénice*. The implication is that the play is something less than a dramatic action designed to generate emotion through a well-constructed plot. [2] This static view of the play can, of course, accommodate a view of "Racine" in which the plot has little part to play. Certainly, for its earliest critic, Villars, *Bérénice* was "a tissue of amorous madrigals and elegies" (516), while Voltaire, who had no trace of animosity against Racine, was equally forthright:

> *Bérénice* […] is not a tragedy. It is, if you wish, a heroic comedy, an idyll, an eclogue with princes, an admirable dialogue on love, a beautiful paraphrase of Sappho and not Sophocles, a charming elegy, whatever you want to call it, but not, I repeat not, a tragedy. (Moland 55: 956)

Curiously, however, *Bérénice* has over the past decades been one of the most successful of Racine's tragedies in terms of theatrical performance. And for Jean Rohou it has been the play by Racine that

---

[2] For critical reception, see Mesnard (Ed. 2: 356-72); Durry 82; Michaut; Hepp, "Le personnage de Titus"; Defaux, "Titus or le Héros tremblant."

since 1970 has generated the most interest (Ed. 969). The following pages will examine this apparent paradox by addressing two related questions. To what extent is *Bérénice* a tragedy of crisis, where mind and emotions are engaged, as in the two previous plays, *Andromaque* and *Britannicus*, through the working of a dramatic machine designed to generate tension and leave the issue in doubt until the very end? Is it possible simply to dismiss the recurring criticism that in *Bérénice* nothing "happens," and that it is less a less a dramatic action than a lament?

To the traditional view of *Bérénice* as a static elegy, one might legitimately respond, as does Michael Hawcroft, with rhetorical analysis, and show that the characters do not simply "lament," but "struggle desperately to make their point of view prevail over that of their interlocutor" (*Word as Action* 151). It is also possible to show, as does Georges Forestier, that the elegiac in Racine's models, Virgil and Ovid, had properly tragic qualities (Ed. 1446). That said, the difference with *Andromaque* and *Britannicus* still appears substantial. The dramatic structure of these two works is based on violent emotional and political conflicts fuelled by ambition, lust, and psychotic jealousy. The plots, which feature abduction, blackmail, and assassination, are both built on suspense, surprise, and sudden reversals. There is a dramatic tension that mounts, with in each case a false lull, until the explosive climax. These plays are in some measure "characterized by sensational incident and violent appeals to the emotions," as the OED defines "melodrama." *Bérénice*, in comparison, whose subject is two lovers who separate, seems bare of incident: no night arrest or poisoned cup, no murder at the altar or Furies waiting in the wings. Can one speak of plot, "a combination of incidents," if there are no incidents to combine? Voltaire's answer was crisp: "there is no crux, no obstacle no plot" (Moland 55: 948). The decision made by Titus, that to be a true Roman emperor he must cut the knot of love tying him to a foreign queen, is something the audience knows about from the beginning of Act II. The whole play therefore seems merely to turn on the communication and acceptance of that decision. There does not seem to be much scope for development. From beginning to end the play's essential parameters seem unchanged: love is love and Rome is Rome. As for the characters, one of them appears to have nothing to do, the second waits for the third, and the third does nothing. It is easy to see why, for Villars (517), this was only enough to fill a single scene.

In addition, in *Andromaque* and *Britannicus* the unities of time and place serve to increase both dramatic suspense and a brooding sense of inescapability: both Andromaque and Junie are literally prisoners, and Britannicus becomes one. In *Bérénice*, on the other hand, these same conventions might at first seem only to encase the play in glass. Absent here are those means of increasing the pressure of time, such as the imminent threat of physical violence, the ultimatum, or the unexpected reversal of a decision, that the playwright used in the two previous tragedies to generate dramatic excitement. Indeed, the productions of *Bérénice* by Michel Grüber and Antoine Vitez have seemed deliberately to emphasize the idea that nothing much happens in it: Jean Mambrino described the first as "a kind of icy, funereal oratorio" in which "everything is already dead even before the play starts" ("*Bérénicei*" 498). Such interpretations can fix the characters as flies in amber, magnifying their immobility and setting them at a further remove from the unpredictable turbulence of violent passion that *Andromaque* and *Britannicus* so impressively re-enact. If proof were sought for Lucien Goldmann's "Racinian timelessness," is it not here for all to see?

The argument that *Bérénice* is less a drama than as an extended piece of poetic writing would not be complete without that most persuasive evidence, the poetry itself. One need only think of the lover's lament by Antiochus:

> Dans l'Orient désert quel devint mon ennui!
> Je demeurai longtemps errant dans Césarée,
> Lieux charmants, où mon cœur vous avait adorée. (234-36)

The shimmering beauty of such verse might seem to exist independently of the play, sustained only by its own dream-like quality. It is at this point that siren voices might appeal, as in Gordon Pocock's suggestion that in *Bérénice* "the essential action is expressed in the poetry" (205). A Valéry or a Brémond hover in the wings, with their own version of "Racine" as "poetry." If *Bérénice* exists in its own right as beautiful poetry, why should anyone worry about a plot? Did John Keats not say it all in his "Ode to a Grecian Urn"?

> Beauty is truth, truth beauty',–that is all
>   Ye know on earth, and all ye need to know. (49-50)

*Is* that all ye need to know about *Bérénice*?

The argument from poetry can of course equally be applied (and by Valéry, Brémond, and Eugène Vinaver has been) to Racinian tragedies other than *Bérénice*. The verse in *Andromaque* and *Britannicus* is equally memorable: one thinks immediately of Andromaque's account of the fall of Troy (992-1012), or Néron's description of Junie's night arrest (385-406). In these the poetry is clearly the servant of the drama. The fires of Troy illuminate the searing dilemma of Andromaque, and bring the audience to the heart of the conflict on which the whole plot is built. Indeed, in the Preface to *Mithridate*, Racine explicitly refuses the idea of including the merely "beautiful" for its own sake:

> You cannot be too careful about only including in a play what is strictly necessary. Even scenes of the utmost beauty might well be found boring, if the dramatic action can progress without them, and if they interrupt its progression rather than driving it forward to its conclusion.

In other words, it is the play as a whole that matters. Everything turns on the dramatist's ability, as Racine says in his Preface to *Bérénice*, to keep an audience's interest for the whole duration of a play by involving it emotionally throughout:

> This is a celebrated event in history, and I thought it very suitable for the theater because of the violence of the passions it could arouse. [...] the final farewell Bérénice makes to Titus, her struggle to leave him, is one of the most tragic moments in the play, and it is also, if I may say so, a relatively good way of giving renewed intensity to those emotions which the play has already aroused in the hearts of the audience.

In *Andromaque* and *Britannicus* it is the plot, the dramatic machine, which arouses that curiosity, uncertainty, surprise, apprehension, and a desire to know that give rise to this emotion. Does it seem credible that in *Bérénice* Racine would now refuse to take this means of reaching the destination of his choice, "the hearts of the audience"?

## A plot at work

It is true that *Bérénice* is a more "interior" play than Racine's previous two tragedies: the dramatic action takes place in a private room essentially within and between two main characters. In all three plays, however, the personal and the political are intertwined. Pyrrhus scorns the pressure of the Greeks, who move against him only at the bidding of a jealous woman, while Néron does what he wishes, despite Agrippine and Burrhus. Similarly in *Bérénice*, if there is a focus on the heart and mind of the protagonists, it is because their most intimate secrets "Sont de tout l'Univers devenus l'entretien" (342). What happens to Titus and Bérénice will affect the destiny of the Roman Empire, just as what happens in Rome crucially affects Titus and Bérénice. The audience is always made conscious of a world outside the tragic couple. Paradoxically, in a play so often seen to be purely about love, this love is situated from the beginning in an essentially political dimension. If the outside world consisted only of passive spectators, such as "Les flots toujours nouveaux d'un Peuple adorateur" (53), it would be easier also to agree with Georges Forestier that this "Rome" has merely an observer status in the play (Ed. 1458). But the representatives of the whole Roman state, while they have no power to decide, still bind Titus with "une honorable chaîne" (1287). They are not just waiting for him to act, but putting pressure on him to act in a certain way:

> Seigneur, tous les Tribuns, les Consuls, le Sénat,
> Viennent vous demander au nom de tout l'État.
> Un grand Peuple les suit, qui plein d'impatience
> Dans votre Appartement attend votre présence. (1237-40)

In *Britannicus* there is no conflict between Néron's love and his desire for absolute power: the one expresses the other. But Titus the lover and Titus the emperor are dissimilar, if inseparable. The conflict between the two roles is fundamental to the play, and confers on it a tragic magnitude.

It is within this unstable setting that the plot is worked out. The result is a dramatic action more complex and unpredictable than might be imagined from a mere acquaintance with the subject and thus the denouement. As is usual, the audience already knows the outcome of the play, or thinks it does. Racine even reinforces that knowledge with the quotation from Suetonius that heads the Preface: Titus sends Bérénice away though neither wishes this to happen. What the audience does not know is how this outcome will be reached. For example, much of the information provided by the exposition lays false trails. Consider Bérénice's initial statement of the position: "Titus m'aime, il peut tout, il n'a plus qu'à parler" (298). As the play progresses, these assumptions become ironically problematical. Does Titus love Bérénice? What can he do? What can he say? Each of these elements is left in suspense until the end.

"Suspense" might seem an odd term to use in the same breath as *Bérénice*. But, as will be seen in a different form in *Mithridate*, suspense comes from suspension, a structure made of uncertainty, indecision, deferment, mistake, and illusion. Not everyone will agree. For example, this "suspension" hardly resembles the pattern identified by Jean Giraudoux in his quest to define what is distinctive in "Racinian tragedy": "Once Racinian tragic heroes have come on stage there is no escape for them, and from the first words they speak they already stand condemned" (47). It will be seen later that this statement does not correspond to what happens in different plays, and not even in *Phèdre*, so often viewed as most perfectly expressing "Racinian tragedy." Nor does Giraudoux's assertion provide an accurate account of *Bérénice*. A clear example is the decision by Titus, revealed in Act II, to leave Bérénice. Philippe Salazar asserts that "Titus hardly weighs up his decision" (582), which if true would break the spring of the whole plot. For the more the emperor ponders the implications of what amounts to saying "Partez, et ne me voyez plus" (522), the less this dismissal seems possible, so that he mentions his determination only to say that it is wavering (548). Montesquieu quite appositely describes an audience's emotions and thoughts as being in a state of "suspension," a term suggesting uncertainty and the inability to predict what will happen (3: 270). It is this suspension that generates suspense, defined by the OED as "a state of mental uncertainty, with expectation or desire for decision, and usually some apprehension or anxiety." Racine exploits the uncertainty created by this suspension to raise the emotional pressure: "Je ne respire pas dans cette incertitude" (644). For the clearer it becomes that Titus must leave Bérénice, and cannot do so, the steeper becomes the curve of emotional tension, and the greater the impact of an inevitable but ironically unpredictable outcome. Put simply, the audience cannot know to what extreme measures either of the main protagonists might resort.

Racine's use of suspension and suspense is evident in his exploitation of the different reactions of characters, oscillating unpredictably between fear, hope, and desire in situations that are volatile and unbearable. An illustration comes in Act III, when the news of Titus's decision is relayed to the queen, who suddenly finds herself in a new and hostile world: "Nous séparer? Qui? Moi! Titus de Bérénice!" (895). With a sense of increased urgency, the dramatic action seems to be moving towards death as the only possible outcome (1189-95). It is another example of Racine's distinctive plotting technique in *Bérénice* that, when this death occurs, it will not be the physical death he has led his audience to expect. In a similar fashion, he focuses its attention on what Titus will do to resolve the conflict. This is especially so in the denouement. In succeeding moments the emperor hears that Bérénice is about to die of grief, and that all the Roman political forces are impatiently awaiting his announcement of their separation. The pressure is on him to act without further delay. "Que veut-il?," asks Antiochus (1298). The emperor's admission of absolute uncertainty (1392-94), and subsequent threat of suicide (1419-20), can only increase an audience's expectation that, just as in Corneille's *Cinna*, and in conformity with the source, some act of imperial courage will cut the Gordian knot. It is a crucially wrong lead. For it is Bérénice, the would-be passive object of the emperor's dilemma, who steps in to resolve it, in what Gérard Defaux calls "an expertly calculated *crescendo*" ("*Bérénice*" 222).

The volatility generated by the plot interacts with and compounds an instability of perception. Characters think that they know each other, and themselves. The audience itself, knowing the subject, may think that there is not much room for development. As Gérard Defaux again shows ("Titus" 280), the whole plot works to undermine this knowledge, and keep characters and audience in a state of uncertainty, where feelings and motives are called into question, while possible reactions and consequences are always in doubt. It is symptomatic that Titus cannot bear to look Bérénice in the face (596). His difficulty in facing up to hard reality is compounded by the illusion that the decision he has taken is behind him, and that the only problem is now only one of presentation and communication (472-76). Michael Hawcroft suggests that the monologue in Act IV, Scene 4 (recalling a similar scene at the same juncture in *Cinna*) shows that Titus is a "basically determined man," because "when alone, he reaches a decision which he starts immediately to put into effect," and only becomes "indecisive" in the next scene, when he has to face Bérénice (*Word as Action* 201-02). It all depends on what is meant by "basically determined." In the emperor's pleading tone to the queen is the voice of a man who can himself no longer act: "Forcez votre amour à se taire" (1051). It might be thought excessive to speak, as does Jean-Claude Ranger, of the "paralysis of will-power that in his case is also power" (105). At the same time, there seems little hard evidence that Titus undergoes some kind of rebirth (Picard, Ed. 1: 457) or conversion (Goldmann, *Racine* 99-106). What seems closer to the mark is that the Cornelian self-exhortations to moral heroism, the reminders of the demands of *devoir, honneur*, and *gloire*, are no longer sufficient to occult the unpalatable truth that he is overwhelmed by his relationship with Bérénice.

There is a history of debate as to whether Titus "really" loves Bérénice.[3] Racine's contemporary, Bussy-Rabutin (qtd. in Michaut 302) was already claiming that "Titus does not love her as much as he says he does." Against this William Evans has counted "no less than twenty-three direct references to his love and devotion to Bérénice" (454). In what is a radically different orientation, Richard Goodkin advances the hypothesis that Bérénice is not in love with Titus, but with Antiochus: "This interpretation [...] is diametrically opposed to what the character repeats *ad nauseam*, but perhaps the lady doth protest too much" (*Birthmarks* 214). These different opinions at least have the merit of demonstrating how widely shared is the uncertainty created by the plot. For Roland Barthes, "it is only force of habit that keeps Titus with Bérénice," and "we only know of one encounter of Titus and Eros, in his reference to the 'belles mains' of Bérénice" (*Sur Racine* 94). Against this genial assertion, however, one may oppose a considerable body of evidence. For it is difficult to ignore the many moments when Eros declares his hand:

---

[3] For differing assessments, see Audet and Kavacovic; Cloonan, "Love and *Gloire*"; Evans; Rohou, Ed. 949; Parent 197-207; Supple, *Bérénice* 72. For a bibliographical guide, see Hepp, "Titus," notes 1-2.

> Soutiendrai-je ces yeux dont la douce langueur
> Sait si bien découvrir les chemins de mon cœur?
> Quand je verrai ces yeux armés de tous leurs charmes,
> Attachés sur les miens, m'accabler de leurs larmes,
> Me souviendrai-je alors de mon triste devoir? (993-97)

The intensity with which Titus evokes the power of love has from the beginning been seen as weakness, a weakness to which the emperor admits (1439). Thus Villars claims he is "infantalized" by his love (513), and Du Bos that he is effeminate (2: 16), while for Voltaire Titus "should not even have to ask why he is emperor" (Moland 55: 954). This view, which has the merit of simplicity, has been countered by many, most recently by Gilles Declercq ("Alchimie") and Christian Delmas ("Histoire et mythe"). There is another reading, one that is consistent with the ironic movement of the plot: to see a man who, prepared for a rough crossing between the fixed points of love and duty, suddenly finds himself alone, with no bearings, in unnavigable seas. This irony surfaces when Bérénice tells Titus that "De tous vos sentiments mon cœur est éclairci" (1173). For at certain moments the emperor no longer knows what his own feelings or motives are, or what to say, or which way to turn:

> Moi-même à tous moments je me souviens à peine
> Si je suis Empereur, ou si je suis Romain.
> Je suis venu vers vous, sans savoir mon dessein.
> Mon amour m'entraînait, et je venais peut-être
> Pour me chercher moi-même, et pour me reconnaître. (1392-96)

The plot of *Bérénice* has thus a crucial importance for any consideration of how an audience's emotions are aroused, and how a tragic effect is achieved. It is a structure created to trap two human beings, and to make them face up to the one thing they cannot even contemplate. In so doing it creates a pathos and irony intensified by the reversal that this involves. At the beginning of the play the emperor is presented as a figure of power, master of the universe (316). The plot works to uncover the trap that this power represents. The words which greet the emperor on his first entrance, "Vous pouvez tout" (349), become, each time the term *pouvoir* is then used, a mocking reminder of his inability to exercise power over himself (722). In the eighteenth century Louis-Sébastien

Mercier among many others denounced Racine's so-called tragedies as not being the real thing, since "real tragedy" was necessarily bound up with affairs of state (27, 39, 289). Indeed, since Saint-Évremond's strictures on Racine's second play, *Alexandre le Grand* (qtd. in Forestier Ed. 181-89), it has been common to see "Racinian tragedy" as an expression of the absolute dominance of passionate love. At least in *Bérénice*, however, it is evident that there is a conflict between political necessity and the dream of a love divorced from the contingencies of life. What is less evident is the relationship between the two. Many critics see the play as showing a man becoming a ruler. There are obviously grounds for this point of view. Against this, however, it might be argued that Racine shows a ruler ruled by a man, a man who finally offers suicide as the only possible exit. Titus had planned to dismiss Bérénice in order to exercise imperial rule. Through the twists and turns of the plot this initial decision can be shown to dissolve in irony: at the end he is a mute and helpless spectator.

This is not a perspective shared by all, or even by many. Christian Delmas maintains, for example, that the ceremonial element in *Bérénice*, exemplified by the famous description of Vespasian's apotheosis (301-16), accompanies what for him is the heart of the play, the solemn enthronement of Titus ("Histoire et mythe" 133). As is only natural, our view as an audience might well be influenced by the emphasis given in a particular production. Indeed, it is for this very reason that this book has argued from the outset that it seems hazardous to speak in terms of a "Racine" that can be analyzed like some inert substance. To that extent, each critic operates as a kind of theatrical director, and any interpretation, as this one, is a sort of mental production. The text of a play will of course always suggest a framework, or limits, within which such interpretations can most persuasively be made. That said, the theatre is not a world of essences and received truths.

This particular interpretation has stressed the way in which the plot works to effect a reversal. It is undeniable that the opening scenes do stress the authority of the new emperor, something that Bérénice is the very first to recognize:

> Parle. Peut-on le voir sans penser comme moi,
> Qu'en quelque obscurité que le Sort l'eût fait naître,
> Le Monde en le voyant, eût reconnu son Maître? (314-16)

The question to be asked, however, is whether this initial manifestation of authority is reinforced by what actually happens in the play. Bettina Knapp (112) sees Titus's decision to renounce his love as a passage from adolescence to manhood. If such is the case, it is Bérénice who confirms the "manhood" in question. For in the end it is the queen who sees what must be done, and does it. As Harriet Stone comments, following Simone Akerman: "she asserts the authority that Titus and Rome would deny her" (*Royal DisClosure* 85).

The structure of the plot could therefore be seen as essentially Aristotelian, one of reversal and recognition. In the reversal of Bérénice's decision to possess Titus totally and publicly, there is a quite formal statement of recognition: "Je connais mon erreur" (1494). This is not just the recognition that Titus can love her and still leave her. It is the realization that no personal desire, however overwhelming, can be an absolute: "Bérénice, Seigneur, ne vaut point d'alarmes" (1496). This accompanies the ultimate reversal, and the final testimony of the power of the plot to move and surprise, in a denouement that, as Louis Racine pointed out (1: 392), no-one could have been expecting. Gilles Declercq calls this "a decision with which both parties in the end agree" ("Alchimie" 146). That is doubtless true after the event: such is the balance between surprise and *vraisemblance*. But it is Bérénice who creates the event: "Adieu, Seigneur, régnez, je ne vous verrai plus" (1506). It is she with sovereign power who decides to leave, and to confer on the moment of leaving the exemplary significance she herself wishes to confer.[4]

In *Bérénice*, therefore, we are gulled by an appearance as we follow the play, as audience and readers. We are caught up in an apparent suspension of activity that in reality is an increasingly unstable development of vacillating and conflicting emotions, crowned with a resolution that overturns expectations. The role of the plot is therefore crucial, and cannot easily be separated from any interpretation that might be made of the play. The emotions generated by the dramatic action produce, not an elegy, but what Georges Forestier describes as "a truly elegiac tragedy" (Ed. 1461). It is certainly quite different from *Andromaque, Britannicus,* or

---

[4] On this decision, see Croquette 120; Durry 87; Landry, "*Bérénice*" 146; Sienaert 28; Stone, "*Bérénice*" 232.

*Mithridate*. In order to make *Bérénice* fit into a unified view of "Racinian tragedy," this difference may be smoothed over. There is no shortage of critical filler for even the most substantial cracks. Or, paradoxically to attempt to shore up the same thesis, *Bérénice* may simply be viewed as "exceptional." However critics might decide to deal with this difference, it is clear that a quite distinctive plot has made for a quite distinctive play.

*A sense of time*

At this point it is easy to imagine some polite protests. "That is all very well," it could be said, "but what then of the reactions of Villars, Voltaire, and many others who for three hundred years have spoken of emptiness and lack of movement?" And indeed, it seems impossible to dismiss out of hand such an established critical reception. Here again it is possible to seek some resolution of this apparent contradiction by pointing to the distinctive nature of the plot, and, especially, to the unique sense of time created by Racine in *Bérénice*. This sense of time is unique if only because, within what can be experienced as a real dramatic movement, the immobile also has a major role to play. In this paradoxical perspective the play may be seen as a particular presentation of the relationship between time and love, and thus as an exploration of that most tenacious illusion of love, so famously expressed by Shakespeare:

> Love's not Time's fool, though rosy lips and cheeks
> Within his bending sickle's compass come;
> Love alters not with his brief hours and weeks,
> But bears it out even to the edge of doom. (Sonnet 116)

It is certain that a sense of immobility is very much present in *Bérénice*. "Suspension" is one name it has already been given. An expression of this apparent lack of movement is the role of Antiochus. At the beginning he decides to leave (33), tells Bérénice that he has never loved her so much (258), and wishes to die (280). This does not prevent him staying until the end, when he tells Bérénice that he has never loved her so much, and wishes to die (1457-59). This passivity has, naturally enough, not always been appreciated. Jean Rohou, for example, finds the character "pathetic and somewhat derisory" (Ed. 957). The role of Antiochus has, however, as Jacques Morel has pointed out (*Agréables Mensonges* 220), a defined function in the plot, allowing Titus and Bérénice to express themselves to each other. In addition, from the point of view of the tragic action as a whole, this elegiac role has a strongly emblematic character. Even if Antiochus does not turn the iron wheels of the tragic plot, his function is quasi-choral, chanting and nourishing the melancholy that pervades the play, as in the lover's lament quoted earlier. As such, this role also contributes to that sense of suspended time that is the great tragic illusion explored in *Bérénice*. Action is for Antiochus one of suspended activity, as for the ships he has waiting in Ostia, "Prêts à quitter le Port de moments en moments" (73). His self-interrogation–"es-tu toujours le même?" (19)–is not important in itself, because his role is not important in itself. But it is a typically choral question, to the extent that it captures the conflict between and within the protagonists, and implicitly poses the problem of mutability.

For Odette de Mourgues, "Racinian passion is outside time" (15). But should "Racinian passion" be confused with what the heroine will realize is an illusion? The opening words of the play, "Arrêtons un moment," aptly prefigure what follows. It is true that love has created for Bérénice, as for that other queen in Shakespeare's *Antony and Cleopatra*, a world out of time: "Eternity was in our lips and eyes" (1.3.35). What has been, and what will be, is what is. Bérénice loves Titus. Titus loves Bérénice. Love is substance, all else accident. The heart that loves is untouched by the contingent:

> Jugez de ma douleur, moi, dont l'ardeur extrême,
> (Je vous l'ai dit cent fois) n'aime en lui que lui-même, (159-60)

This love, rather like *le tragique racinien*, is a world of essences. The aspiration for the *toujours présent* in love may of course be seen as figuring a transcendental dimension of humanity. Existence within the constraints of the world's time is another matter. By definition, that implies action and reaction, birth, growth, decay, and destruction, that continual, self-generating, Heraclitean combustion. If *Bérénice* seems immobile, to be empty of events, it is because of characters' attempts to sustain a weightless world of absolute love, of "éternelle ardeur" (589), a world of the *toujours présent* beyond the gravitational pull of time:

> N'en doutez pas, Madame, et j'atteste les Dieux
> Que toujours Bérénice est présente à mes yeux.
> L'absence, ni le temps, je vous le jure encore,
> Ne vous peuvent ravir ce cœur qui vous adore. (585-88)

To the suggestion that all has changed now that the lover is emperor, Bérénice first replies with an irrefutable absolute: "Titus m'aime…" (298). Her ideal is to live in that timeless state in which Titus "passait ses jours, attaché sur ma vue" (156). This desire involves something other than the debatable thesis advanced by Georges Poulet (112) that "Racinian tragedy" is only ever concerned with past time. Bérénice's repeated "Titus m'aime" sounds a defiant refusal of mutability. The apotheosis passage is in this context eloquent:

> De cette nuit, Phénice, as-tu vu la spendeur?
> Tes yeux ne sont-ils pas tout pleins de sa grandeur?
> Ces Flambeaux, ce Bûcher, cette nuit enflammée,
> Ces Aigles, ces Faisceaux, ce Peuple, cette Armée,
> Cette foule de Rois, ces Consuls, ce Sénat,
> Qui tous de mon Amant empruntaient leur éclat;
> Cette Pourpre, cet or que rehaussait sa gloire,
> Et ces Lauriers encor témoins de sa victoire,
> Tous ces yeux, qu'on voyait venir de toutes parts
> Confondre sur lui seul leurs avides regards;
> Ce port majestueux, cette douce présence. (301-11)

This image of Rome and its emperor, powerful and effulgent, is an important dimension of the play. But this is not the whole story. Here the recurring demonstrative adjective has a consciously arresting, immobilizing effect. It functions as a pointer to scenes in a painting, whose movement is fixed for ever. The account of a transformation is itself paradoxically transformed into the celebration of an unchanging love. The stabbing demonstratives capture Titus as an essence of majesty in a world of ideal forms in which time's corrosions have no place.

There is therefore something ironically fundamental in Titus's plaintive question to the queen: "Quel temps choisissez-vous?" (617). Henry Phillips ("Temps du futur" 156) and Gérald Antoine (80) suggest that before the death of Vespasian both Titus and Bérénice live in conditional mode, excluding the future. Another way of expressing this refusal of reality is to say that love for them is conjugated in the same absolute present that ordinary language uses, for example, to express the unchanging laws of the universe. Bérénice desires to love immutably, as fire burns, or the wind blows. This is the only grammar of love that she can comprehend:

> Vous m'aimez, vous me le soutenez,
> Et cependant je pars, et vous me l'ordonnez? (1357-58)

Titus is equally conscious of this eternal present of love:

> Depuis cinq ans entiers chaque jour je la vois,
> Et crois toujours la voir pour la première fois. (545-46)

Before he became emperor nothing was more natural than to remain thus locked in orbit round the planet Venus, oblivious of a world where things happen and decisions must be taken (455-56). With his father's death he must come back to earth. It is an unwilling return to the world of time, sharply expressed by the necessity to conjugate love in the past tense before the day is out (414). Bérénice cannot understand this necessity:

> *Titus*: Car enfin, ma Princesse, il faut nous séparer.
> *Bérénice*: Ah cruel! Est-il temps de me le déclarer? (1061-62)

"Est-il temps...?" The timeless present to which Bérénice clings with increasing desperation is made to seem increasingly unreal. Its chimerical nature is emphasized by all Titus's references to this love as a time-denying state in which "Mon cœur se gardait bien d'aller dans l'avenir" (1089). It is true that he uses a Past Historic suggesting a narrative of beginning and end: "Bérénice me plut" (509), "Je l'aimai, je lui plus" (531). But his clarion-call of "Ne tardons plus" (1039) is followed by more procrastination, and his only eventual concrete response is to threaten suicide.

What is represented in *Bérénice*, and what is omnipresent, is thus the dream of love, unreal, but achingly pursued. Insofar as the dramatic action recreates this dream, it partakes of the dream's essential immobility. The reality against which this dream will burst is rock-hard and entire: Roman law. This is everything except pretext or fatality (Audet and Kovacovic 354: Chatelain 104). Indeed,

Emmanuel Bury even argues that Titus's place in Roman history is a historical necessity demanding fulfilment ("Mémoire" 392). The recapitulation of important moments in Roman history, with the knowledge that even the most lawless tyrants still respected this one basic law (397-402), means that this unchanging "Rome" always makes its presence felt:

> Rome par une Loi, qui ne se peut changer,
> N'admet avec son sang aucun sang étranger, (377-78)

This is an inescapable *toujours présent* that Bérénice and Titus have no choice but to confront. Love and this law are both present as realities from beginning to end of the dramatic action. For example, never as in Act V does Titus confess so much love, in the fusion of what is now and what always has been:

> Ce jour surpasse tout. Jamais, je le confesse,
> Vous ne fûtes aimée avec tant de tendresse. (1355-56)

At the same time, never does his awareness of the law make him so conscious of the impossibility of staying with Bérénice. Again, his sense of duty to this law is presented in terms of temporal pressure:

> Ma Gloire inexorable à toute heure me suit.
> Sans cesse elle présente à mon âme étonnée
> L'Empire incompatible avec votre hyménée; (1406-8)

The appearance of immobility in *Bérénice* is reinforced by what might be seen as non-activities: waiting, delaying, and frustrated seeking, what Bérénice calls "cette longueur" (957). Titus's response to the conflict typifies this process: "Non, non, encore un coup ne précipitons rien" (1010). The plot therefore shares some of the qualities of the siege of Jerusalem that brought its protagonists together. In this "long and indecisive siege" filled with "futile attacks," Titus's resolution resembles nothing more than the "powerless battering-ram" vainly attempting to breach the unshakeable walls of love and law (105-9). In a play such as *Andromaque* it is possible to identify a dramatic structure of action and reaction, where events gather pace as an impossible deadline approaches. *Bérénice* self-evidently involves a quite different dramatic stratagem, typified by Arsace's advice to Antiochus:

> Laissez à ce torrent le temps de s'écouler.
> Dans huit jours, dans un mois, n'importe, il faut qu'il passe.
> Demeurez seulement. (942-44)

William Levitan has called *Bérénice* "the drama perhaps most extreme in its reluctance to allow the present to evolve into the future" (901). The descriptions or criticisms of the play's "immobility" perhaps spring from the radically different atmosphere produced by this radically different approach. A play is by definition a movement, in Aristotle's terms the imitation not of persons, or states of being, but of an action. The fostering of an atmosphere that seeks to defy the laws of motion is thus as risky as, say, Jane Austen's creation of boring Miss Bates in *Emma*. Novels are meant to entertain, and tragedies to have a beginning, middle, and end.

It is important, however, not to take the part for the whole, to confuse a necessary experience with the real movement. For *Bérénice is* action, *is* movement. As surely as the time-denying atmosphere is created, as surely is it destroyed, through the working-out of the plot. The reason is that at the heart of the tragic action there is not so much a stillness as a dream of stillness. This dream functions as the tragic illusion, which the whole movement of the play painfully uncovers, on a stage where reality comes in the guise of time. A witness is that word so often repeated, the unrelenting *moment* of the tragic action (Soares and Abraham 106), a moment that is also, inescapably, a movement. In *Bérénice* an essential part of that tragic movement is the necessary confrontation of the "always" in love's desire with the unrelenting march of time as expressed in the inexorable progression of the plot. In this dramatic action, "action" is indeed a crucial word. Time is not just symbolized in the character of Titus, as suggested by Jean-Marie Delacomptée ("Majesty and Pleasure" 180). It is the dramatic action as an evolving whole that represents, concentrated in a few hours, the hard, real, disruptive process of time. In his study of Shakespearean tragedy, Northrop Frye sees the very basis of that tragedy as "being in time, the sense of the one-directional quality of life where everything happens once and for all, where every act brings unavoidable and fateful consequences" (3). Both Titus and Bérénice in different ways set their face against the reality of this "being in time." The essence of the dramatic action is the painful coming to consciousness of that reality, as motives are exposed and nerves are stripped bare.

There is thus an ironic tension between the characters' refusal of time and the irreversible movement of the dramatic action which itself renders the experience of time. Lucien Goldmann claims curiously that the wider world in *Bérénice* is represented only by Antiochus ("*Bérénice*" 32). However, from the moment Titus knows that that senate and people will soon be asking him to renounce his love (419), everything is a countdown to the moment in Act IV when an impatient delegation comes requesting his decision (1237-40). In other words, there is an inevitable re-entry into a real world where choices may no longer be postponed. The suicide threats made by Titus and Bérénice are symptomatic. It is as if, having failed to stop the clock, they now desire to smash it.

Those who speak of *Bérénice* as an "elegy," by which they often mean a work becalmed in the still waters of its own poetic beauty, perhaps therefore underestimate the relentless nature of a dramatic movement no less real for being stealthy as the incoming tide, and borne on wave after wave of emotion. For the play moves, both transitively and intransitively. The twists of the plot, characterized by an uncertainty in which Bérénice says she cannot breathe (644), generate expectations which are not always fulfilled, fears that are not always founded, and pity for those caught up in a situation for which they are partly responsible, but which neither an emperor or a queen can completely control. *Bérénice* at least, perhaps paradoxically, is a striking refutation of the contention that "Racine's is essentially a theater of non-evolution," and that "the characters travel over and over the same ground, ending precisely where they begin" (Muratore 114). The increasingly disruptive movement of the dramatic action is accompanied by images of breaking and sundering: terms such as *percer, dévorer, déchirer, arracher, rompre, partir, s'éloigner, abandonner, se séparer, renoncer, quitter, exil, banissement*. This explains Georges Steiner's suggestion that "the close of *Bérénice* should be acted quickly, as if in a race against an approaching thunderstorm" (78).

Examination of the plot is therefore instructive. It shows that it is possible to explain the apparent immobility of *Bérénice* as a necessary part of what is a dynamic, destructive movement. And though critics might quite justifiably enjoy the intellectual challenge of doing so, they do not *need* to reach into the Augustinian or psycho-critical toolkit to prize open the "significance" of this play, unless of course they wish, as for example Jean Rohou, to explain the "evolution of Racinian tragedy" in a certain way (Ed. 965). The plot offers another way in, through the manner in which it works to create and then tear apart the most poignant of human illusions: the dream of love as a *toujours présent*. When faced with expulsion from that artificial world whose light and warmth are provided by the constant sun of love, small wonder that Bérénice experiences everyday temporal markers, such as *jour, mois, an*, as so many lacerations, and *jamais* as a sentence of death. It is for these reasons that it is not easy to agree with Georges Forestier, in his edition of *Bérénice* (133) that the elegiac tone of the poetry in *Bérénice* only concerns the past.

> Pour jamais! Ah Seigneur, songez-vous en vous-même
> Combien ce mot cruel est affreux quand on aime?
> Dans un mois, dans un an, comment souffrirons-nous,
> Seigneur, que tant de Mers me séparent de vous?
> Que le jour recommence et que le jour finisse,
> Sans que jamais Titus puisse voir Bérénice,
> Sans que de tout le jour je puisse voir Titus? (1111-17)

Ironically, the *toujours présent* here is replaced by another, bleaker vision of unchanging time, one of suffering without end. As Thérèse Lassalle stresses (110), the reality that Bérénice is made to confront is empty of meaning for her. The emptiness has its own eternity, stretching out endlessly before her. This is hardly the stuff of the "moralizing bourgeois drama" that draws Alain Niderst's irony ("Préface de *Bérénice*" 323). There is here something more potent, painful, and humanly unacceptable. It is said too hastily that there is no death in *Bérénice*, as in Jean Emelina's suggestion that a heroic finale makes the play less "pessimistic" and thus less "tragic" ("Racine et le mal" 97). The whole question of "pessimism" as a tragic marker is something to which this book will return. But it could be argued that in *Bérénice* there is a death, to the extent that the queen dies, slowly, to what has given meaning to life. By the end, ironically, Bérénice has come full circle, to another type of existence out of time, save that this is now what Ruth Sussman calls "the affirmed consciousness of emptiness, the denial of a future" (248). In her final reference to love, that tearful sense of the forlorn is conveyed, aptly, by the use of the past tense: "J'aimais, Seigneur, j'aimais, je voulais être aimée" (1491). This whole movement ends, in the last words she speaks, with the final, solemn act of severance: "Pour la dernière fois, Adieu, Seigneur" (1518). The curtain falls. Time is up.

In *Bérénice*, therefore, time is of the essence. As such the play obviously invites a multitude of literary associations, not the least of which is the Shakespearian vision of time as a relentless, pounding, all-devouring energy:

> Like as the waves make towards the pebbled shore,
> So do our minutes hasten to their end, (Sonnet 60)

The sense of time created in *Bérénice*, however, is clearly a function of a tightly controlled dramatic structure. It is essentially the mimetic act that affords at every turn a heightened consciousness of those ceaseless vicissitudes that have always seemed to mock our tenacious desire as human beings to live and love in the fullness of an unchanging present. In *Bérénice* mimesis is an intimation of mortality. Time as a experience lived out in this dramatic action predicates the inescapable in life, and takes on the character of a tragic fatality. No work of art is an island, complete unto itself. In *Bérénice*, who can miss the tolling bell?

But this is not quite the last trump. The present has a final card to play. Like *Macbeth,* for all the despair expressed in its "Tomorrow, and tomorrow, and tomorrow," so *Bérénice* too, for all its anguished exploration of time's necessity, is a celebration of living. This is not just because, like any great work of art, it gives form, meaning, and beauty to ideas and emotions that in the everyday can be uncertain, scattered, and gratuitous. It is for pleasure that men and women go to see *Bérénice*, and it is with pleasure that they see it again. Baillet, who had the good fortune to see the first performance, later declared that with every new performance it seemed to be a new play (Parfaict 11: 101). That Augustinian present, in "real" life so elusive, has a reality in the dramatic representation in which Titus and Bérénice alone live, in what Henry Phillips aptly calls "the here and now" (*Language and Theatre* 142). As Arthur Miller puts it, in his *Theatre Essays*: "dramatic form is the art of the present tense *par excellence*" (122). In the theater there can be no question of emotion recollected in tranquility. As John Lyons reminds us, the playwright plays not solely with dramatic time, but with our time, and our experience of it, as audience and readers

("Dramaturgie du temps" 137). In the playing-out of the action, in the playing on our emotions, in all the playing with time that this play affords, there is a cathartic re-enacting of what in everyday life can only be conjugated, with anguish, in the past tense. *Bérénice* is in every sense a tragedy of time.

Plot as suspension: *Mithridate*

For some, *Mithridate* has not been "Racinian" enough. Even admirers of Racine's tragedies have hesitated here. Jean Dubu remarks that it is not often performed ("*Mithridate*" 19), and Jean Rohou concludes from what he sees in the bookstores that it is not often read or studied either (Ed. 1017). Common to many reactions is the idea that as a tragic drama the play is structurally flawed. Whereas for the present Pléiade editor *Mithridate* is an orthodox Aristotelian tragedy based on error, reversal, and recognition (1538), Raymond Picard in the previous edition had deemed it "the least tragic" of the tragedies (1: 159), an opinion shared by critics as diverse as Jean Emelina (*Racine infiniment* 137) and Alain Viala (*Racine* 151), while for Marcel Gutwirth the only tragic thing about the play is its subtitle, *tragédie* ("Problématique" 192). The seeming evolution in Jean Rohou's judgments is symptomatic of this hesitation: in his 1992 biography he judged *Mithridate* to be lacking in tragic quality (285), an opinion he reiterated in 1994 (*Bilan critique* 47), before claiming in 1998 (Ed. 1002) that *le tragique* was at the very heart of the work.

*Suspense and suspension*

Once again, as with *Bérénice*, the heart of the matter is the plot. Unfavorable comparisons are made with the supposedly more "Racinian" plotting techniques of some of the plays that precede it: Donna Kuizenga suggests regret that "it cannot be dismissed as an early effort" (280). *Bérénice*, in which nothing is supposed to happen, presents a sustained, agonizing progression in dramatic tension until the final separation. In *Mithridate*, on the other hand, many have claimed, like Henry Phillips (*Mithridate* 88), that the dramatic action loses its force in Act IV with the reconciliation of father and son. Indeed, Gaston Rudler, in his edition of the play (xxix), declares Act V to be mere padding. While the plots of *Andromaque* and *Britannicus* are intricate knots of conflicting interests, tightened to breaking and then suddenly undone with catastrophic consequences, *Mithridate* is visibly not so tightly strung. With his "inutile courroux" (1413), Mithridate blusters but in the end does nothing, while the two lovers are reunited, all obstacles removed, in what for Charles Mauron (123) is a denouement worthy of comedy. How then does this square with Racine's own dictum, in his Preface, that a play should only contain what is essential for the dramatic action? It is easy to see why so many severe doorkeepers have refused to allow *Mithridate* admission to that select club called "Racinian tragedy."

Implicit in these unfavorable judgments is the idea that there one type of tragedy that is typically "Racinian," and that Racine did not adhere to his own norm. Even Georges Forestier finds *Mithridate* to be "the least Racinian of Racine's tragedies" (Ed. 1527). The following chapter will consider some more general problems associated with common expectations of the "Racinian." As far as plot and time are concerned, however, this chapter has already attempted to show the extent to which the suspension engineered in *Bérénice* represents a "deviation" from the principle expressed by d'Aubignac, that the action of a play, for reasons of credibility, coherence, and dramatic tension, should begin as close as possible to its ending (190). The supposed "Racinian" norm often seems based on the tragic mechanism at work in *Andromaque*: a seemingly irresistible movement from initial crisis to final paroxysm, with a gradual acceleration modulated by delay, panic, and reversal. Following this pattern, time comes in the form of a substance seemingly in short supply. Standard supports of this kind of plot, in *Andromaque*, are phrases such as "il va bientôt revenir en furie" (1046) or "Vous ne donnez qu'un jour, qu'une heure, qu'un moment" (1212). And, as noted even in a play so apparently empty of incident as *Bérénice*, dramatic tension is generated by a sense of time running out.

Attempts have been made to make *Mithridate* conform to this "Racinian" model, from Nadal (Parfaict 11: 256) to Maurice Descotes (*Les grands roles* 114). Throughout the play characters do tell each other that there is no time to lose: "il faut [...] presser notre départ" (237-38), "puisque le temps presse" (244), "Le péril est pressant" (345), "Cours par un prompt trépas abréger ta misère" (751), "partez dès ce moment" (857), "Le temps est cher. Il le faut employer" (1114), "Que dis-je? On vient. Allez. Courez" (1265). The time-markers are there, but is their immediate function obvious? Does their use generate the same kind of dramatic tension and foreboding as, say, Pyrrhus's "Je viendrai vous prendre" (*Andromaque*, 978)? Does any significant action ensue? Negative replies to these questions will suggest that, despite appearances, time in *Mithridate* is not managed in the same way. As in *Bérénice*, this will have necessary consequences for the way in which its identity as a tragedy is evaluated.

In other tragedies by Racine, from the opening lines, the audience is plunged into a rapidly evolving and always escalating crisis. In both *Andromaque* and *Iphigénie*, for example, there is an immediate physical threat. The beginning of *Mithridate*, remarkably, brings the audience to the very end:

> On nous faisait, Arbate, un fidèle rapport.
> Rome en effet triomphe, et Mithridate est mort. (1-2)

In his Preface Racine asserts that the death of Mithridate forms the tragic action of the play, a point both Roland Barthes (*Sur Racine* 105) and Daniel Mesguich (327) qualify by pointing out that the tragedy is played out between his two deaths, imagined and real. This is a quite different dramatic structure from that of *Bérénice*. The word that again suggests itself is "suspension," but of another sort. The quite original dramatic structure of *Mithridate*, involving temporary cessation and postponement, can be apprehended through the dictionary definition already quoted. Without too many word games, this play could be viewed as constructed like a suspension bridge between the death announced in this initial "faithful report" and the physical death at the end. This suspension certainly gives savor to the liminal question: "Il est mort: savons-nous s'il est enseveli?" (298). Throughout the play, however frantic the external action may at times appear, characters are as though suspended between life and death, without being able to live or die.

This suspension is especially true of the king, that would-be source of decisions affecting the lives of all. Just as the end is contained within the beginning, so the movement of the whole play is reflected in the long death-scene at the end. Jean Garapon (137) views *Mithridate* as a hymn to the primal warrior qualities of royal heroism, and this image certainly forms part of the king's rhetoric. But from the terminal beginning the audience is informed already that the reality of his power has gone:

> Et j'ai su qu'un Soldat dans les mains de Pompée,
> Avec son Diadème a remis son Épée. (7-8)

The lost crown and sword are a solemn initial statement of Mithridate's demise as ruler and general. Since these functions constitute his historical *raison d'être*, nothing else remains. Racine twists the knife by adding to these lost sovereignties a final, emasculating defeat: that of any pretence of sexual dominion. Not for nothing is the scene set in the Kingdom of Bosphorus, in a Crimean backwater at the uttermost distance from the center of power. "To have been killed in battle," as Donna Kuizenga remarks, "believing in the illusory allegiance of Monime, would have been Mithridate's personal *belle mort*. Instead, he survives, returns to Nymphée to die less gloriously" (284). In so far as life is movement in time, in *Mithridate* the imitation of an action is played out in a temporal no-man's-land. This creates not so much a sense of unreality as a radically different dramatic reality. Time, therefore, expressed in terms of past, present, and future, is essentially envisaged in this disturbingly suspensive perspective. For Roland Barthes's characteristically bold assertion that "Racinian time" is always circular rather than progressive (*Sur Racine* 58), *Mithridate* at least provides one piece of evidence.

It is widely accepted that in Racine's plays the past weighs heavily on the dramatic action. This cannot, however, be taken as some defining feature of "Racinian tragedy," unless "Racinian" qualities can be found in plays such as *Hamlet* or Corneille's *Cinna*. In *Mithridate* a variant of this idea is the extent to which the present, seen as movement and progression, is as though crushed by things past.

> Ce cœur nourri de sang, et de guerre affamé,
> Malgré le faix des ans et du sort qui m'opprime,
> Traîne partout l'amour qui l'attache à Monime, (458-60)

This inability to live and move in the present time is expressed in different metaphors of denial, such as slavery, imprisonment, unpaid debt, and suffocation:

> [...] de mon devoir esclave infortunée
> A d'éternels ennuis je me voie enchaînée. (643-45)

When, for example, Monime feels able to breathe again, the respite is quite illusory: Mithridate reminds her that a promise made in the past ties them together "Par des nœuds éternels" (1276). Monique for her part vitrifies the relationship in terms such as *reconnaissance*, *obéissance*, and *respect* (1323-27). In the context, it is difficult to agree with Richard Goodkin that she is "the moving element in the play that enables the other elements to move" ("Mithridate" 208). The "nœuds éternels" are embodied in that ambiguous royal *bandeau* which ties her to Mithridate, an asphyxiating presence from the past, sign and symbol of present loss, whose associations are well brought out by Harry Barnwell (*"Mithridate"* 187). When Monime tries to use this for what is a real strangulation, it goes without saying that the attempt is unsuccessful: like Mithridate himself, she manages neither to live nor die. Ironically, Monime and Xipharès exhort each other with a "Vivez," as though this was something they could not themselves manage to do (1213, 1265). This suspension of life is expressed in the "silence éternel" (698) in which Monime has buried her love for Xipharès, himself described by the king as "de tout temps à mes ordres soumis" (465). After Mithridate has tricked her into expressing her real feelings, this silence becomes a choice of death:

> Et le Tombeau, Seigneur, est moins triste pour moi,
> Que le lit d'un Époux, qui m'a fait cet outrage, (1350-51)

This sense of life not lived in the present is acutely rendered in those two elements that paradoxically constitute the staple of the play's action: waiting and fleeing. All the characters wait. They wait to be free, to love, to win, or to die. At the very outset the audience is presented with a Pharnace who "attend tout maintenant de Rome, et du Vainqueur" (26) in order to begin his real life. He is impatiently waiting for Monime, who is herself waiting for Mithridate:

> Jusques à quand, Madame, attendrez-vous mon Père?
> Des témoins de sa mort viennent à tous moments
> Condamner votre doute et vos retardements.
> [...]
> Mais il faut, croyez-moi, sans attendre plus tard,
> Ainsi que notre hymen presser notre départ.
> Nos intérêts communs, et mon cœur le demandent.
> Prêts à vous recevoir mes vaisseaux vous attendent, (224-40)

Monime for her part is still waiting to live and breathe, with "ce triste cœur [...] dont jamais encor je n'ai pu disposer" (161-62). As for Xipharès, he awaits orders from Monime. Indeed, when he is enjoined by her to leave, despite the immediate action he feels is needed, his only action is to wait again. The line quoted earlier, to suggest that there is a whiff of urgency in *Mithridate*, is immediately qualified:

> Cours par un prompt trépas abréger ta misère.
> Toutefois observons et Pharnace, et mon Père. (751-52)

At the very least this is an unusual temporal perspective, not used by Racine in other plays. It strongly suggests that, in *Mithridate* as in *Bérénice*, there is some need to look at the play's dramatic structure in a different light from that of a supposedly more "Racinian" tragedy such as *Andromaque*. Bernard Weinberg finds that *Mithridate* "is more effective as rhetoric than as drama" (212). The implication is that the words spoken by characters do not advance the dramatic action, as in the first scene of Act IV, when Monime waits for Xipharès to appear. Here, as always, care must be taken not to confuse the dramatic action with a series of physical actions that have visible consequences. Action on stage is not always fuelled by what Hamlet calls "the native hue of resolution" (3.1.84). Self-evidently, be it in *Hamlet* or in *Huis Clos*, an inability to act can be the very basis of a dramatic action. In *Mithridate*, similarly, the reality of that action is expressed in phrases such as "Que tarde Xipharès?" (1131). A revealing cameo is when Mithridate, confronted with a Monime who refuses him, responds with "J'attends pour me déterminer" (1357), to which she replies: "J'attendrai mon arrêt" (1373). In the "real" world imagined by Hollywood, this might not be called "real action." It is no less real for that.

## A flight in time

The king crystallizes these disparate elements of refusal and inaction in a single word, *fuite*. To the extent that flight here assumes the proportions of a tragic illusion, it is difficult to accept, as even Charles Mauron seems to do (123), one image commonly given of the king, that of a noble, Promethean figure single-handedly struggling against fate and the might of Rome. Mithridate's illusion is triple: that of past glory where flight is confused with victory, that of a present in which a hopeless cause will become an element of surprise, and that of future conquest, in what is a final flight into unreality.

The prime falsification is that of the past:

> Non plus comme autrefois cet heureux Mithridate,
> Qui de Rome toujours balançant le destin,
> Tenais entre elle et moi l'Univers incertain. (436-38)

It is quite natural to view the King Mithridates of history, like the Pyrrhus of legend, first and foremost as a great warrior. The Pyrrhus and Mithridate of Racine's plays, however, are something different. They are characters created for a distinct and autonomous dramatic action, and existing only through it. Just as the Pyrrhus of *Andromaque* is characterized by a passionate love he will go as far as civil war to fulfill, so in *Mithridate* the eponymous hero is, more than anything else, a busted flush. Past defeats, and a military career spent running away, are subsumed in a single word: *gloire*. The burning presence of the glory days recalls the amputee's sensation of a phantom limb. This is never more evident than in the long speech that begins Act III, whose "incoherent elements" are detailed in the Rudler edition (82-83). Here Roman triumphs are minimized and ridiculed ("gravant en airain ses frêles avantages," 767), his own retreats are presented as triumphs ("l'Ennemi par ma fuite trompé," 765), and his victories are fashioned with imagination and thin air:

> Le Bosphore m'a vu, par de nouveaux apprêts,
> Ramener la Terreur du fond de ses marais,
> Et chassant les Romains de l'Asie étonnée
> Renverser en un jour l'ouvrage d'une année. (769-72)

Just as the king in the kingdom of his mind transforms past retreats and defeats into cunning victory strategies, just so he represents the catastrophic present. The initial "je suis vaincu" (439) is quickly forgotten. He does, it is true, sometimes seem to sail uncomfortably close to the truth:

> Vaincu, persécuté, sans secours, sans États,
> Errant de mers en mers, et moins Roi que Pirate. (562-63)

This picture, however, is only a hypothesis. It allows Mithridate to affirm that, even if this complete shipwreck were to occur, his "naufrage élevé" would be preferred by kings anywhere to their own kingdom (566-69). It is henceforth without irony, and in the service of a rhetoric of persuasion, that "je fuis" is raised as a standard of revolt (759). When Mithridate points again to his past glory to declare that "ce temps-là n'est plus. Je régnais, et je fuis" (1041), the tacit admission of defeat is made only in order to trap Monime: he does not believe a word of it. Whether or not Mithridate's dissimulation is acceptable for a monarch is not here the issue. What matters is the king's desire for Monime to accept the one self-image he will tolerate:

> Ne me regardez point vaincu, persécuté.
> Revoyez-moi vainqueur, et partout redouté. (1293-94)

This flight from the present is paralleled by the king's headlong rush into a literally unbelievable future strategy of re-conquest:

> Tout vaincu que je suis, et voisin du naufrage,
> Je médite un Dessein digne de mon courage. (431-32)

Despite an implied admission of total defeat, Mithridate projects himself into a future of new conquests he sees already to be as glorious as his imagined past (559). Ironically in a play taking place in one particular place on one particular day, the action that concerns him is not in the here and now, but either in a past expressed solely by "Gloire," or in the future, "loin d'ici," "demain":

> Ma Gloire loin d'ici vous et moi nous appelle,
> Et sans perdre un moment pour ce noble dessein,
> Aujourd'hui votre Époux, il faut partir demain. (544-46)

> Demain, sans différer, je prétends que l'Aurore
> Découvre mes Vaisseaux déjà loin du Bosphore. (855-56)

From the play's first performance the temporal fantasies in Mithridate's planned military expeditions have attracted comment (Mesnard Ed. 3.57). The king has ambitious plans:

> Je vous rends dans trois mois au pied du Capitole.
> Doutez-vous que l'Euxin ne me porte en deux jours
> Aux lieux où le Danube y vient finir son cours, (796-98)

It is then difficult to believe, with Raymond Picard, that "the future of the world hangs in the balance," a comment that in any case seems to be at odds with the critic's statement some lines later that "Mithridate's situation is the lost cause of a defeated king who is being hunted down" (Ed. 598-99). These plans are less enlightening about the king's grasp of strategy than about his grip of temporal reality. What he feels he has to do, in his unreal present, becomes something he imagines he can and will do in the future, because he could have done it in the past. In these circumstances it is not so much a question of valour struggling against fate as bravado toying with desperation: "Je vais à Rome, [...] Je le dois, je le puis" (1387-89). Mithridate's portentous "Enfin l'heure est venue" (755), which might at first seem to put the present back on the agenda, in fact relates to this future fantasy. This subversion of present reality by future plans is nowhere better symbolized than by his repeated references to the ships waiting to take him away:

> Mes vaisseaux qu'à partir il faut tenir tout prêts. (622)

> Les Vaisseaux sont tout prêts. (953)

> Tandis que mes soldats prêts à suivre leur Roi,
> Rentrent dans mes vaisseaux, pour partir avec moi; (1273-74)

The king does not yet know that this is an imaginary voyage, not because of cruel destiny, but, more cruelly still, because his soldiers are unwilling to sail. It is a classic irony: the man celebrated for his dissimulation conceals reality from himself.

Between past glory and imagined new conquests, all these temporal references thus translate Mithridate's inability to keep both feet on the firm land of the present tense: "Sortant de mes Vaisseaux, il faut que j'y remonte" (1047). In that present he ends up by doing nothing. Within the suspended life which is that of the play, it is as though all were shadowboxing, and nothing in reality could be done. In that reality, where acts have consequences, he who would set out to march into Rome now finds himself tracked down by the Romans to the extreme limits of what in the real present is the Roman world. The great king and general is unable even to control the parcel of land to which the remnant of his army has withdrawn.

This imitation of inaction does not seem to square with the fact that many things do in fact happen in the play, especially at the end. Maurice Descotes, for example (*Les grands rôles* 114), has counted several *coups de théâtre*: the unexpected return of Mithridate, Pharnace's rebellion and the arrival of the Romans, the unexpected intervention of Mithridate's messenger, the news of the defeat of the Roman army, and the arrival of a dying king. Did Racine not himself declare in his second Preface that he had included in his tragedy most of Mithridate's famous deeds? In addition, is there not a sense of urgency created, as in the other tragedies? Is Monime not almost murdered? Are the Romans not defeated by Xipharès?

In response one might point out that the legacy of Mithridate's "famous deeds" dissolves in a death that leaves Asia Minor more subjected to Rome than at the beginning of the king's military career. It is thus difficult to agree with Noémi Hepp, comparing *Mithridate* with *Bérénice* and *Britannicus*, that Rome in this play just provides background scenery, with a poetic rather than a dramatic role (101). In the real time that exists beyond the palace of Nymphée, as Jean Dubu points out (*"Mithridate"* 25), the present is defined and bounded by Rome, as hard a fact of history as in *Bérénice*. Rome is a measure of concrete political reality. That the king's death is real or reported does not change a lesson of powerlessness and futility delivered, at the outset, in a mocking chiasmus:

> Ainsi ce Roi, qui seul a durant quarante ans
> Lassé tout ce que Rome eut de Chefs importants,
> Et qui dans l'Orient balançant la Fortune
> Vengeait de tous les Rois la querelle commune,

> Meurt, et laisse après lui pour venger son trépas,
> Deux Fils infortunés qui ne s'accordent pas. (9-14)

As for the necessity for hasty action that characters urge on others, one cannot say that this has an obvious effect. If characters move, it is to run on the spot, in a place very different from the terrifying, claustrophobic *lieu* of impending doom depicted in *Britannicus*. It is apposite, for example, that Monime should end up by not taking the poison, just as she has not been able to strangle herself. A sense of suspension and displacement is conveyed in the words spoken, which do not seem to mesh with an outside world of Roman reality. The important thing that happens is that nothing important happens.

This idea of a suspension, and of a death in life paradoxically represented by a dramatic action, is certainly in contradiction with the idea of a "happy ending" conveyed for many by the king's pardon of his son, and the projected union of the lovers. For Alain Niderst, what he calls "*Mithridate* opera" is Racine's "most optimistic play" (136), and Christian Delmas speaks of "a 'sublime' climate of apotheosis" which sweeps all else away ("Stratégie" 124). Terms such as "optimistic" or "positive" abound in many other accounts of the play.[5] Whether one's position here be "optimistic" or "pessimistic" (and the validity of these uncertain descriptors will be considered in Chapter 3), the tragic action of *Mithridate* can be shown to concern a king whose kingdom has little reality, who feigns death to save his life, and who in an ultimate reversal, thereby loses the last little part of the life over which he has dominion, and his last reason for living. Nor is the loss only for one man. Neither the death of Mithridate, nor the survival of Monime and Xipharès, change the nature of existences that from the beginning are a kind of death in life. This is not exactly the "serenity" that Jean Rohou has claimed for the play (*Jean Racine* 285). It is equally difficult to side with what seems to be the majority view, that Mithridate's pardon of his son is a striking demonstration of "moral generosity" and "human heroism" (e.g. Parish 101), if only because there is evidence pointing in the direction of Roland Barthes's con-

---

[5] e.g. Goldmann, *Dieu caché* 296; Parish, p. 101; Phillips, *Mithridate* 68. Between "optimists" and "pessimists," here, Schröder, "Mithridate" 157 (note 24), and Spencer 329, maintain a median position.

tention that the pardon is compelled by *force majeure*, a "gesture of empty absolution" which changes nothing (*Sur Racine* 108). Mithridate will die, and the Romans will eventually triumph, despite the king's prediction of a future Parthian victory (removed by Racine after the first edition). In addition, as Eugène Vinaver suggests (*Poésie tragique* 77), it would seem unwise to place too much reliance on words of forgiveness uttered by someone famous above all for "dangereux détours" and "trompeuses adresses" (369-72), a man who in the play has already faked his own death and the disinterested renunciation of his love.

To see *Mithridate* as a structure of suspension is also one way of addressing the criticism that the dramatic action loses its way when the struggle between father and son is resolved in Act IV. To claim that the play suddenly begins lacking in dramatic interest at this point is to predicate a normative "Racinian" plot as in *Andromaque*. It is also to suppose that the main dramatic structure in *Mithridate* is built from this one interpersonal conflict. If, on the other hand, the focus is placed on the particular temporal dimension given to the plot, it can be suggested that in this play the main conflict is always that between illusion and reality. It is true that Mithridate recognizes his error in suspecting Pharnace, and that this is in strict accordance, as Georges Forestier points out (Ed. 1538), with the Aristotelian pattern of error, reversal, and recognition. It might be asked, however, if the sense of "recognition" engendered by the dramatic action as a whole is limited to a single act of recognition by one character. Racine was, after all, the experienced dramatist who admired the dramatic technique that, in *Œdipus Rex*, allows the audience to discover what is hidden to the character (Mesnard Ed. 5: 235). It could therefore be argued that any "recognition" is primarily for those who watch or read the play. For in the final act Mithridate is still living in those shadowlands where life and time are not invested with the hard reality of stubborn fact. The long death-throes of a king who no longer has any reason to live, but who does not know how to die, neatly encapsulate and crown the whole dramatic action. Even death itself seems to run away

> *C'en est assez*, m'a-t-il dit, *cher Arbate.*
> *Le sang, et la fureur m'emportent trop avant.*
> *Ne livrons pas surtout Mithridate vivant.*
> *Aussitôt dans son sein il plonge son épée.*
> *Mais la mort fuit encor sa grande Âme trompée.* (1604-8)

Some have spoken of "grandeur" and "glory" here. But, as Christian Biet stresses ("Mithridate" 88), the "glory" of this act has an ambiguous quality, since it is a mere substitute for a poison that has no longer any effect. It is also difficult to accept Michael O'Regan's claim that "the Mithridate who sees the approach of death is free of passions, pretensions, and illusions" (10). The king's final words show a blindness that remains complete until the end:

> J'ai vengé l'Univers autant que je l'ai pu.
> La Mort dans ce projet m'a seule interrompu.
> Ennemi des Romains, et de la Tyrannie,
> Je n'ai point de leur joug subi l'ignominie. (1657-60)

A further irony is that Mithridate will finally die at the very moment that his son wins a skirmish with the Romans that would have allowed the father's illusions of success to persist. It is only fitting that Xipharès, worthy son of his father, should at the end stride off into this brave new world of the past: "Et par tout l'Univers cherchons-lui des Vengeurs" (1710). In a tragedy of suspended time, the death of the tragic illusion is, quite literally, interminable.

*Mithridate*, then, is different, as *Bérénice* is different. But it is not so much different from Racine's other tragedies as from a supposed norm of "Racinian tragedy." This difference, however, does not mean that its structure is somehow flawed, or that its tragic quality is thereby diminished. On the contrary, as Micheline Servin witnessed with the 1990 Gillibert production, an audience can witness in *Mithridate* a coherent dramatic action that generates, and is driven by, a truly tragic sense of loss and waste that permeates the human condition itself. It is a play about death and the denial of time. It concerns not just a physical death, but the death of a desire for domination pursued in full flight from that most implacable of enemies: present reality. In both its structure and its vision *Mithridate* is thus a symphony of negation. The dominant chords are those of defeat, retreat, inconsequence, and impotence. If this difference is a "flaw," it is a truly remarkable one, through which Racine allows audiences and readers to experience something of our fractured human condition. Not bad for what François Mauriac calls "the least significant of his masterpieces" (118).

## The Uses of Time: *Athalie*

### The Unity of Time

The attempt to signal important differences between Racine's tragedies will not play well everywhere. "Differences"? For the typical Anglo-Saxon coming to these works for the first time, the fundamental "difference" might well be that separating "French classical tragedy" and the rest. Here "the Rules" can be made to seem like high walls isolating Corneille, Racine, and their colleagues from a freer and more colorful world outside. Add to this perceived uniformization a product such as "Racine," seemingly harmonized by adherence to a rigid aesthetic code, and it is easy to see why talk of "difference" might be greeted with a wry smile. However, *Bérénice* and *Mithridate* have already allowed a glimpse of the original way in which Racine uses the time dimension in his plotting. In this context it seems worthwhile asking whether this expression of difference applies also to his approach to one of those supposedly homogenizing Rules, the Unity of Time, and to ask this question of the "classical tragedy" where this convention is most strictly adhered to, *Athalie*. For in this play, as in *Bérénice* and *Mithridate*, Racine adopts another quite distinctive approach to the use of time, which allows the term "unity" to be seen in a new light.

For the robust Anglo-Saxon, the Unity of Time has traditionally tended to seem a curiosity, if not an absurdity, belonging to a forgotten world of recondite literary quarrels. Even D'Aubignac, High Priest of punditry, admits he finds the Unity of Time difficult to explain, and the quarrels surrounding it slightly absurd:

> In our age no subject has been more controversial [...]. Playwrights discuss it often, and actors for their part talk about it at every turn, as do those who go to the theater, while those women who hold court in their bedchamber invariably set about laying down the law on this matter. (171)

What is the rule? Quite simply ... that the action must take place in one day. It was in this very "simplicity" that some of the quarrels began. For no-one could agree on what exactly was meant by the statement by Aristotle that is the classical authority for the doctrine:

"Tragedy endeavors to keep as far as possible within a single circuit of the sun" (ch. 5). How many hours are in a "normal" or "natural" day? Whatever the precise interpretation, the same fundamental point was being made: the dramatic time of the play's action should not be excessively longer than the actual performance time. The criterion of *vraisemblance* was guarding the premises. For if the dramatic action went beyond a day, the reasoning went, how could it seem true, and how therefore could spectators suspend their restless disbelief? And woe betide the dramatist, such as Corneille with *Le Cid*, who tried to cram too much into that one permitted day.[6]

Faced with this "foreign" convention of time, the Anglo-Saxon man of common sense and no nonsense has traditionally protested against the unnecessary restrictions placed on creative freedom, witness Dryden's "Essay of Dramatic Poesy" (1: 48). Shakespeare's appeal to his audience, in the Prologue to *Henry V*, seems uncontroversial: "On your imaginary forces work" (18), and "Piece out our imperfections with your thoughts" (23). Since everything is in the mind and the imagination, everything within reason can be imagined:

> For 'tis your thoughts that now must deck our kings,
> Carry them here and there, jumping o'er times,
> Turning th'accomplishment of many years
> Into an hour-glass. (28-31)

The author of the anonymous *Discours à Cliton*, composed a few years before Corneille was wrapped over the knuckles for *Le Cid*, showed that such thoughts were not foreign to France:

> The object of Dramatic Poetry is to imitate any action, at any time and in any place, so that nothing can happen in the world, for whatever reason, that drama cannot represent, and this whatever the representation of time that is given, or whatever the country, or however big or distant it is. (qtd. in Pasquier, 115)

---

[6] For Scudéry's attack on Corneille, see Gasté, pp. 94-95. For contemporary reflections on the Unity of Time, see d'Aubignac, 171-91; Chapelain, 113-26; Corneille, *Writings* 71-75. For modern commentaries, see Bray, 253-57; Scherer, *Dramaturgie classique* 110-18; Lyons, *Kingdom of Disorder* 173-87. On the aesthetic implications, see Kintzler 118; Lapp, 38-65; Vinaver, *Entretiens* 48-58.

Why then the Unity of Time? Does it not needlessly pinion the eagle imagination? Here it should be remembered that for d'Aubignac (175), the actual performance time of a play is only one element: within the established convention, the only important sense of time is what is fashioned by the dramatist's own plot and what the audience experiences. In other words, Racine's use of time is perhaps not so far from that of Shakespeare here as some might tend to think. In this context *Athalie* serves well as an illustration of such perennial questions, and as one particular response. The theological implications of the play will be examined in a later chapter. However, in a chapter seeking to illustrate some of the different plotting techniques used by Racine, it is worth nothing how the dramatist renews the relationship between performance time and dramatic time in a Biblical drama where chronological references occupy a self-evidently important place. In so doing he not only exploits an apparent restriction as a powerful emotional weapon. As Judd Hubert has suggested (140), Racine also manages, at the end of a golden age of tragic drama, to expand and enrich the whole concept of Unity of Time.

In the other tragedies the day chosen for the dramatic action is made crucial by an event that sets off a whole sequence: Oreste arrives, Junie is arrested, Hippolyte and Phèdre confess their love. Following a path already signposted by Corneille (*Writings* 75), in *Athalie* Racine chooses a day in itself significant, in this case the Jewish feast of Pentecost. Abner's opening words mark the importance of this day:

> Je viens, selon l'usage antique et solennel,
> Célébrer avec vous la fameuse journée,
> Où sur le mont Sina la Loi nous fut donnée. (2-4)

On this "fameuse journée," "ce grand jour" (159, 377), "ce jour à jamais auguste et renommé" (333), the action starts at dawn and finishes a few hours later (for the debate on exactly when, see Mesnard Ed. 3: 615). Athalie brings the time sequence to an end, when she accuses God of having "vingt fois en un jour à moi-même opposée" (1776). The day, and this particular day, is therefore central. But there is an important difference here between *Athalie* and Racine's other plays: the continuity of action between exposition and denouement, with only the Chorus to play gently with the audience's sense of time. In other words, things are made to seem to happen "in real time." What you see is what you get. For Voltaire this was a dramatic ideal, marrying nature and art (Moland 55: 1052). Jacques Truchet ("*Athalie*" 197) remarks on the quasi-liturgical nature of this correlation of dramatic and performance time. Georges Forestier deftly summarizes its implications:

> This was the only means of perfectly recreating the "mimetic illusion" which the whole of classical drama had been striving to attain: preventing the spectator from remembering that he is at the theater by giving him the illusion that he is witnessing something that is actually taking place before his eyes. This is particularly appropriate in a work that is telling the only really true story, the one spelled out by God. (Ed. 1713)

*Athalie*, therefore, marks quite a distinctive use of time by Racine. It is here, however, that one might object. "Preventing the spectator from remembering that he is at the theater" is a tall order. It clearly depends on other, more important factors, such as the playwright's ability to engage the audience in the action of the play. An audience's sense of time depends primarily on how the play is constructed, that is, on the plot: the imagination is all. If Racine accepts the Unity of Time in the most restrictive way possible, it is because there are good dramatic reasons for doing so.

The first of these is the creation of dramatic suspense. It is true that in tragedies such as *Andromaque* or *Iphigénie* innocent victims seem destined for sacrifice unless decisions are made, and made without delay. But in *Athalie* the pressure of time mounts from within the exposition, with phrases such as "L'heure me presse. Adieu" (295), or "Hâtez-vous" (383). On Athalie's side there reigns at first a certain indecision. The woman who is said to know the price of every second (874) makes her entry giving urgent instructions (436), but then shows uncertainty as to how to deal with the child in the Temple. Her procrastination is abruptly ended, on Mathan's urging, with a demand for the child which is tantamount to a declaration of war: "Les feux vont s'allumer, et le fer est tout prêt" (898). The impression that "Le temps est cher" (1629) is reinforced not just by sudden entrances with dramatic news, but by a whole lexis of alarm, as in references to "notre heure dernière" (1512), and by syntactic devices such the series of short, breathless questions (1557-60). In other words, adherence to the strictest interpretation of the Unity of Time is here no idle ornament, nor does it operate as an arbitrary, external restriction on the dramatist's freedom to create. Racine exploits the short time available to him to generate a sense of urgency and peril, and thus increase the emotional pressure, as Patricia Gauthier points out (231). Compression facilitates combustion.

## *The dimensions of time*

It is not just a fusty dramatic convention that is renewed by Racine. In a significant and original way he also transforms and enriches the very meaning of the phrase "Unity of Time," and this from the opening line: "Oui, je viens dans son Temple adorer l'Éternel." In *Athalie* the dimension of the eternal is essential. This is not just a question of "Un Dieu, tel aujourd'hui qu'il fut dans tous les temps" (126). In this new dramatic dimension time is one. On stage, continuously present, and re-presented, are past and future, memory and promise. In other tragedies Racine does of course use past and future events to colour the dramatic action. An example is the exploitation of the Trojan War in *Andromaque* and *Iphigénie*, or the memory of Augustus and references to Néron's coming tyranny in *Britannicus*. But only in *Athalie* is there the sense of time, past, present, and future, as a real unity of experience. Paradoxically and triumphantly, this sense is conveyed through the playing-out of a single action, in a single place, at a particular moment in time.

For the Chosen People, as Harriet Stone stresses in her study of history and memory in *Athalie*, the past is very clearly a living part of the present. The play's action appropriately takes place in the Temple, within a community dedicated to a daily ritual commemoration, laid down in the distant past for all posterity: "Du Dieu que nous servons tel est l'ordre éternel" (441). Like these religious rituals themselves *Athalie* is filled with references to specific moments in history that are seen to matter now. It is small wonder that Racine took pains in his Preface to outline salient details from the Old Testament. In his play, reference is made, as in a liturgy, to foundational events such as the Law given to Moses on Mount Sinai, the priestly succession of Aaron, Abraham's sacrifice, and, above all, the kingship and inheritance of David: "Souviens-toi de David, Dieu, qui vois mes alarmes" (424). The catechism of kingship, as inculcated by Joad and recited by Joas, is based on a history of good and bad rulers (1285-88). It is true that there is a similar pointing to past models in *Britannicus*: will Néron resemble the model emperor Augustus or the monster Caligula? But in *Athalie* there is no important scene without reference to a past which can be appealed to or regretted, a past never more alive than in the present crisis. The setting of present alarms in this dimension of time is one of the functions fulfilled by the Chorus: in Act I, for example, this involves the Creation, Mount Sinai, the Exodus, the parting of the Red Sea, the water springing from the rock, all in a celebration of the Law seen to be as relevant now as in the time of Moses. *Athalie* is strongly colored with the liturgy of commemoration.

History here is memory, and memory is selection. Each character selects from the past according to desires, needs, and fears, or else forgets it (Hammond 110). For Abner past promises are a utopic reproach to the present time of infidelity and forgetfulness (15-20). Josabeth draws from history the fatalistic idea that the sins of the past always burden the present (235-40). And Joad brandishes past and recent history not just as a triumphant banner of God's power (104-24), but also as a motivating reminder that carnage committed in the name of God can become an obligation and a "noble exploit" (1360-68). For Athalie, on the other hand, history is betrayal and revenge. It obtrudes obsessively on everything she says and does. One of her very first statements, "Je ne veux point ici rappeler le passé" (465), is merely a rhetorical flourish. Her memory of the bloody fate of her own family, seen as an act of blind revenge by this God for an obscure original sin of rebellion (711-16), means that the very mention of the name David evokes a history of injustice (729). It is in terms of this history that she expresses her present animosity to David's descendants, and it is through those same ancestral voices that she expresses her defeat: "David, David triomphe" (1773).

Racine thus expands the dimension of time available to him by making the past indivisibly part of the present. He similarly exploits the potential of future time, in what Nina Ekstein, in her study of this concept in Racine's theater, calls "a complex interplay of futures" that produces "a high degree of dramatic irony" (61). This is not merely the immediate future of the spectator's anticipation with which the dramatist plays in creating suspense, but that future which stretches beyond the immediate dramatic action. Unsurprisingly, the future is judged according to the past, and viewed just as ambiguously. The play is filled with allusions to Joas's coming betrayal, and to the promise of a messiah. This ambiguity is a perfect weapon in the hands of the dramatist, fusing the demands of the plot with all the uncertainties of God and man. It is also a way of binding past, present, and future into one, in a dramatic action that, however it be interpreted, challenges the apparent realities of the here and now.

In chapter 9 of his *Confessions* St Augustine speaks of the unreality of past and future, and of "a present of things past, a present of things present, a present of things to come" (235). It is within this shifting continuous present that Racine constructs the dramatic action of *Athalie*. Paradoxically that present is necessarily a movement, within which are played out the unresolved contradictions, ambiguities, and ironies of past and future. Here an audience can experience a past continually present, a future rooted in the past, both past and future enriching a present that is thereby invested with density and complexity beyond that of the immediate and contingent. This present time is given meaning only by a past and future that by definition do not exist, yet have an overwhelming presence. This unity of time, within an ambiguous vision of the *éternel*, by turns threatening and providential, is compelling, disturbing and, in Racine's work, quite new.

The treatment of time in *Athalie* is thus as complex and original as in *Bérénice* and *Mithridate*. The presumption must be that similar singularities and differences may be found in the plotting of the other tragedies, and thus in the problems posed by each tragic action, and in the way they might be addressed. Is it certain that each particular identity can be respected, and its quiddity registered, in any "Racinian tragic vision" currently on offer? Unless, of course, critics choose to speak in terms of "exceptions." And if so, exceptions to what? It is this question that now deserves some attention.

Chapter 2

EXCEPTIONS AND EXPECTATIONS:
"RACINE" AND *BAJAZET*

OVER the past three centuries, implicitly or explicitly in a vast number of critical works, a series of tragedies by Jean Racine has become a homogeneous body of work called "Racinian tragedy." It can be argued that it was Racine himself who initiated this transformation, in his successive compilations of his "complete" works, each time in a form that rendered the image he wished to give. This metamorphosis of different works into one coherent body is so far from being controversial as to be accepted almost without question. It is all the more persuasive in that "Racine" is seen as the quintessential "classical" author, as though this term itself pointed unambiguously to the uncontroversial aesthetic norms of a clearly defined period of literary history. Even Christopher Braider, though acutely conscious that the term "Racine" is a historico-critical artifact constructed *a posteriori*, can speak in terms that seem to define and thus contain a standardized entity complete unto itself: "The tragedies of Racine are in the strongest possible sense great works of art, displaying the precision and balance, the self-disciplined autonomy and reasoned self-containment classical doctrine prescribes" (326).

However, even those who propose detailed expositions of *le tragique racinien* generally have to acknowledge one small problem: "exceptions." This is a question of a sort once familiar to those prescriptive linguists for whom language *should* be spoken (and often, spoken as it *should* be written) in certain ways. What is not spoken in the prescribed way is therefore treated either an exception to a norm, or a falling away from that norm. Modal verbs, for example, were described and treated, in French textbooks of English grammar, as *les défectifs*, because they lacked the "normal" tenses of "normal" verbs. Ideas of "Racine" and/or "Racinian tragedy" have some similarities with this notion of language. Lucien Goldmann, for example, considered that only three of Racine's tragedies measured up to his standard fit, *le tragique racinien*. Thus *Andromaque* is "*almost* tragic," and tragedy in *Athalie* "is no longer tragic in a proper sense of the word" ("Structure" 259, 264). In the same spirit, *Mithridate* and *Iphigénie* are not classed by Jean Rohou as "authentic tragedies" but as "dramas of love and heroism" (*Bilan critique* 47). The critical recipe here is straightforward, however rich the ingredients. In other words, start with an idea. Support this idea by quotations that, though necessarily selective, are extensive enough to give a sense of pattern. Then link the pattern uncovered by the initial idea to other such patterns, for the final result. Who could complain? The critical procedure is general and uncontroversial. More contentious, however, is the seductively simple objective: totality of explanation. In this way the initial idea becomes the norm against which everything is judged. What does not correspond to the idea is thus, by definition, an "exception."

The problem with "Racine," however, is that there seem to be as many "exceptions" as there are tragedies. As Raymond Picard puts it, "Racine, dites-vous. Quel Racine?" (*Parthénon* 9). In this light, a harmless occupation for a wet Sunday afternoon in the West of Scotland might be to pick out the number of times that different critics have used superlative terms such as "unique" or "exceptional" to qualify Racine's approach in different plays. Thus *Mithridate* has been seen as "a completely unique creation" (Bertaud 182) or as "the least Racinian of Racine's plays" (Dort 12). Similarly, Christian Biet calls *Bérénice* "an exceptional, even experimental play" ("Épique" 131), Georges Forestier finds its treatment of love "unique in the Racinian canon" (Ed. 1444), and Jean Rohou deems it "an exception" (*Évolution* 148). Yet that same play, for Voltaire "the weakest of Racine's tragedies" (Moland 55: 956), has also been viewed as "the most Racinian of the tragedies" (Fonsny 29). *Athalie* is necessarily "exceptional" because of its religious subject, the position occupied by God, because love plays no part, and because of the place occupied by music. For many, *Iphigénie* and *Mithridate* are similarly viewed as "exceptional" because they are considered to have "happy endings." *Andromaque*, naturally enough, is "exceptional" at the very least because each of the two possible endings gives a different coloring to the play. *Phèdre* itself, that tragedy so often considered as most typically "Racinian," is often also set apart from the others, on a higher plane. (Indeed, it is this very conjunction of the "typical" and the "exceptional," in critical studies of *Phèdre*, together with the "unique" status of this play and its heroine, that has motivated the final chapter of this book.) Thus Georges Forestier indicates, for example, that the play at first disorientated Racine's contemporaries, who took some time to realize that "Racine was still Racine," and that Racine had created something completely different "without ceasing to be Racine" (Ed. 1615). A similarly "Racinian" orientation haunts critical approaches to all the tragedies. A paradoxical example comes from René Pommier, in his study of *Britannicus*. With characteristic vigor he denounces Roland Barthes for basing his analysis of the "Racinian Eros" mainly on the character of Néron despite the fact that Néron "is the only character in Racine who finds active pleasure in causing pain" (12). However, he then adds for good measure that, in any case, "*Britannicus* is without a doubt the least Racinian of Racine's great tragedies, definitely less Racinian than *Phèdre*, *Andromaque*, *Bérénice*, or *Bajazet*" (18). In other words, any of the plays can be an exception to the imagined norm of "Racinian tragedy."

Exceptions rhyme with expectations. Certain "classical" qualities are expected from this "Racine," that monument constructed over time that seems always to have existed as such. One thinks of features such as harmony, clarity, logic, proportion. There is, for example, the equation of "Racine" with perfection and a kind of unattainable simplicity of expression, as in Brémond's "Racine simple" (89-123). This, indeed, has acquired the status of a received truth, one that it would be absurd to question. When expectations are not fulfilled, it thus seems reasonable to conclude that the relevant line, scene, play, character, or subject is not quite, or not at all, "Racinian." Racine was not quite himself that day.

*A problem play*

Of all these "exceptions" *Bajazet* is perhaps the most egregious example. Some feel it should be left to one side, while others see it as an archetype. Consider Jean Rohou's attempt to reconcile the admitted particularity of the major tragedies with the centripetal demands of *le tragique racinien*: "While there is a *tragique racinien*, a Racinian vision of the human condition, it is not identical in *Andromaque, Britannicus, Phèdre,* and *Athalie*, and it does not figure so largely in *Mithridate* and *Iphigénie*" (*Bilan critique* 65). For reasons given in the introduction to this book, the omission from this list of *La Thebaïde, Alexandre le Grand,* and *Esther* is, from Rohou's point of view, quite understandable. Curiously, however, *Bajazet* does not figure on the list either. (By a curious coincidence that is purely typographical, Rohou's Pochothèque edition, in its list of Racine's plays, omits *Bajazet*, both on the back jacket and inside the front cover.) Is this play so easily forgotten because, as Eugène Vinaver puts it, Racine in *Bajazet* "seems to forget Racine" (*Poésie tragique* 69)? For Anne Ubersfeld, on the other hand, the play is "one of the summits of Racinian tragedy" ("Auteur tragique" 53), while Georges Forestier declares it to be "one of the most Racinian of Racine's tragedies" (Ed. 1493). In other words, in the midst of "exceptional" plays, *Bajazet* seems to be an exception all on its own. This uncomfortable status suggests questions that are worth some investigation. Why is it *Bajazet* so often considered to be "different"? And does this "exception" shed any light on common expectations of a norm called "Racinian tragedy"?

If, like Molière and Shakespeare, Racine must have his "problem play," then *Bajazet* is an appealing candidate. The problems it presents, however, have not led to it receiving the same degree of critical attention as *Le Misanthrope* or *Measure for Measure*, or indeed as Racine's other "major" tragedies listed by Jean Rohou in his attempt to assess in each case the quality of the *tragique racinien*. Despite having been a thundering success when first performed in 1672, enthusiasm for *Bajazet* soon petered out, and in recent decades performances have been rare. Jacques Scherer suggests that its complications made it difficult to stage (*Bajazet* 295), and Roger Duchêne adds that it is not easy to understand what actually goes on in the play (Cuénin, "Bajazet" 96). This perhaps explains the dismissive tone of Bertrand Poirot-Delpech's review of the 1966 production at the Comédie-Française: "In the stock market of Classical values, *Bajazet*'s share-price has never been very high." In addition, while a trawl through Racinian criticism will bring up many references to *Bajazet*, the bibliography at the end of this book is one witness that there have been comparatively few detailed critical studies of the play as such, with much concentration on linguistic points or on the historical/literary sources. Its absence from the stage of the great Racinian controversies is in itself significant, like Conan Doyle's dog that didn't bark. So what is happening? Is it possible to identify specific reasons for a reception that has been less than enthusiastic? If *Bajazet* does not quite fulfill common expectations of "Racinian tragedy," are there any lessons to be learnt?

Here care must be taken. "Racinian tragedy," for many, represents a kind of perfection. Guy Dumur, for example, called it "the perfect image of a fulfilled literary ideal" (49). It is clear what this implies in practice. "Racine" can often be made to resemble one of those government-designated Areas of Outstanding Beauty, a cultural heritage site composed of matchless masterpieces whose significance may be interpreted, but whose matchless beauty is by definition not open for discussion. Suggest that there are flaws in one particular play, and the heavy artillery is quickly wheeled out: Racine himself in his Preface to *Iphigénie*, Voltaire (Moland 66: 518), Victor Hugo (38) quoting Chateaubriand in the same vein, all of them pouring the writer's holy scorn on nit-picking by would-be critics whose only problem is that they cannot themselves write. François Lagarde has tellingly quoted Théophile Gautier's reaction to this enthronement of "Racine" in the nineteenth century:

> You can turn your back on God, on the Monarchy, on the Family; you can put forward the strangest opinions, the boldest theories; but there is one thing that will make even the most intrepid person tremble, and that is to attempt to suggest even the slightest criticism of Racine. ("Réception de Racine" 119)

Things have moved on, a little. No-one wishes to play the role of Baillet's *chicaneur*, the pathetic quibbler "who only sets out to examine a book in order to find things to criticize in it" (96). And indeed, David Bellos (xxv) with some justice derides the "schoolmasterly" approach of sterile fault-finders like La Harpe. The facts, however, are stubborn. If "the first rule of all" is to appeal to an audience, and arouse its emotions, as Racine suggests reasonably in his Preface to *Bérénice*, it is a fact that *Bajazet* has not quite connected with many audiences and readers. Various terms that are applied to the play, in scattered critical comments, suggest a certain lack of completeness, of finish. *Bajazet* is found difficult material to work with, or to understand. Micheline Cuénin's admission that this play gave her more problems than any other of Racine's tragedies was in direct response to Pierre Voltz's statement that he had tried and failed to find any satisfactory pattern to the plot (Cuénin 94-95). In the past three centuries critics radically different in background and approach have shown reluctance to give *Bajazet* full membership of that star-studded team, "Racinian tragedy." In La Harpe's *Lycée* it figures as "a second-rate work that could only have been written by a first-rate author" (3: 155), while Gustave Lanson's famous formulation is "Anecdote sanglante" (*Esquisse* 110), a phrase leaving the play poised somewhere between an anecdote and a piece of trivia, with blood added. It seems legitimate to ask why. In his 1992 edition of the play Georges Forestier asserts that "*Bajazet* is in absolute conformity with the principles of classic dramatic theory" (25). That, as will be seen, remains very much an open question. This chapter will attempt to show that this hesitant critical reaction to *Bajazet* owes less to prejudice or fashion than to real problems of credibility and coherence, and that these problems also call into question the credibility and coherence of the entity commonly known as "Racinian tragedy."

At first sight *Bajazet* does seem to present some striking differences from Racine's other tragedies. Its subject is contemporary and Turkish, not distant and classical, while the plot is a convoluted construction of twists, turns, and reversals. Some have attempted to keep statistics here: Jean Rohou reaches a total of twenty-seven murders and five suicides (*Jean Racine* 283), while Georges Forestier has counted seven occasions on which the plot suddenly takes the opposite direction to which it has been proceeding, the definitive character of each reversal being underlined with a "c'en est fait" (Ed. *Bajazet* 140). The plot is rounded off by that "great bloodbath" which Mme de Sévigné found so incomprehensible and ill prepared (1: 459). Whatever view may be taken of the play, it certainly takes the audience far from that expected ideal canvassed heavily from the Third Republic onwards, as in Pierre Robert's chapter "Simplicity of Racinian theatre" (74-103). This ideal is at the heart of the rhetoric used by Racine himself to respond to his critics. It is expressed in his very first dramatic Preface, to *Alexandre le Grand*, and he returns to it in his Preface to *Bérénice*:

> Some think that this simplicity shows a lack of inventiveness. They do not realize, on the contrary, that inventiveness is all about making something out of nothing, and that packing a play full of incident has always been the refuge of playwrights who feel they lack the creative strength and genius to keep hold of their audience for five Acts by means of a dramatic action that is characterized by simplicity, and is sustained by the elegant expression of violent passion and beautiful emotion.

A year after this apparent expression of a dramatic credo was written, Racine wrote *Bajazet*, and seemed openly to turn his back on the ideal so flamboyantly stated. This should encourage some prudence in quoting the Preface to *Bérénice* as a manifesto of "Racinian tragedy."

This said, on closer inspection the particular differences between *Bajazet* and the other tragedies do not seem so great. The last chapter stressed that the plots constructed by Racine do not conform to one particular model. Nor is *Bajazet* the only one of his tragedies in which a "melodramatic" element may be found. In Jacques Truchet's words, "Tragedy is not boulevard drama, but we should not turn the two into polar opposites. Even in this high classical age, suspense and surprise enchanted audiences that hungered for emotion, mystery, and spectacle" (*Tragédie classique* 60). As for Mme de Sévigné's celebrated criticism of *Bajazet*, her declared bias in favor of Corneille does not make her the most objective witness. Paradoxically, it could also be argued that Racine's Prefaces, given their polemical intent, should not be used against him. "Simplicity" is part of that idea of the "Racinian" that the dramatist himself was the first to encourage and fashion.

## Credibility and coherence

Is dissatisfaction with *Bajazet* then linked with what is the obvious difference with the other tragedies, the Turkish subject? Is it a plausible subject for tragedy? This brings up the question of *vraisemblance*, that complex mix of what seemms true and what seems right, of what is fitting and what is plausible or probable.[1]

---

[1] On *vraisemblance*, see Barnwell, *Tragic Drama* 72-92; Bray 191-214; Lyons, *Kingdom of Disorder* 83-139; Scherer, *Dramaturgie classique* 367-82.

*Vraisemblance* always seems to have been a good stick for any seventeenth-century French critic to use when seeking to remind a dramatist that accepted dramatic conventions could not easily be ignored. Here Racine was on his guard, and not just against those in the Corneille camp such as Donneau de Visé who insisted that his characters were really French courtiers got up as Turks. In his second Preface, appropriately called "defensive" by Michèle Longino (195), he argues that geographical distance gives a similar perspective to that afforded by classical antiquity, that the subject of the play is based on true fact, and that everything in it is in conformity with Turkish history, habits, and customs. Nowadays this argument hardly needs to be made. Despite Eugène Vinaver's opinion that the failure of *Bajazet* lies partly with the choice of such an exotic subject (*Poesie tragique* 72), Harry Barnwell makes a convincing case that plausibility depends more on treatment than on subject (*Tragic Drama* 79). After all, the other subjects of Racinian tragedy, though not "exotic," are hardly the stuff of common experience, whether they concern an endless chain of love or the cataclysmic forces unleashed by a declaration of incestuous passion. However familiar these classical subjects might have been for his audience, Racine creates new situations with them, and thus always leads his audience into the unknown. While on one level *Bajazet* represents what Jean-Pierre Collinet calls "a genuine change of scenery" (Ed. 1: 12), each of his tragedies brings a new change of scene, and radically new relationships.

To objections of a general nature these are all fair rejoinders. They do not, however, address the questions of credibility and coherence raised by the plot, characterization, and language of *Bajazet*. Credibility and coherence? This is no place to rehearse fine distinctions of seventeenth-century dramatic theory that have been examined at great length elsewhere. It can be tempting to dismiss anything that smacks of the Rules as some old Aristotelian warhorse long since put out to grass. But it seems self-evident that our pleasure as audience or readers depends to a great extent on a need for credibility and coherence that are at the very heart of those mythical Rules. Put at its simplest, if we accept Du Bos's definition, that an event that is *vraisemblable* is "an event that is possible in the circumstances in which it is made to happen" (1: 228), we are also likely to accept that simple credibility is a requirement of the tragic action: without it, our emotions as an audience cannot for long be engaged. When Racine made the same point in his Preface to *Bérénice*—"only the *vraisemblable* can arouse emotion in tragedy"—it must already have seemed a truism, since he was echoing a similar judgment by D'Aubignac (126), who based his critical work almost entirely on the plays of Corneille. In addition, the tragic action demands a certain wholeness: plot, character, and language must serve together to produce a tragic experience that will work on our minds and emotions.

These abstract criteria may be translated into definite questions. For example, does the situation set out in the exposition seem likely? Does what happens thereafter seem a probable and necessary consequence of what has gone before? Is it clear what role characters are playing? Is their behavior consistent with what the playwright allows the audience to know of them? Does it meet the criteria of ordinary experience, in the situation in which they have been placed? Does what they do and say advance the tragic action? Is the language used an appropriate vehicle for that action? Such questions are relevant to any analysis of the uncertain reception of *Bajazet*. They need to be addressed, if only because inconsistencies and improbabilities will necessarily lessen the emotional impact which the plot is designed to create.

This leads to a first area of inquiry, to what is called the *sérail*. In *Bajazet* this can mean either the sultan's palace or what would now be called the harem. Some parts of the text suggest the first meaning (for example 571, 662), while others suggest the second (for example 875-80), as does the 1676 Preface, which describes it as a place of love and jealous rivalry where the only occupation of women was to play the seduction game. Whatever its ambiguities, Racine depicts this *sérail* as an inner palace of enclosure and exclusion. Those inside cannot leave, and those outside cannot, in theory, enter. This has, of course, tragic possibilities: the Sartrean term *huis clos* is a critical commonplace.[2] But there are problems. The obvious one is the simple need for interaction between characters. This dramatic necessity means that there are important differences between the *sérail* created by Racine and a real or theoretical exclusion zone. "Is it plausible," asks Jacques Scherer, "that the action

---

[2] For different interpretations of the *sérail*, see Dubu, *Racine aux miroirs* 137-48; Scherer, *Bajazet* 187-89; Starre 92-97. On the *huis clos*, see Dort 8; Hepp, "Bérénice, Bajazet, Athalie" 63; Gillibert 50.

should take place where it does? Hardly. It is obvious that Racine was rather troubled by this point, and that he started trying to explain it all" (*Bajazet* 61). And indeed the playwright does expend much energy answering the questions that arise from this initial implausibility. Of these the very first is access:

> Et depuis quand, Seigneur, entre-t-on dans ces Lieux,
> Dont l'accès était même interdit à nos yeux? (3-4)

Acomat at first brushes aside this natural question. An implicit response comes later, in his exposition of the Roxane-Bajazet situation: "Voilà donc de ces Lieux ce qui m'ouvre l'entrée" (201). In other words, there is a need for communication between characters For a start, there can be no love interest without it. Du Bos said it all:

> It follows from the rules of our theatre, and the accepted practice in our political plays, that women always have a major role in the plot, and that love is treated from our own perspective: this in turn prevents us from conforming to the customs and behavior of foreign countries. (1: 149)

In other words, there is reason to doubt Racine's declaration, in his 1672 Preface, that his main endeavor was "not to change anything in Turkish behavior and customs."

This new type of sultan's palace, or harem, where men and women can meet and express their love when the need arises, is doubtless legitimate: dramatists may do what they wish. On the other hand, the slightly incredible nature of this *sérail* necessarily reduces the sinister quality of what is depicted elsewhere as a prison-like environment where secrecy and oppression are absolute: Racine cannot have it both ways. The reality of his *sérail* hardly corresponds to Noémi Hepp's evocation of an oppressive environment "where no-one can reach the light of day" ("*Bérénice, Bajazet, Athalie*" 62), or Sabine Gruffat's judgment that it is "one of the most confined and stifling worlds in Racinian theatre" (121). The possibility of love in a place where Roxane and Bajazet have theoretically not the right even to meet gives rise to potential problems of credibility that Racine is obliged to address at an early stage. He thus plants the question that might naturally come to mind–"Mais pouvaient-ils tromper tant de jaloux regards?"–and then answers it: false rumor of sultan's death, guards bribed, the sultan's spies compromised, a rendezvous achieved (143-64). But another question might then be raised: would people not suspect something if such meetings should continue? Racine attempts to resolve this problem through the bizarre but necessary expedient of using Atalide as a go-between for Roxane and Bajazet. This is necessary for basic dramatic reasons: the eternal triangle has eternal demands. But it is no less bizarre for that. There seems no reason why Atalide should be able to see Bajazet any more, or any more easily, than Roxane herself. And indeed Roxane does see Bajazet, not once but twenty times (277). This leads to a question that to many will appear preposterous, but which is worth asking: why was Atalide necessary in the first place? After all, if Roxane and Acomat, or Atalide and Bajazet, can be alone in a place set apart, where they can speak freely and openly (207), why not Roxane and Bajazet? This "artifice" (353), of having Roxane express her love for Bajazet via Atalide, thus appears artificial indeed. The contrivance seems to exist less for Roxane than for Racine.

This difficulty comes straight from the *sérail*, and the uncomfortable partnership between dramatic requirements and the subject dramatized. A related problem is the co-existence of the harem with traditional ideas of love and marriage. On one side there is the place crammed with beautiful young women from all over Europe and Asia (98-99). On the other, but as though hermetically sealed from the very idea of a harem, is a concept of exclusive romantic love on which Racine's plot is built, with the sultan's choice of Roxane and her own desire for marriage. This cohabitation is, at the very least, a curiosity, unless one accepts Harriet Stone's argument in *Royal Disclosure* that the play's coherence comes from "the Oriental accommodation of mutually exclusive conditions" (107). It demands an initial statement by Amurat–"elle seule a fixé son Amour" (100)–and a somewhat contrived explanation by Roxane to explain the anomaly: "Je sais que des Sultans l'usage m'est contraire..." (290-306). There is then a further summary by Roxane of historical details with which Bajazet is presumably just as familiar, and to which his response is the wooden "Il est vrai" (455-71). These different "explanations" can only hinder the progress of the dramatic action, without achieving any major gain in credibility. As Jacques Scherer has pointed out, suspension of disbelief is not bolstered by the way in which Roxane is shown to fall head over heels in love with Bajazet from the mere description she receives of him from Acomat, a man who claims to know nothing about love (*Bajazet* 55).

The questions asked about the integration of subject and plot may be extended to Racine's handling of time in *Bajazet*. In other tragedies this is complex, varied, and surefooted, and should serve as a warning against using a term such as "stasis" (Muratore 124) as a general descriptor of "Racinian tragedy." The last chapter considered some examples: the use of the ultimatum and the race against time, as in *Andromaque*, the blending of history and time in *Britannicus*, the fusion of past, present, and future in *Athalie*, or the crafting of a suspended time, as in *Bérénice* or *Mithridate*. The plot of *Bajazet*, on the other hand, seems to lose its way somewhere between ultimatum and suspension. It is true that the need to act quickly is often affirmed:

> Peut-être en ce moment Amurat en furie
> S'approche pour trancher une si belle vie. (265-66)

As the play progresses, the necessity to act is rendered even more pressing by the news that the sultan has won his battle, and that Orcan, his avenging minister, is stalking the palace:

> Le temps presse. Que faire en ce doute funeste?
> Allons. Employons bien le moment qui nous reste. (1117-18)

In principle, therefore, the audience is given to believe that there exists a situation of terror and impending death. In practice, despite the various plans, plots, threats, and changes of mind that occupy most of the play, the initial situation does not change within the palace, until the final convulsion. An illustration is the reaction of Roxane. She does nothing, even when she knows that the dangerous Orcan is seeking her "avec impatience" (1105), and when she has discovered Atalide's hidden love for Bajazet (1209). It is easy to see why Acomat seeks a reason:

> Que faites-vous, Madame? En quels retardements
> D'un jour si précieux perdez-vous les moments? (1335-36)

It is more difficult to find a reason that is plausible. Does an audience know why Act V still finds Roxane pressing Bajazet to decide, even though Act II has begun with her warning him that "l'heure fatale est enfin arrivée" (421)? Equally, it seems implausible that her admonition, "Les moments sont trop chers pour les perdre en paroles" (1474), should in fact preface the most extended scene in the last three acts of the play. Thus Roxane's "Pour la dernière fois, Perfide, tu m'as vue," towards the end of Act V (1573), would be more disquieting if it were not a reprise of the scarcely less menacing threat uttered in Act I, "Pour la dernière fois je le vais consulter" (259). Indeed, after this final threat, with crisis and danger supposedly cranked up to the highest possible level, Atalide is still able to deliver to Roxane what is the longest speech of the play outside the first expository scenes. Given that Roxane has, four scenes earlier, prevented Atalide from speaking, and has nothing more to learn from her, the possibility that such a long speech could be delivered somewhat strains belief.

No play of Racine is more crowded with incident than *Bajazet*. And yet these "incidents" do not form part of a logical cause-and-effect structure that brings about the denouement. Those futile acts and declarations that compose the plot, Raymond Picard's "squabbles between prisoners on death row" (Ed. 1: 523), could of course be seen as predicating some bleak Augustinian or pre-Sartrean world where decisions made by characters are absurdly irrelevant to a predetermined outcome, "no more than the dreams of people condemned to death" (Ratermanis 214). After all, the battle has already taken place when the play opens (223), and Orcan is on his way. For Jean Rohou it is a case of purely melodramatic ploys, "derisory games played out in the antechamber of death" (*Jean Racine* 278), while André Blanc (193) finds the subject to be one of the most tragic in Racine's theatre because of the primary importance of events external to the interaction between characters. Perhaps. Here again, however, it is important not to stray too far from the credible and the probable. The characters do not know any more than the audience that the sultan has won the battle, and Orcan's arrival comes as a genuine surprise, a "malheur imprévu" (1109). In addition, they do not see themselves as on some kind of death row, and it is always open to them to take decisions that will change the course of events. Though they act in ignorance, they naturally feel that something can and must be done: they are not "forsaken creatures" (Gillibert 50).

In circumstances of imminent murder, a rhetoric of urgency is understandable. What jars is the unexplained discontinuity between this rhetoric and the inaction that accompanies it. Put simply, the sultan's decision to have Bajazet executed makes it difficult to see what most of the activity is for. This point Forestier seems to have conceded:

> [...] everything we saw happening on stage, and in particular everything concerning the conflictual relationship between Roxane, Atalide, and Bajazet, had no bearing on the direct and mortal relationship that links the sultan Amurat and his brother. It was just an interlude. (Ed. 1500)

It is easy to understand Richard Goodkin's quip that "Roxane and Atalide seem to spend most of the second half of the play reading each other's mail out aloud" ("Performed Letter" 95). This is not the realm explored by *Hamlet* or *Bérénice*. Delay and suspension are not, in *Bajazet*, obviously rooted in some self-tortured exploration of a moral or metaphysical predicament.

The conduct of the plot arouses many similar questions which, taken together, go some way to explaining why *Bajazet* has not managed to hold the interest of many critics as much as the other tragedies. Why, for example, does Roxane suddenly become suspicious of Bajazet? Atalide asks this question (267). Though Roxane explains that she does not find in Bajazet the "trouble" and "ardeur" promised (274-86), the audience does not know why today happens to be the particular day when she notices this reserve. Other questions follow. Does it seem likely, with Bajazet remaining unmoved after six months of pressure, that Roxane, the former slave-girl, should entertain no doubts about the relationship between her intended lover, the sultan's brother, and the chosen go-between, an Ottoman princess, who has been providing rapturous reports so much at variance with Roxane's own experience? This again strains belief, especially in a context where male-female meetings could not be ordinary events. Jules Brody explains this curiosity by suggesting that she has "the psychology of a slave" ("Bajazet" 283), while Michèle Longino asserts that she "lucidly opts for blindness." Such apparent blindness, for Jacques Scherer "highly implausible" (*Bajazet* 81), seems even odder when Roxane's suspicions are awakened by Bajazet's refusal to explain his lack of ardor:

> Quoi donc! Que dites-vous? Et que viens-je d'entendre?
> Vous avez des secrets que je ne puis apprendre!
> Quoi! de vos sentiments je ne puis m'éclaircir? (561-63)

There is a marked contrast between the person who asks such piercing questions and the persona of a totally credulous Roxane seemingly created to explain her strange inability to understand what is going on in front of her very eyes (373-76).

An audience's sense of what is natural and thus believable in human behavior is not accentuated by the next twists in the plot: Bajazet's re-arrest, followed by Roxane's decision to forgive and forget when he seems to promise to marry her. Bajazet's sudden personality change might awaken some doubts even in a person with no reason to be suspicious or jealous. But Roxane only declares, credulously, how wonderfully incredible it all is:

> L'auriez-vous cru, Madame, et qu'un si prompt retour
> Fît à tant de fureur succéder tant d'amour? (1019-20)

In the context of impending catastrophe it would be improper to speak of the gullibility that so often holds center stage in Molière's comedies. That said, could Roxane's credulity still be presented as tragic blindness? It is true that Hermione, for example, believes Pyrrhus's conversion to love in *Andromaque*. But Pyrrhus, unlike Bajazet, is not threatened by instant execution for a refusal. Blinded by passion though she is, Hermione has some reasons to say that a king in his kingdom "veut tout ce qu'il fait; et s'il m'épouse, il m'aime" (*Andromaque*, 850). If Roxane's behavior is to be dismissed as merely foolish, despite the constraints of the tragic genre, it becomes difficult to explain the sharpness of some of her questions. There is certainly a vast and curious gulf between the easy acceptance by a nominally suspicious woman of Bajazet's surrender to love eternal (1039-40), and Bajazet's own embarrassment at her sheer credulity (991). But then, can an audience even get to know what happens in this reconciliation scene between Bajazet and Roxane?

Here it is worth paying attention to the evidence put forward by Nina Ekstein, in her *Dramatic Narrative*. An expert witness, on this occasion she is also a skeptical one. For she points out that three contradictory narratives are given of what happens between Bajazet and Roxane, that not even the spectator finally discovers what has occurred, and that these narratives, by uselessly obscuring the dramatic action, represent "the most complete breakdown of the *récit*'s reliablitity in Racine's theater" (104). This central relationship between Roxane and Bajazet is therefore problematic. Its development is too riddled with inconsistencies and incongruities to be entirely convincing, and thus moving. Coherence and *vraisemblance* are first cousins, and together allow the emotions to be engaged: quite simply, as Boileau observed in his *Art Poétique* III, "we are not moved by what we do not believe." In the circumstances, Will Moore's judgment of *Bajazet* has therefore a paradoxical logic: "There is so little to the dramatic action that we would be bored stiff if we didn't find what happens between Bajazet and Roxane deeply moving" (79).

In the construction of the play what happens between Bajazet and Atalide is perhaps equally important, since Roxane is absent from the whole central section (between Act II Scene 3 and Act III Scene 6). This relationship seems to be equally flawed, however, though for different reasons. There is, first, something incongruous about the plot these two characters hatch, a point well made by Pierre Voltz:

> Their plan seems to be a ramshackle affair. [...] It appears inconceivable that Atalide could draw up the following scheme: Roxane falls in love with Bajazet, Roxane gives the throne to Bajazet, Bajazet marries me and remains grateful to Roxane. All of this is just about possible if we do not know the extent to which Roxane is in love. (94)

A second disconcerting factor is the strange opposition between the supposed situation of terror and what actually happens in the play. For Bajazet, theoretically, this should be a moment of extreme threat. There is, for example, Roxane's injunction "que tout rentre ici dans l'ordre accoutumé" (572), a phrase justly praised as an understated and therefore even more threatening expression of terror. In practice, however, the play's characters meet as before, and the two lovers more than ever. There ensues, as La Harpe pointed out, an uncomfortable disparity between, on the one hand, "the daggers, the cords, the dumb slaves," and, on the other, "love's little anxieties and refinements, the things that could provide one of those scenes in a comedy where characters have it out with each other" (*Lycée* 3: 137). Atalide's successive crises take on a wearisome familiarity, ironically justifying Zatime's reaction: "Quoi, Madame? Quelle est cette nouvelle alarme?" (805). Raymond Picard refutes the idea of any "psychological quirkiness" in Atalide's successive fits of jealousy and repentance, on the grounds that the audience knows that she can be jealous, from a stray remark in the first Act (*Parthénon* 82). This discreet "preparation," however, does not change the reaction of many to the behavior of the two lovers, which appears too inconsequential to be moving. Jacques Scherer recalls one comment on the 1937 Copeau production: the subject of *Bajazet* is "two lovers flirting" (*Bajazet* 293).

As the following chapter will show, *Iphigénie* has often been accused of "domesticity," because the conflict is within the family, even though that is exactly what Aristotle recommended for tragedy. In *Bajazet*, however, it is the content and tone of some of the dialogue between Bajazet and Atalide that too often stray from the emotional world of tragedy into the household drama. A good example is provided by the reproach and counter-reproach that fill Act II Scene 5. Bajazet arrives with an "I told you so" agenda: "Je vous l'avais prédit. Mais vous l'avez voulu" (671). The brave Turkish prince suggests that Atalide does not understand his self-esteem, to which she replies in the same vein (733-75). Her instruction that he should convince Roxane of his love is followed, after his departure, by another fit of jealousy, and her decision to commit suicide, a decision that she conveys to the hapless Bajazet when he returns to say that he has done what she has told him to do (961-62). Audiences might here recall *Andromaque*, and Hermione's celebrated "Qui te l'a dit?" to Oreste (1583), when he returns for his reward after the murder of Pyrrhus. There is, however, a crucial difference. In *Andromaque* promise and rejection are part of a pattern of tragic reversal and discovery that unfurls murderously in a mounting crescendo of emotion. Atalide's "mille soins jaloux" (682) go nowhere in particular, save back to a room with two quarrelling lovers. It is typical, for example, that Bajazet should respond with a petulant "after all I've done for you" to Atalide's announcement of her intended suicide:

> Cependant quand je viens après de tels efforts
> Chercher quelque secours contre tous mes remords,

> Vous-même contre moi je vous vois irritée
> Reprocher votre mort à mon âme agitée. (999-1002)

The play loses nothing by this being their last dialogue. Not everyone will agree. Michael Hawcroft, for example, says of the play's concluding scene, involving Atalide, that "monologue, judicial oratory, and recognition combine most successfully to prompt feelings of pity in the audience" (*Word as action* 207). This is debatable. Atalide accuses herself of having caused Bajazet's death, which might well be a cause of pity. But for Georges Forestier, quoting the following lines, the play is tragic precisely because her transgressions have no influence on the course of events (Ed. 1503):

> Et par mes artifices,
> Mes injustes soupçons, mes funestes caprices,
> Je suis donc arrivée au douloureux moment,
> Où je vois par mon crime expirer mon Amant. (1729-32)

The previous chapter attempted to show that it is by engaging the emotions that the plot plays a central role in involving the audience in the tragic action. The level of that audience's response depends in great measure on how well the plot works, and, in particular, on the strength of the chain of the probable and the necessary. Whim and artifice are not the strongest links in that chain. A similar artifice is the late appearance of Orcan. Jacques Scherer (*Bajazet* 157) suggests that this serves the sole purpose of allowing Racine to dispose of Roxane, while for Raymond Picard, on the other hand (Ed. 1: 524), Orcan's intervention does not alter the tragic outcome. This leaves an unenviable choice between the arbitrary and the unnecessary.

In other tragedies Racine creates a probable and necessary sequence of events. There is an initial error–for example, Oreste's decision to put pressure on Pyrrhus, Néron's arrest of June, the refusals by Bérénice or Mithridate to admit the reality of change, or the initial confessions in *Phèdre*–that precipitates a reversal of intention and some form of recognition or discovery. It is difficult to identify any such sequence of the probable and necessary in *Bajazet*. For Erec Kock, "the event that is awaited, the event that will determine the fate of all" ("Bajazet" 103), is Bajazet's declaration to Roxane. Reality, however, does not quite square with this idea of determination from within. The outcome of the action, and the future of the whole Ottoman empire, does not depend, as in these other plays, on what characters might do, and on the cascading, interlinked consequences of these decisions. It hangs on the result of a battle that has already taken place (53-54). When, in Act IV, we learn as an audience that "la fortune est changée" (1169), and that the sultan is returning to Constantinople, we know that potentially mutinous officers will now crush any attempt at rebellion "avec une aveugle et basse obéissance" (62). A battle far away therefore functions as the quintessential *deus ex machina*. This outside event may of course be viewed as "tragic," in the sense that it represents a harsh, unyielding fatality: thus Christian Delmas speaks of "a fatal pattern made up of a series of chance events" (*Tragédie* 155). There is a strong argument, however, of which Aristotle is the fountainhead, that in tragedy the chance event is not likely to move an audience as deeply as an ironic reversal of intention.

This distant battle is not the only intervention of fortune. Jean Prophète has asserted, quoting Madeleine Defrenne, that "objects have no role to play in Racinian theatre" (77). While it would be interesting to hear them both on Monime's *bandeau* and Hippolyte's sword, there is also in *Bajazet*, much more crucially, the discovery of the letter lost when Atalide faints. "No device in any of Racine's plays has drawn more severe criticism," admits Jules Brody, who curiously defends the letter episode by asserting that it achieves nothing (284-85). This is not the strongest argument for the coherence of the tragedy. For Raymond Picard, on the other hand, "this one moment of physical weakness determines the outcome" (Ed. 525), pushing Roxane to her decision either to eliminate Bajazet or to allow him to watch Atalide's execution. This thesis seems convincing, but hardly lets *Bajazet* off the same hook of coherence, if only because the fainting-fit possesses the characteristics of what Aristotle calls "a stage-artifice" (ch. 15), an unconvincing way of provoking the denouement. Hélène Baby reminds her readers that both the letter and the fainting-fit are common features in tragicomedy, and do little to add plausibility (94). For a properly tragic action to be advanced through a purely physiological lack of consciousness is something quite out of the ordinary, and not just in Racine's theater. Indeed, in Jacques Scherer's view, "*Bajazet* is the only important play in the seventeenth century in which a fainting-fit plays an important role" (*Bajazet* 219). Evert van der Starre (58) proposes an original defense of this fainting-fit: far from being accidental, it has the properly Aristotelian character of the probable and the necessary, since it is the direct consequence of Atalide learning that Bajazet will die. In that case one wonders what our reaction would be as an audience if, in similar circumstances, Andromaque were to faint, or if Hermione were spurred to vengeance by the chance discovery of a love-letter from Pyrrhus to his Trojan prisoner.

Some might speculate as to why Racine chose to include in *Bajazet* what Phillip Yarrow calls this "contrived and artificial episode" (60). As seen in the previous chapter, this does not correspond with his practice in other plays, one founded on a rigorous cause-and-effect structure, with characters victims of decisions they and others have taken, or failed to take. Jacques Scherer suggests that Racine had invested Roxane with such an extraordinary degree of blindness that she needed written proof of her misfortune (*Bajazet* 91). Whatever the playwright's motivation, a chance fainting-fit, or the accidental discovery of a piece of paper in another character's clothes, hardly enters into the accepted categories of the necessary and probable. It is as if Racine had painted his plot into a corner, and could only find a way out by knocking a hole in that tragic convention. He thus surrenders to an *invraisemblable* he had previously denounced as unacceptable in tragedy. In *Bajazet*, for Terence Cave, "the arbitrary, the conventional, and the accidental are made to seem *vraisemblable*" (358). This must remain a matter of opinion. The ordering of the plot in *Bajazet* certainly seems at a remove from the preference, stated with such brio in the first Preface to *Britannicus*, that is so often quoted as a manifesto of the quintessentially "Racinian." Here Racine implicitly sets out a dramatic ideal by ridiculing what he alleges he would have to do to satisfy critics of his plays:

> Instead of the simplicity of a dramatic action not weighed down by detail, which should be the case if it takes place in one day, instead of a dramatic action that progresses by degrees towards the ending, one that is sustained only by the interests, feelings, and passions of the characters, you would have to pack the play with an accumulation of incidents that would need a whole month to take place, and where the effect of surprise would depend on the degree of implausibility of countless theatrical ploys [...].

This is not to suggest that Racine resorts to melodrama in *Bajazet* in a way he refrained from doing in other, more "Racinian" tragedies. An example is Thésée's unexpected reappearance in *Phèdre*, a play so often seen as the most "Racinian" of all. There is, however, a difference. In *Phèdre*, as in other tragedies, the use of techniques of suspense and surprise, such as the *coup de théâtre*, only reinforce the impression an audience retains, after the event, of something plausible that has arisen from elements already present. Thésée's reported death, in retrospect, can be seen to have been too readily accepted, because it suited characters trembling on the brink of a confession that would have been impossible had he been alive. The letter in *Bajazet*, on the other hand, is a bolt from the blue. It is clear even in the case of *Bérénice* that Racine plays on the emotions by placing his audience in a state of uncertainty. No audience here can safely predict what will happen, or how characters will react, even if, after the event, it can sense why what happened was inevitable. Such are the workings of dramatic suspense and tragic necessity. In Aristotle's words, "incidents arousing pity and fear [...] have the very greatest effect on the mind when they occur unexpectedly and at the same time in consequence of one another" (ch. 9). *Bajazet* hardly conforms to this Aristotelian pattern.

Here it might be objected that the outcome of *Iphigénie* turns on such a *deus ex machina*. But in this play, apart from anything else, Ériphile is present from the beginning, as is the audience's knowledge of what will placate the gods. This enables Racine to say in his Preface that "the denouement of the play springs from the very heart of the play." It would be difficult to sustain the same claim for *Bajazet*. In *Andromaque*, it is the unrelenting combination of suspense and necessity that confers on the tragic action such a degree of emotional intensity. In *Bajazet*, on the other hand, events are determined as by the toss of a coin: the sultan could have lost the battle, Atalide might not have fainted, and the letter might have remained undiscovered. In the circumstances it is hard to share Jean Rohou's judgment that this play, which follows *Andromaque*, *Britannicus*, and *Bérénice*, represents "a deepening of Racinian tragedy" (Ed. 987). What can this "Racinian tragedy" mean, and how can it possibly be "deepened" here? Lucien Goldmann, wielding the keen blade of paradox, suggests on the other hand that the arbitrary letter incident is absolutely essential, simply because it is arbitrary, since for him *Bajazet* is clearly a melodrama, not a tragedy:

This accidental occurrence is inconceivable in a tragedy, but *is necessary as such in drama*, and underlines, better than any critical analysis could do, the distance separating *Bajazet* from the three plays that precede it. (*Dieu caché* 392)

Whether or not one accepts the Goldmann distinction between what he calls "tragedy" and "drama," it seems clear that in *Bajazet* the intervention of fortune necessarily weakens the emotional charge that is created and intensified by the spectacle of characters hurtling to their doom through decisions that spring from within the constraints developed through the dramatic action itself. It certainly seems legitimate to ask whether the plot in *Bajazet* corresponds to the standard ideal of the seventeenth-century French tragic plot, an ideal, here outlined by Bénédicte Louvat, that for many would be at the very heart of "Racinian tragedy":

> The ordering of the play's material into a system has a corollary: the need to respect an unbroken pattern of cause and effect, so that everything that happens flows from something that has happened before. The inner coherence of the dramatic action depends both on plausibility (the sequence of events must seem probable, and grounded in reality) and necessity (the same events must be linked together within the play). (*Poétique* 68)

*Strange roles*

These problems of credibility and coherence may be regarded dismissively as mere grains of sand on the vast foreshore of *le tragique racinien*. But they are sufficient, in *Bajazet*, to impair the effective conduct of the plot, that unseen dramatic engine built to generate emotion. They also grate in the characterization, which like the plot raises questions. A prime example is the role of Acomat. In the first place, why has he stayed in Constantinople, knowing that his sultan wants to eliminate him (85-86)? If such a ruthless ruler as Amurat is ready to have Roxane sacrifice a popular royal prince "à ses moindres soupçons" (132), why then, before embarking on a dangerous period of absence, did he not suppress this potentially troublesome nuisance? As for Amurat's plot, for Jean-Marie Apostolidès "undermined by too many contradictions" (*Prince sacrifié* 108), is it really credible? How could Roxane and Bajazet possibly close the gates of the city to an all-powerful sultan, returning victorious with a compliant army (225-50)? If Acomat's strategy is motivated by his personal survival, it appears risky in the extreme. But can an audience easily comprehend what his motivation is? Is he driven by concern for his own safety (85)? Does it seem likely that he acts out of some "juste colère" at the way Bajazet has been treated (133), despite knowing that Bajazet would betray him if ever he had power (648-50)? Is it credible that, in the face of the evidence, he can praise the "courage inflexible" of a vacillating Bajazet (655), only to wonder later why he has followed that prince's "conduite imprudente" (1386)? And is it ever clear why, as the situation deteriorates, Acomat refuses advice to flee, opting to die gloriously and save Bajazet "malgré lui" (1409)?

These nagging questions make it difficult fully to accept the role of Acomat. It has a lack of coherence that, again, might sap the readiness of an audience or reader to engage with the tragic action. A symptomatic incident is the swing from despair to elation that has him, at one moment, on his ship ready to sail away, and the next, rushing back to the palace (871-76). It is hard to situate this within the parameters of the probable and necessary. One source of difficulties is perhaps the removal of this character's sexual desire, which tends to confuse rather than simplify (177). Even Acomat's confidant Osmin, at a late stage in the action, believes that his master must be motivated by love, simply because he can think of nothing else to explain his conduct (1370-72). All of this means that he has an uncertain role in the play, aptly crystallized in Atalide's instruction that he should leave, but not go too far (661-63). It thus seems inevitable that having gone off to help Bajazet, Acomat cannot find him, arrives too late to save him (1663), and flees when the others are dead, or about to die, without his actions having any apparent effect.

If the role were a minor one, this apparent incoherence would matter little. But, as Jacques Scherer has said, there is a paradox here: "Acomat seems to have no great part to play in the plot, and does not really connect with the audience, but it is still a big part in the play" (*Bajazet* 83). In fact, the role of Acomat has more lines than that of Bajazet. It is here that Aristotle beckons:

> The story, as an imitation of action, must represent one action, a complete whole, with its several incidents so closely connected

that the transposal or withdrawal of any one of them will disjoint and dislocate the whole. (ch. 8)

Racine nowhere dissents from a criterion so massively central to the dramatic theory of the age. Indeed, in his Preface to *Mithridate* does he not emphasize that a dramatist must only ever include in a play what is strictly necessary? And yet Acomat seems a good illustration of the part, in both senses, that weakens the whole. If an audience begins to question what exactly this part contributes, it is no wonder that the emotional effect of the whole play is diminished.

Paradoxically, the role of Bajazet is equally difficult to fit into the play that bears his name. If, of the four main characters, he has the fewest lines and scenes, then plausibly, as Jacques Scherer suggests, "it is because he does nothing and can do nothing" (*Bajazet* 97). The difficulties inherent in this role are, as with that of Acomat, compounded by problems of credibility and coherence. At the very outset it might be asked why the sultan, a supposedly jealous brother, should have first allowed Bajazet the opportunity for military glory (117-22), and then left him behind with Roxane during his prolonged absence. Scherer supposes that Bajazet would have been a poor tragic hero if he had been kept in the *sérail* since childhood, and that he needed some military glory to fit the role: "So Racine gives him the military successes he needs, but without any great degree of plausibility" (*Bajazet* 54). There is, in addition, an unresolved contradiction between two versions of this character. On the one hand there is the Turkish warrior as touted by Racine in the 1676 Preface: "Though in love he still retains the fierceness of his Nation." And so he is duly pictured fighting to the death, with courage and resolution (1708). On the other hand, there is the seemingly helpless character caught between the demands of two indecisive women. This hero will depend for everything on the army and the population (481), and sometimes needs his role scripted for him: "Mais quels discours faut-il que j'emploie?" (786). These two starkly contrasting forms of behavior do not cohabit happily in the same role.

This lack of coherence extends to the language that accompanies the uncertain role Bajazet is made to play. This character is not depicted as are Andromaque or Junie, sustaining the honor of family or nation in a refusal as morally absolute as the despotism that threatens them. Bajazet does, it is true, brandish the language of moral grandeur, in phrases such as "Je ne puis plus tromper une Amante crédule," "Je me parjurerais?," "bassesse," "indigne détour" (742-55). But it is a rhetoric that sits strangely with a long-accepted reality of deception and compromise. For example, his supposed courage, pride, and dignity have not prevented him promising Atalide to Acomat (176). Though Bajazet is no Matamore or Don Quixote, there is nonetheless a hint of empty swagger, of the *rodomontade*: his words tilt at windmills. When Bajazet denounces any possibility of cowardice on his part, Acomat is thus understandably skeptical, as was La Harpe:

> When you see, on the one hand, Bajazet caught between the Empire he is being offered and the death that hangs over him, and, on the other, the fit of scruples he has about deceiving Roxane, on whom his life depends, we are moved to ask once more: what proportion is there between the two? (*Lycée* 3: 135)

This lack of proportion mirrors the other contradictions of what is a puzzling role. There is an impression of parts fitting together badly, of a picture that does not stay in focus. Once again, what can suffer is the reception of the play as a whole, at least on the part of some audiences and readers.

## A "Racinian" language?

Here the critic enters dangerous waters. For it is easy to accept, almost as an article of Racinian faith, that what is felt to be the absolute, musical beauty of Racine's verse will stay splendidly aloof from any impertinent questions asked about credibility and coherence. After all, ever since the eighteenth century there has been a pervasive notion that "Racinian" language is something perfect, eternal, and absolute: Gilles Siouffi sees it being given a mythical status, and describes this process as a "sacralization" (435). To a request that he should write a book on Racine, Voltaire is supposed to have replied: "You only have to write at the bottom of every page of his works: 'beautiful,' 'moving,' 'harmonious,' 'admirable,' etc." (Fontanier 31). Even La Harpe, his bag always bursting with quibbles, had no desire to tarnish the Racinian ideal:

> His language is such a seamless web that you can move nothing, add nothing, remove nothing. It is a complete whole that seems to exist out of time. Even his inaccuracies—and these are very few in number—are almost always, when you look closely at them, merely sacrifices that are made to good taste. Nothing would be so difficult as to rewrite a line of Racine's poetry. [...]
> ONLY WHAT IS TRUE IS BEAUTIFUL. If you always want to be in the presence of this beauty and truth, read Racine, read him again and again. (*Éloge* 21, 51)

Michèle Rosellini has shown that the "musicality" of Racinian poetry was something invented or conceded very early by Racine's critics to compensate for a supposed lack of dramatic skill (280). Clinging to his "style" as a model of the "Racinian," and thus of "poetry" itself, seems also to have become a major critical temptation when the Romantics began to scorn classical dramatic conventions, and Racine's plays began to seem dated, as Sainte-Beuve acknowledged:

> While being quite ready to agree that nowadays Racine's plays are not the center of the theatrical universe, people fall back on his style, and some maintain that this Racinian style is, and must remain, the one essential core of French poetry. This is the model and example to which they invariably refer when appraising any poetry. (3: 571)

The beauty of Racine's verse has been enough to keep this image intact. Solange Guénon, for example, declares that Racine's works, however controversial in other respects, "have commanded consensus on one point: the precision of his language, the aptness of the words he uses, the power, efficiency, and economy with which they are organized" ("Monime" 113). In other words, whatever questions may be asked about other aspects of the play, is the sheer imaginative force of the poetic expression not sufficient to break through the iron gates of admiration?

It is evident that Racine's poetic genius did not suddenly desert him in *Bajazet*. As in other tragedies, he can give renewed energy to the familiar, and invest the apparently simple with a disturbing resonance. For example, he succeeds most persuasively, at some moments, in presenting the palace as a prison, where silent hovering warders will unhesitatingly execute orders:

> Et moi, vous le savez, je tiens sous ma puissance
> Cette foule de Chefs, d'Esclaves, de Muets,
> Peuple, que dans ses murs renferme ce Palais,
> Et dont à ma faveur les âmes asservies
> M'ont vendu dès longtemps leur silence et leurs vies. (434-38)

Unsurprisingly for a playwright who has already created Hermione and Néron, Racine displays the same vision and economy in projecting the volatile passion of Roxane:

> Qu'il meure. Vengeons-nous. Courez. Qu'on le saisisse.
> Que la main des Muets s'arme pour son supplice. (1277-78)

In *Bajazet* there are lines whose telling dramatic effect is universally praised, such as "Rentre dans le néant dont je t'ai fait sortir" (524), or the hissing "Sortez" (1573). Racine even increased the intensity of the terror dispensed by Roxane, between the 1672 and 1676 editions: for the syntactical tangle of "De ton cœur par sa mort viens me voir m'assurer" (1548) he substituted the chilling clarity of "Dans les mains des Muets viens la voir expirer" (1544). Some of these lines, taken separately, must rank with the most felicitous that Racine ever composed.

The problem is that they cannot be taken separately. However tempting it may be to consider "Racine" as essentially "poetry," it is difficult to consider any of Racine's tragedies in this manner. Georges Forestier makes the point firmly:

> There is not a single line of poetry in Racine's tragedies, however, pure it might seem, that has not been composed, with as much "elegance" as possible, to account for some aspect of the dramatic action, or else to "express" a passion or feeling related to that action. (Ed. liv)

In other words, the "poetry," just like plot or character, must first and foremost be a servant of the tragic action. Take for example this magnificent quatrain:

> L'imbécile Ibrahim, sans craindre sa naissance,
> Traîne, exempt de péril, une éternelle Enfance.
> Indigne également de vivre et de mourir,
> On l'abandonne aux mains qui daignent le nourrir. (109-12)

In La Harpe's view these lines are amongst the most beautiful in the French language (*Éloge* 81), while Boileau is supposed to have said that they showed Racine to have been a better satirist than himself (Mesnard Ed. 2: 485). Unfortunately neither Ibrahim nor satire has any part to play in the tragic action. In Aristotle's words, "one may string together a series of characteristic speeches of the utmost finish as regards Diction and Thought, and yet fail to produce the true tragic effect" (ch. 6). In his Prefaces to *Mithridate* Racine himself declared: "The most beautiful scenes may be found boring, if they be separated from the dramatic action, and interrupt it instead of driving it onwards to its conclusion." This is an explicit refusal of the idea of including beauty for beauty's sake. There is little point scouring the text, like la Harpe in his *Lycée*, distributing stars for "genius" or giving bad marks for "incorrect usage." It is the effect of this poetic part on the dramatic whole that matters.

What is striking in *Bajazet* is the number of elements that impair the emotional impact of the whole: language that sometimes seems too conventional or out of register, and thus chafes with the dramatic body it seeks to clothe. One recurring false note, perhaps paradoxically, is the intervention of what one might call the language of high tragedy. An example is the use of the apostrophe, when a character addresses abstract qualities, such as Atalide with her "Sentiments trop jaloux" (818-21), or other such examples (1382-86, 1446-48, 1465-72, 1733-34). It may be objected that this rhetorical figure is simply part of the baggage of tragedy, though d'Aubignac did suggest that such apostrophes be limited to two lines at the very most (478). One thinks immediately of the opening lines of Corneille's *Cinna*, and Émilie's address to her "Impatients désirs." *Bajazet*, however, does not possess the consistently elevated tone of Corneille's play. The intervention of such high rhetoric may thus jolt expectations, in a way that distracts rather than enriches. The expected register in *Bajazet* is set at a simpler and more natural level, as exemplified in the shiver of terror communicated in Roxane's question to Atalide:

> Madame, j'ai reçu des Lettres de l'Armée.
> De tout ce qui s'y passe êtes-vous informée? (1165-66)

As Pierre Larthomas has stressed, the high tragic register must be maintained, if it is to be credible and effective (295-307). This is simply not the case in *Bajazet*, stigmatized by La Harpe as not having a suitably "Racinian" language: "the only play by Racine where love is expressed in a language that is beneath the dignity of the tragic genre" (*Lycée* 139). The apostrophe, therefore, which Leo Spitzer calls "this rather stiff stylistic device" (89), is sometimes simply unbelievable in *Bajazet*, as Michael Hawcroft has pointed out ("Apostrophes" 407). It seems doubly inappropriate in a work filled with what Eugène Vinaver describes as "amorphous verse" (*Poésie tragique* 71). Indeed, the language used can recall that of the melodrama, as when Atalide and Acomat attempt to compel Zatime to say what she knows: "Malheureuse, réponds" (1673).

For Lucien Goldmann it is this disparity between tragic and melodramatic elements that makes *Bajazet* the weakest of the tragedies. A striking example occurs in Act V. Here, with death seeming to threaten on all sides, Roxane is to be found, as though in a *salon*, reproaching her would-be *galant* with having "Feint un amour, pour moi, que vous ne sentiez pas," to which Bajazet replies with a "Qui? moi, Madame?" (1484-85), like a schoolboy accused of cheating. These are not isolated cases. Throughout the tragedy there exists an uncomfortable conjunction of the language of high tragedy with the banal lexis of love's minor accidents. An example is the monologue by Atalide that opens the final act:

> Hélas! je cherche en vain. Rien ne s'offre à ma vue.
> Malheureuse! Comment puis-je l'avoir perdue?
> Ciel, aurais-tu permis que mon funeste amour
> Exposât mon Amant tant de fois en un jour,
> Que pour dernier malheur, cette Lettre fatale
> Fût encor parvenue aux yeux de ma Rivale? (1433-38)

Here *ciel*, *funeste*, and *fatal* seem curiously out of place. An enlightening comparison is the stabbing, almost prosaic character of the monologue that opens the final act of *Andromaque* (1401): "Où suis-je? Qu'ai-je fait? Que dois-je faire encore?" Hermione is seeking reason, coherence, identity: Atalide is looking for a lost letter. A similar example is when Atalide's "Funeste aveuglement! Perfide jalousie!" is followed by "Zaïre, s'il se peut, retourne sur tes pas" (1150-55). The dissonance produces an effect of chiasmus, undercutting the attempt to convey emotional intensity through the traditional vocabulary of tragic blindness.

Some might seek to advance a theory of subversion here. Bajazet, for example, can at times use a vocabulary typical of a hero of high tragedy: "lâcheté" (596), "un beau désespoir" (634), "d'un lâche désespoir ma vertu consternée" (734). Since this high tragic mode corresponds ill with the hapless character represented, is it not possible, one might ask, that Racine is using inappropriate language to force a parallel between an appearance of vaulting moral ambition and a reality of broken-backed passivity? This hypothesis hardly seems likely, however, if only because language used in such a subversive manner would assume something of that satirical function used so adroitly by Molière. "Éloignement fatal! Voyage malheureux!," cries Arnolphe in *L'École des femmes* (2.1.385), and the highfalutin language makes the audience laugh. It would be odd for a practiced dramatist such as Racine consciously to devalue a linguistic currency used elsewhere for tragic effect.

This said, the failure in *Bajazet* to maintain an even register, and the disproportion in some cases between rhetoric and reality, is necessarily corrosive of the delicate relationship between language and emotion in tragedy. When that link is broken, when such language loses its emotive force, the ordinary can seem faintly ridiculous, as though dressed up in fancy clothes: "Je sais de Bajazet l'ordinaire demeure" (1429). Then the hyperbolic can suggest less an intensity of feeling than an inflation from experience:

> Et ne m'exposez point aux plus vives douleurs
> Qui jamais d'une Amante épuisèrent les pleurs. (699-700)

And in that case the conventional of tragic expression will remain coldly conventional, stuck in the frigid banality of a rhetorical ploy heard once too often. This must remain, of course, a question of personal taste. Of the Infante's line in *Le Cid*, "Ma plus douce espérance est de perdre d'espoir," Georges Scudéry used the term *galimathias*, "gibberish" (qtd. in Gasté 97). But Georges Forestier, three and a half centuries on, finds Racine's replication of this line, in Atalide's "Mon unique espérance est dans mon désespoir" (336), to be "of an exceptional poetic density" (Ed. 1514). *De gustibus non disputandum est.*

Appositely, therefore, since the ingredients cook in the same pot, the questions asked about the credibility and coherence of the language mirror those that have arisen over plot and character. In all three there reigns an intercommunicating degree of uncertainty, a lack of co-ordination that sometimes occasions a hiatus between tragic purpose and dramatic means. John Bayley speaks of the playwright's "Apollonian clarity of speech" (qtd. in Ricks 253). This has become one of the standard identifiers of "Racine." Here it is perhaps reassuring to note that Racine is not always "Racine." For example, at what should be the very tensest moment of *Bajazet*, when death hangs on each word the doomed hero speaks to Roxane, it will takes a reader some time, and probably some help, to work out what the words mean. An audience has less time, and no help:

> Et même votre amour, si j'ose vous le dire,
> Consultant vos bienfaits, les crut, et sur leur foi
> De tous mes sentiments vous répondit pour moi. (1502-4)

As Volker Schröder puts it, in a different context, but with a similar desire to question an accepted view of the "Racinian": "How can we find here the legendary classical 'transparency,' the mythical 'Racinian simplicity'?" (*Britannicus* 241). After *Bajazet*, it is tempting to agree at least in some measure with Michèle Rosellini, that the supposed "Racinian harmony" is simply "a prejudice that has become an institution" (295).

## Expectations

*Bajazet*, then, is different. Though it clearly shares many elements with other tragedies by Racine, it is all put together less well. Samuel Johnson's harsh assessment of Shakespeare's *Measure for Measure* could thus more fairly be applied to Racine's play: "the grave scenes, if few passages be excepted, have more labour than elegance. The plot is rather intricate than artful" (7: 216). This is not just negative carping. On the contrary, the observation of difference is a positive and revealing exercise. First, it clearly shows up the dramatic ideal implicit in common expectations of Racinian tragedy. These are crisply expressed in the entry under "Racine" in the *Petit Larousse*: "He achieves the ideal of classical tragedy in the simplicity and limpidity of a dramatic action whose twists and turns come from the characters' own passions." And that most subtle and delightful of commentators, Lytton Strachey, described what many think of as an essential "Racine" with equal economy:

> His conception of the drama was of something swift, simple, inevitable; an action taken at the crisis, with no redundancies however interesting, no complications however suggestive, no irrelevancies however beautiful. (93)

This is certainly a widely shared conception of "Racinian tragedy." On the evidence adduced in the preceding pages, it is hardly an accurate representation, each time for different reasons, of *Bérénice*, *Mithridate*, or *Bajazet*. There is obviously a question of taste here. Many find that *Bajazet* works as a drama, and that it provides a powerful representation of terror. At least for some critics, however, and for reasons that this chapter has attempted to present, this play achieves only fitfully the ideal of an intensity engendered by unity of tone, single-mindedness of purpose, and concentration of means. What is found missing is that harmony of plot, character, and language which alone can spin an unbroken thread of emotional, intellectual, and aesthetic engagement with a play.

A necessary corollary to these disappointed expectations is the need to be wary of the potentially exclusive nature of terms such as "Racine" or "Racinian" when their use is more evaluative than nominal. Eugène Vinaver, for example, declares that in *Bajazet* "no Racinian voice may be heard" (*Poésie tragique* 71). And Bernard Weinberg, because of what he calls the play's "multiplicity of circumstances, episodes, and moral characteristics," concludes that *Bajazet* "is not 'Racinian' or neo-classical in any sense" (181). The suggestion is that this particular Racine is not the *real* Racine who composed the *truly* "Racinian" tragedy that corresponds to a collective ideal, and is thus fully deserving of critical attention. A similar thought is perhaps implied in Harriet Stone's idea that "the American Racine responds to different demands than his French brother" ("Millennium" 5), in other words, that the significant "Racine" exists beyond the individual plays, and can be truly identified through the debates and theories that this particular body has engendered. In this light, a certain wariness about "exceptions," and the expectations these imply, should perhaps be extended to the recurring desire to distill "Racine" into a neat series of patterns, be these of the psyche, gender, class, or any socio-historical determinism.

Victor Bourguy speaks of the "illusory authenticity" of what he calls "the "Shakespearean," which he defines as "something that makes you think it is by Shakespeare although it's not" (30). Can the "Racinian" not be viewed in the same light, as essentially the synthesis of certain expectations? These expectations often involve a view of "Racinian tragedy" that involves elements such as "pessimism," "Jansenism," and a certain image of the role played by "God" or "the Gods." This *tragique racinien* or "Racinian tragic vision" is often seen to culminate in *Phèdre*. The following chapters will examine these matters more closely. But the questions remain. Does a term such as "Racinian tragedy" point to anything more solid than accumulated expectations of what the tragedies of Racine *should* be? Is it an ideal world cleansed of plays, scenes, lines, characters, and language deemed insufficiently "Racinian" or "tragic"? It is a useful term. But does it mean very much?

CHAPTER 3

"PESSIMISM" AND THE "RACINIAN TRAGIC VISION"

IT is not uncommon for the terms "tragic" and "pessimistic" to be used to describe the same corner of the wood. A waste wood, perhaps, and one that "Racine" is commonly supposed to inhabit. Those who begin to ask questions about the identity and coherence of "Racinian tragedy" are soon confronted with some variant of what is often called the *vision tragique racinienne*. This "vision" supposes a set of identifiable markers that might differentiate it from, say, a *vision tragique cornelienne*, as in Jean Rohou's comparative study of *Pertharite* and *Andromaque* as "two visions of the human condition" (59). A traditional marker of the "Racinian tragic vision" is taken to be its "pessimism" (e.g. Lapp 192), with Corneille's "optimism" existing in neat opposition. "Racine is a pessimist," asserts Anne Ubersfeld, "because although those with power are overcome, the hero dies: destruction has the upper hand" ("Auteur tragique" 65). A powerful ally of Racine's supposed pessimism is his supposed Jansenism, to which the next chapter will return. "Racine is a Christian pessimist," declared Jules Lemaître, speaking appropriately enough on the site of Port-Royal: "His plays are those of a man who believes neither in the goodness of human nature nor in the ability of the will to overcome on its own the temptations of the flesh and the heart" (qtd. in Alemany 253). Thus, in that most perfect of critical circles, the Jansenism is used to demonstrate the pessimism, and the pessimism to demonstrate the Jansenism. Luzius Keller's claim is a typical one: "Nowhere can Racine's Jansenism be seen more clearly than in its pessimistic vision of Creation" (57).

Despite its easy acceptance, and the critical tradition that supports it, this "tragic vision" begs questions that merit some response. For example, is "pessimism" an unambiguous marker of late seventeenth-century French literature, of an age that has its own narrative coherence? Or else, as Giovanni Dotoli puts it, "does the seventeenth century exist?" (25). Are terms such as "pessimistic" or "optimistic" adequate or reliable descriptors of Racine's tragedies? Is an utterly bleak vision of the human condition a necessary constituent of "Racinian tragedy"? To what extent might one speak, as some critics do, of "happy tragedies"? If such works exist, how do they correlate with the apparently "pessimistic" identity of this "Racinian tragic vision"?

These questions have recently been the subject of some debate. Or rather, it might be more accurate to say that "the pessimism of Racinian tragedy" has for some time been the standard view, and that voices are sometimes raised to contest it. The amiable sparring of Jean Emelina and Jean Rohou, which recently reawakened this debate, in so doing provided a useful synthesis of some common twentieth-century perceptions of French seventeenth century "classical" literature. Of the papers they have published on this subject, the very titles give a flavor of the arguments. Rohou has written a series of well-documented works seeking insistently to demonstrate the "Augustinian" and therefore fundamentally "pessimistic" nature of *le tragique racinien*. The Emelina approach is reflected in titles such as "Can one imagine a happy Classicism?," "Happiness in the non-religious tragedies of Racine," or "Are the 'Classics' happy or unhappy?" He is skeptical about the whole "pessimism" thesis:

> We are expected to believe that, once we have left the reassuring waters of rhetoric and dramatic theory [...], we are suddenly sucked into terrifying maelstroms, in which there is nothing but poison of the soul, man's inhumanity to man, crimes, cruelty, misery [...]. ("Le bonheur" 343)

Rohou's detailed reply, in a lengthy article on the "pessimistic anthropology" of French classical authors, is itself an anticipation of his 2002 book, *Le XVII$^e$ siècle: une révolution de la condition humaine*.

This exchange is a microcosm of what has been a long-running debate. The questions at issue turn on fundamental and controversial aspects of history, society, theology, and literature, which it would be absurd to attempt even to summarize in one short chapter. The aim here is simply to set this important debate in context, and then very briefly to look at the evidence provided by *Britannicus* and *Iphigénie*, two plays that have often been used as examples of "pessimism" and "optimism."

"Pessimism" and "Tragic Vision"

Jean Rohou is the most energetic contemporary representative of the "pessimistic" camp, as can be seen from his numerous publications on the work he calls "Racinian tragedy." This point of view lies within a tradition articulated in the past century most notably by Paul Bénichou and Lucien Goldmann. The general thesis is that, for various social and political reasons, a seventeenth century that began "optimistically" saw a swing to "pessimism" in the later decades. Bénichou famously refers to what he calls "the demolition of the hero" in works produced in that period, an idea to which Philippe Sellier returns:

> For a hundred years, the renewal of Stoicism had left its mark on a considerable part of writings of a literary and philosophical nature, from Montaigne's *Essays* to Corneille's tragedies and Descartes's *Correspondance*. Then, in the middle of the seventeenth century, there was a complete change of direction: what in literary works is often a confident tone is replaced by the orchestration of suspicion, the denunciation of appearances, and a demystification. (*Port-Royal et la littérature* 2: 261)

This is a neat pattern. It seems legitimate to ask whether it is not a bit too neat. Some, such as René Tavenaux or Marc Fumaroli ("Melpomène" 198), certainly contest the idea that heroism, or representations of it, somehow died out in the middle of the seventeenth-century. One might also wish at least to debate the easy association of Stoicism and "optimism." It is true that both imply a degree of control by will and reason. But the Stoics also insist on the fortitude necessary to confront inevitable suffering and the inescapable pain of death. It was after all in his early work, heavily influenced by Stoicism, that Montaigne wrote the essay "That to philosophize is to learn to die," whereas the later essays, when this influence has waned, celebrate the desire to live life rather than meditate on death.

It is in the context of this general debate that Jean Rohou's "Anthropologie pessimiste des classiques" provides a valuable summary of what has been an influential current of thought. In line with the established tradition, he views the second half of the century as a pessimistic parenthesis, between the "heroic optimism of Corneille" and the desire for "a reasonable happiness" which he sees as marking the beginning of the eighteenth century (1530). Following on Lucien Goldmann, he sees a clear reason for this change in mentality:

> The exceptional output and quality of French literature in the period 1660-80 seem to me to be fundamentally due to the fact that, at that particular moment in history, the social elite—uprooted by royal absolutism and yet involved in the initiatives that would later occupy it—could not solve its problems either by economic or political action, or by critical reflection, or by an escape into religion. It could only solve them by putting them on stage, in the structural and stylistic perfection of self-contained works that enclosed and sublimated them. (1549-50)

An immediate objection here is that other critics, such as Pierre Ronzeaud in his "Racine et la politique" have considered factors such as Louis XIV's absolutism to help explain the literary works of that time in a quite different way. In addition, not everyone will accept the very basis of the claim that there is a necessary link between Jansenist theology and the interests of the educated middle class. An example is the celebrated theologian Leszek Kolakoski:

> Goldmann's attempt to establish this link and to prove that Jansenism was no more than an expression of this particular interest is ingenious but unconvincing and artificially concocted; it starts with the assumption that every ideological movement of any importance must reflect the aspirations of a specific social class. (93)

There can be little doubt about St Augustine's pessimism, if this word is to have any meaning at all. This is especially so in that, as A. H. Armstrong has put it, "his pessimism about man became a pessimism about God" (19). Critics can speculate at their leisure as to whether a necessarily pessimistic Augustinian theology, as popularized by Jansenist authors, was a symptom or a cause of the change of mind or mood that Jean Rohou describes. For Rohou himself, the influence of this "pessimism" on the great French "classical" authors seems self-evident. In particular, he sees what he calls the "Racinian tragic vision" springing from this Augustinian source as clearly as a stream from a mountain:

> For some years now I have been suggesting that we read Racine's tragedies, not as if they were peculiar stories that were foreign to us [...] but as poetic fables that express, through the singular tales they tell, a vision of the human personality and condition. [...] Having through original sin turned aside from the perfect Being who alone can fulfill our desires, we experience intense frustration and are tortured and carried away by the overwhelming desire for union with the ideal. In the children of Adam and Eve, however, that overwhelming urge becomes concupiscence and self-love. When we encounter a representation of our ideal, this perverse and frustrated desire is immediately fascinated, but its attempt to conquer the ideal is absolutely inadequate, since it views the ideal as an erotic object and aims to possess it by violence. [...] Racine transforms the stories he borrows to adapt them to this pessimistic Christian anthropology. ("Anthropologie" 1528-29)

No-one doubts that Jean Rohou's works are well-researched arguments for a point of view he sees as the most credible explanation as to why the little orphan Jean Racine became "Racine." This explanation, however, has its own problems. For a start, the evidence for the "Racinian tragedy" whose characteristics Rohou identifies is only taken from some of Racine's tragedies, and from some parts of them. At the same time he seems to be asking his readers to believe that this playwright adapted his sources, perhaps unconsciously but systematically, to fit in with a single, obsessive, meta-theological model. This Jean Racine is the same tortured soul who, apparently without effort or inner disturbance, withdrew from the theatre the moment he received the social advancement that he had always sought.

Some might also choose to take issue with the manner in which Rohou, in this same work, draws conclusions from what is a very rapid overview of complex issues, such as the theology of grace, or the relationship between biography, literature, and a necessarily incomplete and subjective historical viewpoint. For example, it does seem quite a simplification to assert that "from 1645 there was one dominant idea: there is a fundamental split between mankind, deeply tainted by original sin, and God" ("Anthropologie" 1536). Nor is there any easy parallel, as the following chapter, will attempt to show, between the situation in which the characters of tragedies are placed, and the lot of fallen humanity. In tragedy, as Leszek Kolakowski remarks, "what produces the tragic impossibility of a morally good choice is the situation, not inherited guilt; and the actors have a choice, even though any choice is morally wrong for one reason or another" (196).

These will remain matters of debate. For the purposes of this present work, one particular point deserves some attention. This is the commonly received idea, articulated by Jean Rohou, that Racine, consciously or not, adapted his materials to conform to a "tragic vision" which, because it is Augustinian, can only have one view of humanity: "the distinctive feature of the human condition is its state of inevitable and insuperable misfortune" ("Anthropologie" 1540). This "tragic vision" is certainly coherent, a closed circle. It is worth asking, however, to what extent such a perfect shape is achieved through the exclusion of elements that might have prevented such an intellectually satisfying closure. For this striking coherence does appear to come from a careful selection of historical facts and literary works, those very ones, naturally enough, that are seen to reflect the same vision. The question then arises: what of the thousands of works produced in the same period that, self-evidently, do *not* concord with this "tragic vision"?

This is a point seized on by Jean Emelina to underline the severe process of exclusion by which Jean Rohou's "pessimistic anthropology" is constructed. For example, only some parts of La Fontaine's works can seriously be considered: *The Wolf and the Lamb* will play better than *The Two Pigeons,* those necessarily unrepresentative birds "who loved each other with tender love, and found happiness only with each other" ("Les Classiques" 635). Rohou's response is to categorize poems such as this as "entertainments, works that are good fun but propose an existential attitude rather than a vision of humanity" ("Anthropologie" 1524). And how could Racine's tragedies be "entertainments" in this sense, since, as Luzius Keller has expressed it, their subject is the "revelation of monstrous creatures" (49)?

The argument will convince if the terms of the argument are

accepted. But what if this "vision of humanity" cannot be seen everywhere in the tragedies of Racine? What "monsters" are revealed in, say, *Mithridate* or *Iphigénie*? As already mentioned, the answer here was suggested by Lucien Goldmann. Quite simply, some of these tragedies, or parts of them, are to be blackballed from the tragic club, as not being "tragic" enough, in the particular and anachronistic sense he gives to that word. For example, he finds *Iphigénie* too "providentialist," so that only the role of Eriphile is seen to merit the *appellation contrôlée* of "tragic" ("Structure" 256). Jean Rohou makes a similar distinction in his "Anthropologie" (1526-27). Thus *Iphigénie* is "optimistic," and by definition therefore cannot be "tragic," since tragedy and pessimism are one flesh: "do we have to look for Racine's tragic vision in his weakest plays, the ones that most readily conformed to the fashion of the time, in other words, his most personal ones?" *Britannicus* and *Phèdre*, on the other hand, fulfill the necessary conditions.

To uncover the underlying structures of what may properly be called "Racinian tragedy," however, it is not enough to choose the right plays. These plays must also be looked at in the right way. The Rohou "Anthropologie" again illustrates this procedure. For example, there is no point highlighting the tender love of June and Britannicus: they have "no substantial autonomy" because Néron is the subject and the driving force of the play (1527). As for *Phèdre*–it is a point to which the final chapter will return–the "Racinian tragic vision" can be seen in its most concentrated form if the focus is placed on the character of Phèdre, since the expression of her sentiments is deemed to be somehow more "real" than that of the other characters:

> Phèdre has as much importance by herself as the seven other characters. [...] the beautiful, pure love of Aricie and Hippolyte cannot be seen as representing the Racinian vision of reality [...] because it is has no reality, not having had the time to exist. (1527)

This orientation prompts Jean Emelina to ask a searching question: "Why is it only pessimism that counts for anything?" ("Les Classiques" 635). The answer is doubtless contained within the immemorial desire, when pen is put to paper, to confront the problems of the human condition. An example may be found in any library catalogue, where titles containing the term "pessimism" greatly outnumber those with "optimism." By the same token, however, there is nothing to indicate that either of these features is a distinctive, identifying mark of any particular period or work, one that sets it off from any other. The same sample of titles from the catalogue will also show that "pessimism" is associated with authors as diverse as Sophocles, Thucydides, Ecclesiastes, Dr Johnson, James Thomson, Novalis, Schopenhauer, Leconte de Lisle, Thomas Hardy, Miguel De Unamuno, Graham Greene, and Samuel Beckett, as well as with the Bible, atheism, the Enlightenment, irrationalism, romanticism, and postmodernism. One does not have to be Sherlock Holmes to deduce that "pessimism" can hardly be a specific marker of a supposedly Augustinian French "classical" literature.

The most surprising candidate in this list might seem to be the Enlightenment. That is, until it is remembered that the title of Voltaire's *Candide ou l'optimisme* uses a term first recorded in 1737, while its sister term, *pessimisme*, only appeared in 1759: both referred specifically to the philosophy of Leibnitz. This in turn suggests that there is always a risk of inserting into a seventeenth-century context an ideology, or a way of considering experience, with which that century was not familiar. Since the same phenomenon has been noted with regard to the terms *classique* and *le tragique*, the association of either with *pessimisme* only magnifies the anachronism.

All of this has implications for what might seem to be a natural correlation between "pessimism" and tragedy. As Georges Forestier puts it, "our contemporaries expect to find in tragedy a vision of the human condition that is one of utter despair, and it is in such a vision that they believe they recognize Racine" (Ed. 1527). Examples abound. "In these plays no opening is provided for anything like an Aristotelian fault," asserts Albert Cook, "Fault lies in the total condition" (xiii). And Marie-Odile Sweetser sees Racine in *Britannicus* as "a precursor who has explored what will become the domain of modern theatre, that of the absurd, of the disappearance of the natural, rational and moral order, of the unhappiness of the individual left only with his instincts" ("Racine rival" 30). The playwrights and critics of the seventeenth century, however, made no such automatic link between "pessimism" and tragedy. Heinsius, for example, declared that "the purpose of Tragedy is the imitation of the happiness or unhappiness of mankind" (139) and D'Aubignac was even more specific:

> A play bears the name of Tragedy only because of the events and the lives of persons represented within it, and not because of its outcome. Thus we note that, of the nineteen tragedies Euripides wrote, many have a happy end. (211)

Despite these caveats, many may still be inclined to stick with a view that became prevalent in the twentieth century, and make "Racinian" synonymous with "pessimistic," with both in turn referring to some "tragic vision of man" of the sort proposed by Lucien Goldmann and Jean Rohou. It is a secure, well-trodden path, along which those who seek to understand Racine's tragedies will find much to reassure them that they are on the right track, especially if they confront the matter of which these plays are made. It will comfort any sense they have that "Racine" is a coherent unit of experience with a number of clear identifiers. But at the very least there should be some awareness that there is no necessity to stick to this one path, and that there are some reasons for choosing other ways of encountering the tragedies of Racine.

## BRITANNICUS: PROOF POSITIVE OF "PESSIMISM"?

From the beginning this play was judged bleak, too bleak. Rather like Samuel Johnson faced with Shakespeare's *King Lear*, Saint-Évremond judged that *Britannicus* was not fit for the stage, and that the horror that it inspired destroyed the play as such (Mesnard Ed. 2: 230). The title of Françoise Jaouën's article provides an apt summary: "*Britannicus*, or the eulogy of cruelty." Thus Alain Viala sees the play as projecting, as does Machiavelli, "the universal decline of humanity," and finds the treatment both of politics and humanity "profoundly pessimistic" ("Périls" 108). Harold Ault summed up what seems to be the majority verdict on *Britannicus* with the phrase "unrelieved gloom" (19). Both subject and treatment have occasioned a welter of interpretations, none of which need restatement here. The "pessimism" debate, however, does allow me briefly to return, perhaps less stridently than in an earlier work on the play, to two vexed questions that are at the heart of the matter: what is the subject of *Britannicus,* and what moral perspective, if any, does it offer?

In his book on *Britannicus* Volker Schröder has followed other critics by closely comparing the fall of the tyrant Néron with the model of virtue presented by the Auguste of Corneille's *Cinna* (77). It seems only natural to compare two plays, by the two great French tragic dramatists, that question the nature of absolutism. But does such a comparison also provide evidence for a thesis concerning the anthropological "pessimism" that is supposed to have held sway in the second half of the seventeenth century, and thus in 1669, when *Britannicus* was first performed? Jean Rohou entertains no doubts on the matter:

> [...] in 1642, when *Cinna* came out, the dominant tendency was still the belief that human beings were able, by a heroic effort, to control their passions and forgo revenge. By 1669, however, people had been convinced for a long time that the passions were totally in control. (Ed. 914)

It is not just the sweeping nature of the historical generalizations that raises questions here. Just on the narrow comparative point, if such comparisons are to be made, one might ask why is there no mention of Corneille's *Horace*, performed in 1640, just a few months before *Cinna*. Does the earlier play, in which a hero kills his defenseless sister, show the "control of passions"? Given the impunity granted the murderer by a king who needs him for reasons of State, can the political lesson of *Horace* be viewed as easily reassuring, or "optimistic" in any commonly accepted sense of the term? It is hardly controversial to see the tragic action of Corneille's *Horace* as representing what happens to a man who crosses certain limits bounding the acceptable in human behavior. If that be so, the same process can be seen at work in Racine's *Britannicus*. Where then does that leave the historical generalizations that use such comparisons as evidence?

It is not just different interpretations of history that lead to more or less "pessimistic" appraisals of *Britannicus*. It is different notions of what constitutes the subject of the tragedy, or—to borrow the title of Marcel Gutwirth's article—of whose tragedy it is. Many focus on Néron's path to tyranny. Racine's description of the emperor in his Preface, as a man just beginning his transformation into a monster, is used as evidence that the play is about that metamorphosis: in Raymond Picard's phrase, "Néron must become Néron" (Ed. 1: 378). This emphasis on the monstrous, and its triumph, leaves little room for hope, and places the tragic action in a necessarily "pessimistic" perspective. The outcome of the play seems to lend support to this view. Britannicus is murdered, Junie has to flee, Agrippine's murder is projected, and Néron's mad descent into bloody tyranny is the only future left open. This leads Picard to say that "the dramatic action is one of the most violent and inhuman conceived by Racine" (Ed. 374).

A different perspective is naturally offered by a different idea of what constitutes the tragic subject. Here Racine provides another lead. In his second Preface he also contends that "my tragedy is no less the downfall of Agrippine than the death of Britannicus." Is this not a way of saying, as others have pointed out, that the subject is first and foremost the death of Britannicus? In a perspective in which the Junie-Britannicus couple figures more prominently, the audience's emotions will be more aroused by the threat to two powerless victims from someone who is beginning to act as though there were no limits to his power. This will lead to a greater focus on the resistance of the two victims, on the values Junie embodies, on reactions to the death of Britannicus, on Junie's flight to safety, and to what is predicted for Néron at the end. Each of these elements moderates or challenges the view that the tragic action is an expression of unalloyed despair.

### A moral dimension?

It is at this point that the moral dimension of the play, or its absence, takes on a certain importance. The caveat to enter, as hastily as is decent, is that Racine was no teacher of morality. Few now openly adopt the didactic approach that characterized, for example, even such a subtle critic as Samuel Johnson: "we learn from *Othello* this very useful moral, not to make an unequal match; in the second place, we learn not to yield too readily to suspicion" (Boswell, 745). That there is a moral content to the tragedies of Euripides, Shakespeare, or Racine is self-evident. But need it be said that evident moral content does not necessarily mean evident moral purpose? In addition, the centuries of discussion as to the "morality" of certain characters bear witness, if nothing else, to the ambiguities and uncertainties inherent in the encounter between ethical and aesthetic judgments, as Ronald Tobin shows in his recent study of "Andromaque's choice."

In this context some prefer to avoid the quicksand of moral didacticism by avoiding as much as possible the use of the word "moral." Like Georges Couton or Volker Schröder, for example, they may prefer to concentrate on the political and historical dimension of *Britannicus*. The question that might be asked, however, is whether the moral and the political can be separated as easily as the yoke and the white of an egg, especially in this play. Pierre Ronzeaud, in his "Racine et la politique," asserts "the primacy of politics in Racine's works" (136), and deplores the absence of research on the playwright's political vocabulary (143). But can it be said with any certainty that the political vocabulary of *Britannicus* is without any moral resonance? One example that springs immediately to mind is Junie's refusal of Néron's *empire*, his *désirs* and *plaisirs*, in the name of a love stripped of any desire for power or worldly pleasures:

> J'aime Britannicus. Je lui fus destinée
> Quand l'Empire semblait suivre son hyménée.
> Mais ces mêmes malheurs qui l'en ont écarté,
> Ses honneurs abolis, son Palais déserté,
> La fuite d'une Cour que sa chute a bannie,
> Sont autant de liens qui retiennent Junie.
> Tout ce que vous voyez conspire à vos desirs,
> Vos jours toujours sereins coulent dans les plaisirs. (643-50)

For Raymond Picard, certainly, while the love-interest in *Britannicus* is minimal, and the caveat about didactic literature must be entered, the moral dimension is still essential: "This tragedy would be incomprehensible to anyone who did not have the scale of moral values constantly in mind. [...] every action is given a certain moral weighting" (1: 375).

Here one encounters two radically different understandings of the "moral," either of which can support "pessimistic" readings. In the first perspective, "morality" can be explained in empirical terms: norms and taboos arise from the constraints of ordinary social existence, and are thus heavily dependent on the contingent and contradictory phenomena of life. This point of view tends to be stressed by those who read the play, mainly if not entirely, as a politico-historical lesson. Richard Goodkin, for example, in *Birth Marks* (173), suggests that the ambiguity about how power is transmitted reflects the changing nature of French society. He sees "virtue" in genealogical and even Darwinian terms:

> Néron, unlike Phèdre, has a deranged father as well as an unscrupulous, power-hungry mother. Perhaps this is why Néron's period of virtue lasts a shorter time than Phèdre's struggle against her fatal love for Hippolyte. (176)

The opposing idea of the moral, one that insists on the reality of categorical imperatives independent of everyday contingencies, can also favor "pessimistic" readings, by showing *Britannicus* to be a representation of fundamental moral infringement. Jean Rohou, for example, in what he calls "the Machiavellian conflict recounted by Tacitus," finds that Racine substitutes "a moral antimony absent from his sources" ("Anthropologie" 1529); Alain Niderst sees in this play "an almost bestial world, abandoned by God" (*Tragédies* 72); while for Raymond Picard, "characters move around in a repulsive world of scheming and raw appetites, a world denied the warmth of any unselfish sentiment" (Ed. 1: 373).

However, these same two fundamental and fundamentally different views of the moral are also the basis of interpretations that refuse to see the world portrayed in *Britannicus* as entirely devoid of hope. In his book on *Britannicus*, for example, Volker Schröder suggests that terms such as "pessimistic" or "optimistic" are inappropriate for what is a lesson in history and politics, an expression of support for absolute monarchy that shows the kind of tyranny from which France has escaped. He wishes to go beyond "morality and psychology," and sees Junie's "virtue" as the genealogical continuation of that of Augustus (179). In this same perspective he suggests that strength also includes the ability to resist strength, which is what Junie does: "this virtuous resistance indicates the limits, and, in the end, the failure of the tyrant's power" (188). Despite this abstinence, Schröder finds himself at the very threshold of the "moral" by pointing out, as many had done previously, to what extent Néron at the end is an isolated figure, while speaking of "the triumph of Junie" as "not just a moral victory but also a political one" (277).

Once again, and perhaps paradoxically, the opposing perspective, with its open espousal of moral criteria, also supports readings that see hope and light. Examples already mentioned are the stress laid on the love of Junie and Britannicus, on the values represented by Junie, and on the reversal that attends Néron. Thus David Maskell (215) mentions the "transcendental dimension" suggested by Junie's heavenward gaze in line 387, while Marie-Claire Kerbrat suggests that Racine "is calling less for political vigilance than for metaphysical reflection" (143), a statement that echoes Thomas Pavel's assertion that "in all Racine's tragedies, political motivation is secondary to metaphysical reasons" (135). Georges Forestier contends that the bleakness of Néron's monstrosity must be set beside the purity and innocence of Junie and Britannicus, and that this moral dimension counter-balances the political one (Ed. 1413). This reading of *Britannicus* is stressed by Anne Ubersfeld, with typical vigor: "Nowhere will you hear more clearly the pure song of the love that triumphs over violence and death, the love that is the very basis of resistance to the tyrant" ("Auteur tragique" 49). Such interpretations are reinforced by efforts to set the play in its properly mimetic dimension: in Arthur Miller's words, "we forsake literature when we are content to chronicle disaster" (*Theatre Essays* 10). In other words, it is not necessary to view *Britannicus* primarily as a chronicle of what has already happened, or as a history lesson. Nor does it seem scandalously naive to follow the lead of Aristotle, for whom tragedy was a credible imitation of what could happen, a mimesis performed by actors primarily to act on the emotions:

> The distinction between historian and poet is not in the one writing prose and the other verse [...]; it consists really in this, that the one describes the thing that has been, and the other a kind of thing that might be. (ch. 9)

For many, it is the play's ending, seen as the triumph of Néron's totalitarian designs, which conclusively steers the tragic action in the direction of total pessimism about humanity. Jean Emelina and Jean Rohou again speak with one voice here. Rohou, unsurprisingly, sees the ending as "confirmation of the worst" (Ed. 937). But for Emelina, too, despite his aversion to "pessimistic" interpretations of *le tragique racinien*, this play is different:

> The most unbearable thing–and here the sense of the tragic is absolute–is when the evildoer continues to live on happily and with impunity. This is the case, quite uniquely, with Néron. [...] *Britannicus* is without doubt the bleakest of Racine's tragedies. ("Le mal" 107)

It is true that Néron does "win," in a very material sense, unlike Pyrrhus or Hermione in *Andromaque*. Burrhus's account of the death of Britannicus does not seem to leave much reason for hope. He weeps not just for the dead prince, but for the demise of the Emperor he had tried to form, and "tout l'État" (1654). The certainty of future horrors is written in what he sees as Néron's amorality:

> Néron l'a vu mourir, sans changer de couleur.
> Ses yeux indifférents ont déjà la constance
> D'un Tyran dans le crime endurci dès l'enfance. (1730-32)

There is, however, a different way of viewing the ending. First, the number of murders or of horrors committed is not a sure guide to the impact of a play as a whole. As Christopher Gossip reminds us, "a tragedy without deaths does not necessarily indicate the triumph of virtue, any more than the destruction of one or a number of characters may be sufficient to suggest that vice reigns supreme" (*Introduction* 165). In addition, is it possible to choose to overlook the impact of the final scene?

> Il rentre. Chacun fuit son silence farouche.
> Le seul nom de Junie échappe de sa bouche.
> Il marche sans dessein, ses yeux mal assurés
> N'osent lever au Ciel leurs regards égarés.
> Et l'on craint, si la nuit jointe à la solitude
> Vient de son désespoir aigrir l'inquiétude,
> Si vous l'abandonnez plus longtemps sans secours,
> Que sa douleur bientôt n'attente sur ses jours. (1775-82)

These concluding lines clearly show an isolated figure with madness and suicide waiting on the road ahead. It is hard to visualize this ending as the triumph of evil, or as the expression of some "pessimistic anthropology." As his readers have come to expect, Jean Rohou solves this problem by Procrustean surgery. Indeed, he has little choice in the matter, if he wishes the body of the play to fit the bed of his theory. The audience, therefore, is simply not to take any notice of these "cringingly conventional lines" which cannot be used to imagine "a brighter future" ("Anthropologie" 1534). This response does not answer the straightforward point made by Phillip Butler in his edition of *Britannicus*: "If Racine's purpose was only, as he tells us in his Preface, to show the first stirring, then the birth, of a monster, why then had he not left us with the terrifying impact of Burrhus' message?" (59). On the face of it, at least, Rohou's appeal to ignore the ending somewhat underestimates the manner in which, openly from the second Act, the worlds of Néron and Junie, and the values sustaining them, have been brought into conflict.

In all of this there is little agreement. It is hardly surprising that *Britannicus*, like *King Lear*, should attract strongly held and contradictory views. But the very existence of these views at least shows that the "pessimism" thesis is very much open to question. This division of opinion implies once again that the identity of the "Racinian tragic vision" is not quite so easy to recognize and describe as might sometimes appear, even in a play that, at least for Jean-Pierre Miquel, is "transparent, even luminous, telling a story that is precise and clear" (150). It seems correspondingly difficult to obtain any clear and fixed idea of what constitutes that body of plays called "Racinian tragedy," an identification that might be thought desirable before the work of dissecting the body begins.

### Tragedy between "Optimism" and "Pessimism": *Iphigénie*

Another way of challenging the widely accepted identity of "Racinian tragedy" is by examining the case of *Iphigénie*. This play's "optimism" is often seen as contributing nothing to a "Racinian tragic vision" almost invariably defined as "pessimistic" and deemed to be fully on display in *Britannicus*. Is *Iphigénie* then a tragedy in name only? Does the "commun bonheur" referred to in the last scene (1790) give the play a "happy ending"? In other words, is the play either "Racinian" or "tragic"? Is this yet another "exception"?

Formulations such as "happy tragedy" or "optimistic tragedy" are commonplace in respect of *Iphigénie*. In Jean Emelina's words,

"Despite the tears the heroine sheds for Ériphile, it is the only denouement that celebrates a 'commun bonheur' and gives an impression of general jubilation" (*Racine infiniment* 137). Raymond Picard considers that "*Iphigénie* is a tragedy that ends well" (Ed. 1: 1143), while for Daniel Achach, in his edition of the play, "The atmosphere of the tragedy demanded another outcome than this 'happy end' where goodness triumphs and wickedness is severely punished" (22). Indeed, well before the denouement, is *Iphigénie* really a tragedy? It can be argued that a certain tragic pomp and circumstance are only dressing up what Jean Rohou calls "a drama of pathos" (*Avez-vous lu Racine?* 326). Obstacles placed between two young lovers, squabbling parents, the unexpected denouement reuniting all in happiness and marriage: are these domestic conflicts not the stuff of boulevard drama, if not of comedy? Pierre Brisson saw the dramatic action as springing from nothing more serious than "anxiety about the weather" (127). Roland Barthes felt able to assert, with that touch of provocation that is one of the enduring charms of his writing, that "If it were not for Ériphile, *Iphigénie* would make a very good comedy" (*Sur Racine* 115). And Alain Niderst is simply dismissive of the tragic subject: "We sense, we foresee, that all these sharp exchanges of words will not have too serious consequences" (*Tragédies* 120).

The following pages will attempt to put forth another point of view: that the conflicts at the heart of *Iphigénie* are not minor, or domestic, and that the dramatic action generates real tragic emotion, and poses some fundamental questions, conferring on *Iphigénie* a tragic dimension within which the final expression of "shared happiness" is tinged with irony.

Expressions such as "happy tragedy" or "happy end" suggest that, with the necessary resolution of the conflicts engendered by the plot, the audience's questioning is stilled. But is such the case? Take, for example, questions of power and identity. *Iphigénie* begins in almost total darkness, appropriate for the "funeste secret" (144) borne by the king. But is the physical identity of the sacrificial victim the only discovery that will be made as this dark secret comes to light? Agamemnon is identified at the beginning as "Roi, Père, Époux heureux" (17), but do these identities remain stable? In the first Act the audience may well be informed that "Les Dieux ont à Calchas amené leur Victime" (374), but can it be sure what sacrifice is made in *Iphigénie*, and who or what is the victim? At the center of *Iphigénie*, as in *King Lear*, is the trial experienced by a king and father, and his loving daughter. In both plays, in a reversal effected by tragic plot, there is a subversion of these identities, and the apparently stable relationships they imply. Can the "commun bonheur," like Lear's reconciliation with Cordelia, make an audience simply shrug off the intense emotional charge which the tragic plot has generated? Are expressions of suffering, injustice, and barbarity to be left to one side? And in the ending is there a simple dissolution of the searching questions posed by the tragic action?

*The tragic plot*

The reversal in *Iphigénie* concerns the exercise of power, and the possibility, or impossibility, of reconciling kingship and humanity in situations where no palatable choice is on offer. The first words of the play focus attention on Agamemnon's function: "Oui, c'est Agamemnon, c'est ton Roi qui t'éveille." This monarch, with the richest kingdom, and twenty other monarchs at his command, seems to have more than ordinary power. Could such a king, as Ulysse is quick to point out, sacrifice "honneur...Patrie...Peuple...Rois...l'Empire d'Asie," and indeed, "tout l'État," simply to save his daughter's skin (74-77)? Will he be a "Roi sans gloire" (78)? These questions beckon to a traditional motif, connected with the servitude of power, perhaps familiar from Shakespeare's history plays. In *Iphigénie*, however, there is a sustained emphasis on the subversion of kingship. Through the agency of this king the audience is brought into a tragic kingdom of error, reversal of intention, and, perhaps, to a heightened consciousness of what it is to be human. It is, after all, by assembling the Greek armies, and assuming command, that Agamemnon has assumed a power beyond that of ordinary mortals. It is Agamemnon who, as Achille puts it, seeks in war a glory that will make gods of them: "Ne songeons qu'à nous rendre immortels comme eux-mêmes" (262). Through his active pursuit of this power he has closed a trap on himself: to achieve the glory he must now exercise the power by extinguishing the life of the person he most loves (79-82). In other words, more than continuing some pursuit of an elusive "tragic vision," Racine first and foremost, once again, crafts a tragic plot designed to have the greatest emotional effect.

An early example is how the picture of quiet command given in the two opening lines is almost immediately transformed by the image of the king weeping. Agamemnon's reaction to Calchas's decree, that he must condemn his own daughter–"Je sentis dans mon corps tout mon sang se glacer" (64)–is a line Racine was shortly to adapt in Phèdre's description of the fever which takes hold of her, "Je sentis tout mon corps et transir et brûler" (*Phèdre*, 276): both characters are traversed by forces that seem to overwhelm them. The permission Agamemnon gives to sacrifice Iphigénie is thus presented as arising not from a decision but a surrender:

> Je me rendis, Arcas; et vaincu par Ulysse,
> De ma Fille en pleurant j'ordonnai le supplice. (89-90)

Since the warrior-king is unwilling to confront his wife Clytemnestre directly (92), any decision or failure to decide by Agamemnon will now be seen to spring from an inability either to act or to face the consequences of his actions. The first Act ends, for example, on the king's admission of helplessness (389). Georges Forestier expresses the situation with typical clarity and force: "The tragic hero is here the most powerful of kings, thrown into a situation that leaves him powerless, and this invests the subject of the play with an extraordinary intensity" (Ed. 1567). It is difficult to overlook the sheer emotional pull of this primal conflict.

The king's helplessness casts an ironic light on the "grandeur" and "splendeur" that are evoked by Clytemnestre to remind him that "tout vous est soumis" (803). This "grandeur" is also put in its place by Achille's curt dismissal of any pretension Agamemnon might have to the divine right of kings. He reminds the king that it was he, Achille, who had schemed to have him put at the head of twenty other kings (967). In this context it is difficult to agree with André Cheyns that "Agamemnon always manifests his authority" (31). On the contrary, this putative king of kings is reduced to clothing his impotence as resistance (1227), and his failure to decide as a self-immolation (1232). Indeed, an important part of the rhetoric he uses, to convince his daughter that she must submit to sacrifice, is that his hands are tied by the prospect of mob rule:

> Ne vous assurez point sur ma faible puissance.
> Quel frein pourrait d'un Peuple arrêter la licence,

> Quand les Dieux nous livrant à son zèle indiscret,
> L'affranchissent d'un joug qu'il portait à regret? (1237-40)

The reversal that attends Agamemnon, in the unwinding of his kingly authority, reaches a climax in Clytemnestre's furious assault on her husband's very humanity (1249-1316). The terms of moral repugnance she chooses ("Race funeste," "Bourreau," "Barbare," "horreur," "inhumain") are sharpened by reminders of his deception ("artifice," "feindre," "fausse tristesse"). Agamemnon's values are stripped bare by irony as by a whip: to defend the honor of his brother's wife he is willing to hand over his defenseless daughter to be publicly slaughtered. André Cheyns is one of many to judge Clytemnestre's language here excessive (30). It is visibly extreme, as extreme as that of Camille's celebrated condemnation of Rome in Corneille's *Horace*: neither case is strengthened by hyperbole. But both are the expression of an emotion fuelled by a sense of outrage and injustice. And in both, the outrage is understandable, and the sense of injustice equally so. Clytemnestre overturns any idea of glory, present or future, attaching to the whole Trojan enterprise, and rejects any idea of divine will, by relating all to her husband's pride, and to the desire for a power he is willing to purchase with blood (1289-92). This attack is followed by Achille's disdainful rejection of Agamemnon's accusation that he is a warmonger: was it not the king who had sought war, and who had brought all the armies together to that end, in order to avenge a jilted brother?

> Seul d'un honteux affront votre Frère blessé
> A-t-il droit de venger son amour offensé? (1391-92)

*Iphigénie* was staged as part of celebrations for the victories of Louis XIV. Solange Guénoun, for example, suggests that the play was composed mainly to prop up the supposedly failing authority of that monarch (*Archaïque Racine* 192). Whatever weight may be placed on such necessarily speculative hypotheses, it is a fact that in *Iphigénie* searching questions are asked of kingship itself, its power, authority, and sacred nature. It is by no means certain that positive answers are given.

The dramatic action in *Iphigénie* is therefore driven by a recognizably tragic plot, structured to uncover the consequences of the trap that Agamemnon has unwittingly set for himself. And once the machinery is set in motion, all the efforts he makes to halt the catastrophe only increase the speed with which it arrives. In his dilemma the king pronounces phrases of a sort used in earlier tragedies, such as "Que vais-je faire?" (1433), and "Que dis-je? (1445). He is the very first to present himself as victim, using as cover the servitude theme and the harshness of fate, as in, for example, "Triste destin des Rois! Esclaves que nous sommes" (365), or "Je cède, et laisse aux Dieux opprimer l'innocence" (390). But to what extent is this self-spun image true? For it was Agamemnon, as Ulysse reminds him, who single-handedly had insisted they all obey the oath they had given to pursue the war whatever the personal cost:

> Vous seul nous arrachant à de nouvelles flammes
> Nous avez fait laisser nos Enfants et nos Femmes. (309-10)

Agamemnon presents the impending sacrifice as a fatality: "Ma Fille, il faut céder. Votre heure est arrivée" (1241). Manifestly, however, he is a victim, not of circumstances, but of an earlier act of ambition that, in the end, forces him to concede to Ulysse, or appear to:

> Seigneur, vous le savez, j'ai donné ma parole,
> Et si ma Fille vient, je consens qu'on l'immole. (329-30)

The situation in which it is he who must decide, and not the Gods, is a reversal consequent on his initial error: "Ah! quels Dieux me seraient plus cruels que moi-même!" (1450). The fate of Ériphile is not in the end sealed by any royal fiat. The army wants its campaign, and Ériphile only chooses suicide when life is no longer an option for her (1768-70). This army is, however, the embodiment of Agamemnon's desire for kingship, and its decision here originates in his initial desire to seek glory in Troy, however much he may have attempted to extricate himself from the consequences of his own actions.

It is in this traditionally tragic context that it seems appropriate, as later in *Phèdre,* to set the various references to flight. The entrapment of characters is the more poignant in that, from the beginning, they are presented as seeking to escape, and their flight leads them into the jaws of the monster they are seeking to escape from. All Agamemnon's attempts to flee his responsibilities, to flee the sight of his daughter (533), to flee confrontation with Clytemnestre (1053), lead him to rush headlong into making the very sacrifice he feels he cannot humanly make. "Vous vous cachez, Seigneur," exclaims Iphigénie (552): but there is nowhere to hide for Agamemnon, nor for any other character. The king's "Fuyez" (1479) comes too late, when all paths are closed except that which leads to sacrifice (1498).

This plotting device is closely linked with what another traditional structuring element of tragedy, that of characters resisting the truth. In *Phèdre* this is presented in the heroine's inability, when she first comes on stage, to face the light of day, her desire to "dérober au jour une flamme si noire" (*Phèdre*, 310). Similarly, *Iphigénie* begins with an image of first light, which is not to be found in the Euripides text from which Racine otherwise draws extensively in these opening lines: "A peine un faible jour vous éclaire et me guide" (5). Once the chariot of the tragic action, driven by the plot, begins to spread its light, nothing can halt its course. In the word *jour* are fused the day on which the tragic action will take place, and the disquieting light of truth that this day will bring, despite Clytemnestre's plea to the sun (1689-92) that recalls a famous couplet from Racine's first play:

> O toi, qui que tu sois qui rends le jour au monde,
> Que ne l'as-tu laissé dans une nuit profonde?
> (*La Thébaïde*, 23-24)

When, therefore, Ériphile recalls the oracle's verdict that "sans périr, je ne me puis connaître" (430), words that seem to spring from the very depths of the tragic genre, one wonders whether a figurative sense of the phrase might not be applied to Agamemnon and to Iphigénie, as much as to Hermione and to Phèdre. The rhyme *périr/découvrir* (1491-92) reinforces this sense that the revelation of identity is linked to a mortally wounding discovery. In its revelation of the moral identity of actions, the tragic plot leaves no-one unscathed, leading Agamemnon to tell Iphigénie that her sacrifice is also his death, and worse: "Du coup qui vous attend vous mourrez moins que moi" (1244). Though the first scene ends with the realization that "Déjà le jour plus grand nous frappe, et nous éclaire" (158), there is an ironic relationship, characteristic of tragedy, between revelation and a blindness exemplified in the "bandeau fatal" that prevents the Greeks seeing what is before their eyes (1735). Are characters themselves conscious of this revelation? In this context the case of Agamemnon is again emblematically ironic. Anna Ambroze (192) sees him as being involved in a process of enlightenment. This is open to debate. At the outset only he bears the burden of a terrible secret, yet he embarks on a journey where knowledge is replaced by uncertainty, identities are dissolved, and reality is too painful to be contemplated. This is not the ordinary path of enlightenment of the tragic hero. In the last image given of the king, as he sees Achille ready to kill and be killed to defend the daughter he himself has been unable to protect, it is for the audience to decide whether, like Œdipus, he is unable to contemplate the consequences of his own actions, whether he is overwhelmed by an emotion he does not wish to show, or whether emotion and aversion are inseparable:

> Le triste Agamemnon, qui n'ose l'avouer,
> Pour détourner ses yeux des meurtres qu'il présage,
> Ou pour cacher ses pleurs, s'est voilé le visage. (1708-10)

## A family drama?

At this point the "happy" camp might respectfully point out that reversal and discovery, and the dialectic between growing awareness and a flight from it, are also features of boulevard drama. Already in the eighteenth century voices were raised suggesting that *Iphigénie* belonged to the banal everyday. Thus Mercier declared that Clytemnestre was "basically just a majestic variety of middle-class woman" (286), while Joubert drew the approval of Monthérlant (3) with his view that Racine was admirable for having made poetry out of middle-class attitudes. If the evidence were to support Derek Connon's assertion that *Iphigénie* is "a domestic plot with a happy ending" (251), would these features not disqualify the play as a tragedy?

Any study of the vocabulary of this particular tragedy will certainly show that family relationships figure largely in the dramatic action. Gustave Lanson (*Histoire* 544) has not been the only critic to suggest that one could extract "domestic dramas" not only from *Iphigénie* but from *Britannicus*. This element, however, is hardly enough to allow a generic distinction. It was Aristotle, after all, who opined that the poet should seek after situations where the tragic deed is done within the family, on the basis that it is this very closeness of the relationship that arouses the emotions (ch. 14). That pinnacle of English tragedy, *King Lear*, is the most obvious expression of this principle: as Mary Dahl has put it, "the congruence of political violence and kinship is uniquely distressing" (2). In addition, as William Howarth points out (129), "le sang d'Atrée et de Thyeste" referred to in line 1250 is not some ordinary family, nor is the subject of *Iphigénie* an everyday story of family life. Deeds of horror within this family are inseparable from acts of violence within and between whole tribes and nations: hanging in the balance here is the whole Trojan war, itself provoked by nothing more than the theft of a wife from her husband. On this basis alone *Iphigénie* cannot be regarded as a drama confined to the domestic sphere. As a dramatic action it is based on a plot typical of the tragic genre: passions spurring decisions that, once taken, have consequences of a violence totally disproportionate with the original act.

The treatment of the father-daughter relationship is the most signal example of the properly tragic perspective in which the actions of this particular family are viewed. Set against terms such as *Père*, *Fille*, *tendresse*, recurring more often here than in any other play of Racine, is the bare fact that, in order to pursue a war, the *Père* feels obliged to have the *Fille* ritually slaughtered, despite their mutual *tendresse*. These three words are thus from the beginning used to express, not some domestic quarrel, but a relationship of tragic irony. An example comes from the first dialogue between father and daughter, in the admiration expressed by the still unknowing Iphigénie: "Quel bonheur de me voir la Fille d'un tel Père!" (546), "N'osez-vous sans rougir être Père un moment?" (560). It is difficult not to be moved by the emotion that charges the father's reply, "Ah! ma Fille!" (568), a simplicity paralleled in Iphigénie's reaction when the truth of her intended sacrifice is revealed: "Mon Père!" (913). Iphigénie's last words in the play–"Ah Mon Père!" (1481)–thus place an appropriate final emphasis on the intimate link between tragedy and family. The monosyllabic starkness of the language expresses the almost unspeakable horror of the deed to be done, and the intensity of an emotion that almost stifles language itself. On the one hand the *tendresse* characterizing the relationship between father and daughter is very real, so real that eminent critics have suggested an incestuous dimension. The father and daughter's agonizing awareness of each other's dilemma contrasts strikingly with Achille's obsession with his own injured honor: in one particular burst of 14 lines, he makes 15 self-references, and not one to the potential victim herself (949-62), whom he is nonetheless energetically seeking to marry. But if the father-daughter *tendresse* is real, the horror too is real, and closing in. For Clytemnestre this horror becomes inseparable from the whole idea of family:

> Ô Mère infortunée!
> De festons odieux ma Fille couronnée
> Tend la gorge aux couteaux, par son Père apprêtés. (1693-95)

It somewhat stretches credibility to believe that these same family relationships are miraculously restored in Act V. The denouement can hardly wipe from the mind the brutal violation of a sacred bond of trust and love that, at the very moment of impending violation, reveals and reaffirms its intensity:

> C'est mon Père, Seigneur, je vous le dis encore.
> Mais un Père que j'aime, un Père que j'adore, (1001-2)

The fact that Agamemnon is torn apart by a dilemma that is of own making, and that is contrary to what he most desires, only increases the emotional impact of the tragic action, and indeed confers on it, as Georges Forestier expresses it in his unequalled commentary on this play, true tragic sublimity (Ed. 1574). Here one hypothesis might be advanced. Iphigénie's acceptance of death may be hastened by Achille's preoccupation with the achievement of glory, and by her father's pursuit of it. If she chooses to die to life, it is perhaps also because, like Bérénice, what she values in life has already died. What can "happiness" mean, after the horror, and the tearing of bonds, and the sense of waste so powerfully recreated in the dramatic action as a whole? Iphigénie could well exclaim, with Lear after the storm: "You do me wrong to take me out o' th' grave" (*King Lear* 4.7.45).

*And the Gods?*

Another important constituent of *Iphigénie* that does not sit easily with terms such as "happy" or "domestic" is the role assigned to the Gods. This is an aspect of the play that has attracted considerable attention. Thus Anne Ubersfeld expresses the long-standing view that Iphigénie is already condemned when the play starts ("Auteur tragique" 55), and Revel Eliot (85) that the characters are just the playthings of the Gods. However, the organization of different tragic plots in other plays has already demonstrated the preponderant place given to human decisions, hesitations, and failures to decide. Against the "playthings" thesis one must set Ronald Tobin's reminder that "few transcendental forces operate in classical tragedy" (*Racine Revisited* 19), and André Cheyns's well-argued case (18) that it is men, not Gods, who take the decisive action in *Iphigénie*. "C'est à ces Dieux que vous sacrifiez," cries Clytemnestre, of Agamemnon's pride and thirst for power (1292). Georges Forestier (Ed. 1575) adroitly manages to combine both approaches, noting that Racine keeps his audience in a state of uncertainty by suggesting at one and the same time that the Gods run everything and that human beings are responsible for their actions.

Without calling the human agency of events into question, however, one might still suggest that the motiveless sacrifice of an innocent young woman, as the price to be paid before war can be waged (920), inevitably gives rise to certain questions. For the anonymous author of the *Remarques sur les* Iphigénies *de M. Racine et de M. Coras*, that followed the publication of *Iphigénie* in 1675, the role of the Gods lacked credibility: "why on earth would the Gods demand such a great reparation without any crime having being committed to justify their anger?" (qtd. in Forestier Ed. 797). The questions asked in more recent times have tended to be more of an ethical or metaphysical nature. Put simply, if an innocent person is sacrificed, what then of justice, love, and human worth? This questioning is sharpened rather than diminished by the nature of the sacrifice demanded in the name of a power beyond human appeal (922), by the way in which the supposed will of the Gods is exploited for reasons of politico-military expediency (369-88), and by the support given to the bloodletting by a feverish population that is ready to take divine law into its own hands and tear Iphigénie limb from limb to get its war (135-38, 293-96, 1238, 1499). This unease has led some, such as Jean-Marie Apostolidès (151), to suggest that *Iphigénie* represents a vindication of state violence, in which any means are justified to attain a perceived common good. Part of the unease concerns the figure of Calchas, the person who demands the sacrifice and will wield the knife. The priest could hardly have a more disquieting role, in a way that seems to foreshadow the Joad of *Athalie*. While not present on stage, he seems, Big Brother, to know everything (458), and to manipulate everyone at his will:

> Ce n'est plus un vain Peuple en désordre assemblé.
> C'est d'un zèle fatal tout le Camp aveuglé.
> Plus de pitié. Calchas seul règne, seul commande. (1623-25)

In this kingdom of disorder, who is the king? Or rather, who or what rules? Visibly not Agamemnon, who expresses his powerlessness in his denunciation of an arbitrary vengeance exacted blindly on an innocent victim (122, 361, 390, 1225). True, he himself is implicated in the drive to war, and his attempts to save his daughter are too little and too late. Equally, however, it is humanly difficult not to share some of his anguished puzzlement at a malevolent universe, if only because his puzzlement rejoins that of human beings from our first stirrings as conscious subjects seeking reasons for the wrong done by irrational forces beyond our control. Paradoxically, the sacrifice might finally be accepted by Iphigénie, but not by the person who allows it to be perpetrated:

> J'ignore pour quel crime
> La colère des Dieux demande une Victime.
> Mais ils vous ont nommée. Un Oracle cruel
> Veut qu'ici votre sang coule sur un Autel. (1221-24)

This mix of bewilderment, anguish, and anger finds expression in Greek tragedy as in the Book of Job, and nourishes contemporary musing on the problem of evil. This leads to the age-old question: "why?" No readily convincing answer has been found. This is doubtless why *Iphigénie* can be read as "an allegory of the problem of evil" (Périvier 148). It is a context that explains Roland Barthes's phrase that "tragedy is essentially about putting God on trial" (*Sur Racine* 54).

## A happy end?

This gnawing sense of metaphysical unease is a substantial objection to "happy tragedy" views such as those of Christian Biet, for whom "suddenly and miraculously, justice and morality win the day" (*Racine* 141). The denouement has obviously a considerable role to play in the idea that, because *Iphigénie* is deemed to finish on an "optimistic" note, it can therefore be denied the quality label of "real" tragedy. This denouement is deemed to be "happy" because, while Iphigénie escapes death, the concluding lines celebrate her marriage and the departure of the Greeks for Troy. For Jean Emelina, the ending plays the decisive role in any attempt to classify Racine's tragedies: "in his 'optimistic' tragedies, it is in the denouement that real happiness breaks out, grows, and spreads" ("Le bonheur" 351).

There is, however, another point of view. This is not just, as Maurice Descotes points out ("Le dosage" 238), because Racine invariably spared his "virtuous" heroines, sensitive as he was to audience expectations and prejudices, and aware of the threshold of horror he could not cross. A serious disadvantage of the "happy" approach is that it underplays the conflicts that form the basis of the tragic action. It also takes little account of the fact that it is not the subject that is either comic or tragic, but the perspective in which it is placed: it is the whole play that counts, a point made strenuously by D'Aubignac (211), and echoed by Raymond Picard (*Parthénon* 67). In this perspective, may *Iphigénie* be reduced to some *tragédie galante*, in which justice and morality arrive in the nick of time to rescue the doomed maiden? If the overall perspective is kept in mind, is it possible to accept the view, expressed for example in Barbara Woshinsky's "Ipighénie Transcendent," that "Racine concentrated all the evil in the play within one infernal character" (92)? Is an audience that has supped with horror easily reassured by Arcas's claim that "un Dieu combat pour vous" (1700)? Is it at ease with the restoration of an order of affairs which accommodates violence and injustice, and in which human appetites are satisfied by inhuman means? Are the unease and questioning that surround issues of innocence and evil in this play suddenly removed by the "commun bonheur" reported by Ulysse at the end (1790), when priest, army, and people get their victim? It is questions such as these that lead Richard Goodkin to conclude that, whatever the appearance of final happiness in *Iphigénie*, "in tragedy there is no final conclusive escape from–or taming of–disorder" ("Iphigenia" 101).

The "shared happiness" of the ending is in any case curiously insubstantial. First, it is not as "shared" as Ulysse would have the audience believe: the play's heroine is last glimpsed weeping at Ériphile's suicide. More importantly, this "happiness" can hardly be removed from the dimension of irony in which the dramatic action has moved from the beginning. In *Iphigénie* part of the irony lies in the reminder, stressed by Bernard Magné (250) and Nina Ekstein ("Weight of the Future" 61), that the day of the play's action is the prelude to other days. For what is this "happiness," but to kill and to be killed, in Troy and after? The glory sought by the Greek heroes is always invested with an uneasy ambiguity:

> The army had to be given what it wanted. The men had to be sent to Troy and immortality. So they have to believe that the Gods are holy. This rather ambiguous ending is doubtless in tune with the very nature of the problem of evil, for which we can never find any rational solution. (Périvier 168)

As the next chapter will show, there will be a parallel in *Athalie*, in which the "happy" restoration of the "rightful" and "innocent" king will later provide a tyrant as murderous as the deposed queen. In *Iphigénie* the audience is reminded that Achille is rushing to his death (226), and that Agamemnon, returning victorious from the final butchery, will himself be butchered by Clytemnestre, who will in turn be butchered by her own children (1661-62). If, in addition, that audience knows *Andromaque*, it will not easily forget Racine's other famous evocation of the Trojan War, and the terrifying picture Andromaque paints of "heroism" and "glory" on the night Troy fell:

> Figure-toi Pyrrhus les yeux étincelants,
> Entrant à la lueur de nos palais brûlants;
> Sur tous mes Frères morts se faisant un passage,
> Et de sang tout couvert échauffant le carnage. (*Andromaque*, 1003-6)

In *Iphigénie* the image given of the looming conflict, though seen from the Greek side, is no abstract evocation of future glory:

> Et la perfide Troie abandonnée aux flammes,
> Ses Peuples dans vos fers, Priam à vos genoux, (382-83)

In Nina Ekstein's phrase, "The Trojan War looms large before the entire dramatic universe, drawing the characters inexorably forward" ("Destabilization" 919). These images of a war still to take place are heightened by Racine's decision to highlight Achille's punitive expedition to Lesbos, evoked in terms such as *malheurs, ravagée, épouvantent, débris, fureurs, sang, morts, cendres, flamme* (233-36, 679-81). It is in this carefully chosen context that the playwright situates a coming war for which the entry price is ritual slaughter. There is nothing here of the rational humanism of Goethe's *Iphigenia*, with its appeal for happiness, tolerance, and civilizing values. Racine's Iphigénie wonders how, in a single day, thoughts of war could have replaced normal human emotions (615-16), as though the human norm were love and fellowship. It is ironically this gentle heroine, when urging Achille to go for glory, who speaks of Troy in more uncomfortably harsh terms than any other:

> Allez, et dans ses murs vides de Citoyens,
> Faites pleurer ma mort aux Veuves des Troyens.
> Je meurs dans cet espoir satisfaite, et tranquille. (1555-57)

We the audience have one advantage over the celebrating Greeks: we know that the ethnic cleansing did take place. There was no "happy end" for Troy, and images and thoughts of the final massacre suffuse the whole play, suggesting an inexorability that leads John Lapp to say (65) that we witness here the process by which things become "fatal." Equally, the "shared happiness" of the denouement excludes Ériphile, a Trojan prisoner driven to commit suicide before she is ritually slaughtered in public, and Iphigénie herself, driven to tears by what she has witnessed. This moment seems more than just "a gesture towards pathos" by the playwright (Worth-Stylianou 202). Indeed, it is difficult to integrate any feminist reading of the play, as Véronique Desnain has suggested, with the notion that *Iphigénie* is not a tragedy ("Altar" 164). That the victim sees herself as a patriot ready to sacrifice herself for her country (1134-40), and at the end is no more than a helpless orphan surrounded by brave Greek soldiers baying for her blood, makes her the worthy object of Iphigénie's tears. In addition, this denouement is not some rabbit from the hat, but the final element of a quintessential tragic structure that has many other examples: Ériphile makes a fatal mistake, out of jealousy, that rebounds on her, and leads to a literal discovery of identity. The creation and depiction of this character, the picture given of war and its agents, the tears of Iphigénie, the rush to Trojan slaughter by those same Greek heroes who have been rushing to slaughter her: in such a context, Jean-Marie Delacomptée's description of the ending as a "happy family reunion" (*Racine en majesté* 198) seems strange, even when the ending is taken in isolation.

The fact is, of course, that no audience can easily take this ending in isolation from the remainder of the tragic action in which its emotions have been involved. First of all, in what tragedy by Racine is the temporal perspective limited to the single day on which the action takes place? In all these plays the past hangs like a weight, or the future casts its forbidding shadow: on thinks for example, in *Britannicus*, of the past of Agrippine or of the future crimes of Néron. *Iphigénie* is no exception, as Jean-Pierre Collinet reminds us, with its different time-frames presented by family history and the looming war. To ignore this dimension is to dull all those emotions that are sharpened by that sense of irony created by Racine's use of the larger temporal perspective. Furthermore, those emotions spring from a plot built on a conflict that is anything but everyday and domestic, though involving those close to one another. This conflict involves a threat leading to an impossible choice, deeds of horror committed or portended, a bloody sacrifice that in the end does take place, substantial victims such as fatherhood, kingship, and a sense of divine justice, and consequences that far outreach the private lives of the persons involved. These fundamental elements, mediated through the emotion created by the plot, confer a truly tragic identity to *Iphigénie* as surely as to *Andromaque*, where another threat forces another impossible choice, makes horror a pressing reality, and engenders murderous passions. In neither play is this tragic identity challenged by the final removal of the initial threat. In both, the plot creates inextricable situations which test to destruction some of the most sacred and intimate bonds of humankind, and through its twists and turns, in a language of unmatched dignity, it generates intense emotions not normally aroused by the domestic and the everyday.

Happily, this is not the end of the matter. To affirm that

*Iphigénie* is of truly tragic grandeur is not to say that this play, or *Britannicus*, or any tragedy as such, creates the unhappiness it portrays. In the end, terms such as "pessimism" and "optimism" may be a diversion. *Iphigénie* and *Britannicus* operate at another level, as aesthetic experiences. It is true that this, more than any other, is a realm of personal taste, interest, and conviction. But what these plays at least propose, to different people in different ways, is a renewed experience of human relationships, and of the hidden constraints that surround them, an experience that perhaps allows a greater focus than is readily available in the everyday. This heightened consciousness, in *Iphigénie* and *Britannicus* just as in *Œdipus Rex* or *King Lear*, cannot be a negative experience. There is also, simultaneously, that happy paradox in which the foulest thoughts and deeds are transformed by the emotions so aroused, in the act of dramatic representation. As Jean Dubu points out, this at least is the domain of which Nietzsche spoke, "where dissonance and the terrifying spectacle of the universe are resolved in beautiful harmonies" (*Racine aux miroirs* 275). This is the real pleasure for us as spectators. Violence and violation, laid bare before us, are as though transfigured by a language that, as we the audience follow the dramatic action, strews our path with flowers of exquisite pleasure:

> Un Prêtre environné d'une foule cruelle,
> Portera sur ma Fille une main criminelle?
> Déchirera son sein? Et d'un œil curieux
> Dans son cœur palpitant consultera les Dieux?
> Et moi, qui l'amenai triomphante, adorée,
> Je m'en retournerai, seule, et désespérée!
> Je verrai les chemins encor tout parfumés
> Des fleurs, dont sous ses pas on les avait semés! (1301-8)

Whatever dark deeds are represented on stage, any audience might wonder about the semantic consistency or coherence of words such as "pessimism" when it hears lines such as these, in *Iphigénie* as in *Britannicus*, when it is caught up in the emotion and beauty of it all. How easy to understand the rare degree of hyperbole and emotion with which Voltaire, no misty-eyed admirer of anything, could respond to *Iphigénie*: "O truest tragedy! Beauty of all ages and all nations!" (Moland 17: 411)

Happy tragedies indeed. Some will doubtless conclude that Voltaire was naïve. It is true that he believed that Racine's tragedies were written to be performed for pleasure. Emotion and beauty do not seem to have impinged much, for many critics of the past decades, on what has been their principal task, that of identifying the structures of "Racinian tragedy." The following chapters, which seek to question some critical certainties, will not make this task any easier. Emotion, beauty, and uncertainty are not easy to pin down. They are no less real for that.

## Chapter 4

## THE GOD QUESTION

"THE God question," as Martin Henry formulates it (14), keeps resurfacing, at least in connection with Racine's tragedies. This question was alluded to in the previous chapter, and will be in the following one. The role that the divine is often seen to play becomes an important part of that "Racine" so conveniently packaged as a single brand. The God-related questions constantly raised by critics thus tend to reflect accepted ways of interpreting Racine's tragedies. This chapter examines two such questions, important not only in themselves but for any attempt to seek identifying features of "Racinian tragedy." First, to what extent can Jansenism be seen as a clearly defined and defining characteristic of the "Racine" that criticism has constructed over the centuries? Second, does the God presented in Racine's most celebrated religious drama comfortably belong to the type of tragic universe commonly associated with an easily identifiable "Racinian tragic vision"?

### JANSENIST TRAGEDY?

Despite periodic attempts at refutation, what is called "Jansenism" remains for many one of the surest markers of the entity called "Racine." A recent example, taken from many other such, is Christopher Braider's contention that "*Athalie* exhibits the dark Jansenist bite we associate with Racinian tragedy" (346). The "associate" here implies a link it would be naïve to ignore, and the "we" suggests a near-consensus. Quite simply, the playwright's upbringing, in the shadow of Port-Royal, is felt to have left an indelible Jansenist imprint. His work is seen to contain a latent Augustinian message, a code waiting to be deciphered. This reading accords neatly and naturally with a view of "Racine" as a single text. It also supports the equation of the "Racinian tragic vision" with alienation and determinism. In particular, Racine's treatment of love, viewed as something irrational, obsessive, and destructive when it is *truly* "Racinian," is traditionally considered to be symptomatic of his Jansenist sympathies and/or subconscious leanings.

Are Racine's tragedies thus "Jansenist"? The very concept deserves some pause for thought. After all, the theology of grace is notoriously controversial and slippery, and the relationship between grace and human freedom is a problem still awaiting resolution, as Karl Rahner admits (Jeffrey 317). In addition, Bernard Beugnot (54) has reminded his readers gently of the almost irrecoverable complexity of religious life in seventeenth century France. No less complex is the history of how many hundreds of subtle minds in that century addressed the issues raised by a burning question: how can divine love, foreknowledge, and omnipotence co-exist with human responsibility for evil, in a context where happiness is an aspiration and suffering a reality? Such are the eternal riddles of theology. Paradoxically, however, for many the addition of literature and biography to the mix seems magically to make it more transparent. This is despite what is already an uncertain relationship between literature and biography, and the paucity of biographical evidence in the case of Jean Racine. In essence this whole approach turns on the following equation: Racine's Jansenism explains the fundamental pessimism of his tragic world, and the pessimism of his tragic world confirms his Jansenism. This gives an alluring coherence to "Racinian tragedy." Love, fatalism, tragedy, Racine, Port-Royal: pick any one, and it will lead to the others. Unsurprisingly, therefore, the Jansenism of the dramatist's "tragic vision" has almost acquired the status of a received idea. So much is apparent, for example, from the entry "Racine" in a well-considered everyday work of reference such as the *Petit Robert des noms propres*:

> By conceiving of love in fatalistic terms, as a passion from hell that generates hatred and destruction, by presenting it as the most possessive and egoistical instinct of the human soul [...], Racine shows himself not only to be a disciple of Port-Royal, but to be the playwright who has got closest to the heart of the tragic experience [...].

This uneasy amalgam of theology, biography, and tragedy has been around for some time. Voltaire, for example, mentions in 1760 that the idea of a Jansenist Phèdre was already common currency in his own childhood (Besterman 106: 404). Since at least the middle of the nineteenth century, with Sainte-Beuve, the link between Jansenism and "Racinian tragedy" is one that an overwhelming majority of critics seem to have made, or implicitly accepted. Gustave Lanson's judgment, for example, leaves little room for nuance: "it is quite certain that there is a perfect harmony between Racine's ideas of psychology and the dogma that characterizes Jansenism" (*Histoire* 545). In the first part of the twentieth century this approach was relayed by hugely influential critics such Charles Brunetière and Paul Bénichou. It was then immeasurably strengthened by critical works influenced generally by structuralist currents, and inspired particularly by readings of Marx and Freud. The emblematic mid-century figure here was Lucien Goldmann. Indeed, so convinced was he that Port-Royal provided the key that he even maintained that to understand Racine's work "account must be taken of the genesis and internal structuring of the Jansenist group" ("Structure" 252). Counter-arguments, in detail from Maurice Delcroix, or from such an acknowledged authority on Jansenism as Philippe Sellier, seem to have had little effect on what often passes for critical orthodoxy, an orthodoxy of which Jean Rohou has become the most vigorous contemporary advocate.

In all of these critical works there is often an initial acceptance that "Racinian tragedy" may best be deciphered, or may only be deciphered, if Augustinian theology is used as a codebook. Depending on the strength of the individual critic's desire to embed creative writing in the immediate historical context, this may or may not involve the establishment of further links between the plays and the Jansenist movement as such: in the words of Albert Gérard, "there is much to commend interpretations that rely on our knowledge of the dominant ideology in Racine's own circles" (103). In this spirit, even a practical man of the theatre such as Jean-Louis Barrault, in an article appropriately named "Connaissance de Racine," can insist that "if we want to try to understand Racine, it is essential above all else to take account of the irresistible links that tie him to Port-Royal" (22). It is unsurprising that an eminent Pascal scholar such as Jean Mesnard should consider that Racine drew from his childhood days at Port-Royal "the main elements of his work" (369). But Christian Surber, for example (216), even situates his work on the language of the plays in a context evidently regarded as uncontroversial: the Jansenism of "Racine."

This view can be accepted almost as something given, like the Englishness of Shakespeare. It is strengthened by the uncontroversial opinion that a writer's work cannot stand in splendid isolation from its historical context. From this, it is just one jump, which to some appears small, to the idea that the work in question can best be interpreted through the prism of what is, nonetheless, a selection of biographical and historical details. In this perspective, for example, the Racine who was orphaned at a tender age, and then educated at Port-Royal, can quite naturally be seen to produce characters and situations that replicate the absent-but-severe Father/God figure necessarily springing from a psyche that, three centuries on, some feel confident enough to read like a book. Thus Lucien Goldmann can assert with confidence that Racine was someone "the structures of whose mind were completely determined by Jansenism" ("Structure" 258). Add a dash of Freudian superego, and it then becomes easy to explain, say, the character of Hippolyte's love for Aricie: "Nowadays we know," opines Claire Nancy, "that the 'primal scene' of such a mortal love is that of the relationship between Racine himself and his father-figures, the Jansenist monks of Port-Royal" (47). It is therefore common enough to see Racine described, for example by Thomas Braga, as "the seventeenth-century Jansenist playwright" (297). As description slips towards definition, and hypothesis to certainty, so Racine becomes "Racine," laid out like a corpse in William Harvey's anatomy theatre, with Jansenism exposed as the blood that circulated round the plays seen as a body, a dead body.

In the circumstances, it seems reasonable to ask what this "Jansenism" implies. Since the emphasis, in the case of a creative artist, is primarily ideological, the identity of the term is inevitably bound up with St Augustine. Indeed, Leszek Kolakowski, in his pellucid analysis of the relationship of Jansenism to Augustinian theology, frequently uses the term "Augustinian-Jansenist." It would, of course, be injudicious simply to equate Port-Royal Jansenism, a heterodox expression of seventeenth-century Catholicism, with the complex spiritual, philosophical, and literary inheritance left by the Father of the Western Church. Already in the ninth century Isidore of Seville (qtd. in Brown 311) declared that anyone who claimed to have read all of St Augustine's works was a liar. In addition, this vast inheritance has spawned what Bruno Neveu calls "thorny controversies, which for centuries have exercised the subtlest minds, and filled the libraries of Europe with interminable Latin treatises" (29). These are daunting objections to any attempt at a simple overview. Deep waters are reached very quickly, but it seems that few theological vessels have the necessary ocean-going qualities: Neveu takes Kolakowski himself to task for oversimplification. On the other hand, whereof we cannot without oversimplification speak, thereof must we be silent? This is especially true in relation to the stuff of Jansenism. If there is a divinity that shapes our ends, he cannot be left to divines, rough-hew him how we may.

In the present case the main features of this Augustinian landscape, as mediated by its Jansenist interpreters, are well known. Humankind is a mass of lost souls, St Augustine's *massa perditionis*. From birth men and women are contaminated by an original sin for which we must all pay the price. In Pascal's formulation, "mankind without God is in a state of absolute ignorance and inevitable unhappiness" (fr. 75). Without that grace that is granted only to a few, that unfortunate mankind remains unavoidably sunk in the corrupt pit of a fallen nature. Most human beings, by the very fact of being human, stumble around a fallen world whose depravity is expressed in the passions that consume them. Blind, helpless, but no less guilty for that, they can only await the eternal torment it behoves divine justice to apply. On this point, St Augustine's *City of God* is refreshingly clear:

> That the whole human race has been condemned in its first origin, this life itself, if life it is to be called, bears witness by the host of cruel ills with which it is filled. Is not this proved by the profound and dreadful ignorance which produces all the errors that enfold the children of Adam, and from which no man can be delivered without toil, pain, and fear. [...]
>
> And if the true philosophy–this sole support against the miseries of this life–has been given by Heaven to only a few, it sufficiently appears from this that the human race has been condemned to pay this penalty of wretchedness. (2: 643-46; *City of God* 22.22)

On reading passages such as this from St Augustine, it is easy to understand Leszek Kolakowski's contention that "Pascal's religion [...] was a religion for unhappy people, and it was designed to make them more unhappy" (197).

This Augustinian vision of the world is commonly seen as the bridge between Racine's upbringing and the fundamentals of his tragic universe. Two recent works provide examples of the bridge-builders' work:

> His Augustinian education [...] had taught him a deep sense of the degradation and helplessness of human beings, who are overwhelmed by a deadly concupiscence. [...] It was at Port-Royal that the decisive part of Racine's development took place, intellectually, ideologically, and psychologically. (Rohou, *Jean Racine* 123-25)

> From the Jansenists he had already learnt that human nature was corrupt, and was given over to the darkest forms of unreason: it was perhaps this that gave him his sense of tragedy. To show men and women their passions in all their coarseness, as in a mirror, he needed the theatre and its magic. (Vincent 162)

In this context it seems legitimate to ask whether Racine's tragedies, experienced as living dramatic entities, correspond at least with the outline of this Augustinian-Jansenist scenario.

USING THE EVIDENCE: *ANDROMAQUE*

It would be possible to pursue this enquiry by looking at a selection of possible Augustinian influences in all of Racine's tragedies, despite the fact that Maurice Delcroix has already performed that particular task with some thoroughness. But the apparent advantage of comprehensiveness is outweighed by the disadvantage of dealing with selected extracts from a work called "Racine," and therefore admitted to have a certain homogeneity. When critics do examine one particular tragedy commonly taken to be Jansenist in inspiration, the choice tends to fall on *Phèdre* and thus on Phèdre, so effortlessly taken to be typical of "Racine" as a whole. However, other related aspects of *Phèdre* are to be examined at some length in the following chapter, including the very basis of this supposed typicality. And this one play has hitherto received the lion's share of comment on the supposed Jansenism of "Racine." For these reasons, the test case chosen here is *Andromaque*.

It may appear paradoxical to consider Augustinian influences in a work written just after the playwright's break with his Jansenist educators and mentors. But in order to scrutinize the idea that the Port-Royal of childhood is somehow translated into an adult vision of the world, *Andromaque* seems a good place to start. Three of its characters–Pyrrhus, Hermione, and Oreste–are amongst the five ordinarily quoted to illustrate what is intrinsically Jansenist in "Racinian tragedy" (e.g. Delcroix, *Le sacré*, 362). In addition, no less an authority than Lucien Goldmann has enthroned *Andromaque* as "the literary transposition of Jansenist thought" ("Structure" 259), and Jean Rohou in his book on the play sees its very structure as "the expression of Augustinian anthropology" (35). In other words, if in this supposedly Jansenist play doubt can be cast on the idea that Augustinian thought is a fundamental component of "Racinian tragedy," the same hypothesis will necessarily be undermined in the other tragedies, including *Phèdre*.

*The Jansenism of "Racine": a case in favor*

At first sight, the proponents of the association between Jansenism and "Racine" seem to have easy pickings. The most obvious parallel is characters' subjection to forces which cripple their freedom to decide, to act, and thus to escape. This seems to accord with the Augustinian-Jansenist theory of grace, according to which, in Leszek Kolakowski's formulation, "we are, all of us, so hopelessly corrupted that we are incapable of being saved by our own forces" (32). (It was one of St Augustine's adversaries, the British monk Pelagius, who maintained the opposite and received the eternal reward of having the heresy named after him.) The shackles worn by Racine's characters engender a degree of suffering and a sense of doom that it can be tempting to see in anti-Pelagian terms, as characteristic of a world where nothing can be done to avert the catastrophe to come.

If this determinism is accepted as an important part of Racine's "tragic vision," its most obvious ambassador in *Andromaque* is Oreste, the character most dependent on others' decisions. As indicated in the Introduction, a change made to one of his speeches in the play's final edition transforms passion into destiny (98), to reinforce and perhaps ennoble his rhetorical stance that he has no control over what happens to him. He presents himself as the passive victim of an alienating passion driving him on to an unknown destination:

> L'Amour me fait ici chercher une Inhumaine.
> Mais qui sait ce qu'il doit ordonner de mon Sort,
> Et si je viens chercher, ou la vie, ou la mort? (26-28)

The mysterious force that saps human will equally involves Pyrrhus and Hermione. The language of domination and enslavement is a constant, as here when used with stinging irony by Hermione to describe Pyrrhus's inability to leave Andromaque:

> Tout cela part d'un cœur toujours maître de soi,
> D'un Héros qui n'est point Esclave de sa foi. (1331-32)

This point of view seems to be reinforced by Racine's transformation of this Pyrrhus, the great hero of the Trojan War, into "un Cœur, si peu maître de lui" (120), "le jouet d'une flamme servile" (633). As Maurice Delcroix remarks, Racine's insistence on human weakness "is evidence enough, for some, [...] of an embedded reference to Jansenist thought, and for others it is a direct and obvious product of it" (*Le sacré* 337). A standard example comes from Anne Ubersfeld, concluding that Hermione's own enslavement "expresses the Jansenist theory of the passions, which was always that of Racine" (*Andromaque* 41).

The suggestion made in the first chapter was that the plots Racine created implied a certain degree of freedom of choice for characters. This point will be further stressed in the next chapter in connection with *Phèdre*. That said, anyone really desiring to see "Racine" as intimately bound up with what is held to be the Augustinian world-vision might feel encouraged by the plot of *Andromaque*, which seems structured to generate a sense of helplessness and loss of control. Oreste, whose arrival in Epirus has set the murder machine in motion, pleads that he had been the victim of a force greater than himself: "De moi-même étais-je alors le maître?" (729). Thereafter three characters' fates are suspended on the decision of Andromaque, a blackmailed prisoner to whom is given a choice so unpalatable as not to merit the name. Ironically, her jailer Pyrrhus, whose own future hangs on her impossible decision, has a sense of constraint all the sharper for his theoretical power to do what he wishes (974). In these circumstances, each use of the word *vouloir* is attended by irony, as in Hermione's description of Pyrrhus: "Il veut tout ce qu'il fait" (850). In the final Act this disjunction between desire and act is brought to a paroxysm by Hermione, from her opening "Où suis-je? Qu'ai-je fait? Que dois-je faire encore?" (1401), to the dismissal of Oreste's claim that he murdered Pyrrhus only to carry out her wishes: "Quand je l'aurais voulu, fallait-il y souscrire?" (1589). *Vouloir* is pictured almost as an entity exterior to the self:

> Qu'il meure, puisqu'enfin il a dû le prévoir,
> Et puisqu'il m'a forcée enfin à le vouloir.
> A le vouloir? Hé quoi? c'est donc moi qui l'ordonne? (1427-29)

It might seem natural to relate this to the view expressed by St Augustine, that "no-one is known to another so intimately as he is known to himself, and yet no-one is so-well known to himself that he can be sure as to his own conduct on the morrow." P. R. Brown, quoting this last phrase, follows with a summary of St Augustine's thought that many will see as applying equally to *Andromaque* in particular, and "Racinian tragedy" in general:

> [...] man is so indeterminate, so blind in his intention and haphazard in his attempts to communicate, that he must be determined by some forces outside the horizon of his immediate consciousness. (313)

Associated with this lack of freedom one might find another Augustinian theme, that of human beings locked together inextricably, and irreparably damaged, by a past catastrophe that determines the present. There is no need to insist on the central place occupied in *Andromaque* by the Trojan War, recalled even in the way characters are identified, in relation to Agamemnon and Achilles, Hector and Helen. In this context, Helen's one initial act of defiance could be seen to function as a kind of original sin, its consequences crippling those uninvolved:

> Ses yeux pour leur querelle, en dix ans de combats,
> Virent périr vingt Rois, qu'ils ne connaissaient pas? (1487-88)

Astyanax may be innocent, but is guilty nonetheless: "Oui, les Grecs sur le Fils persécutent le Père" (225). When Helen plucked the apple from the tree of forbidden love, generations yet unborn would suffer. Her one act caused the fall of Troy, and the *nuit cruelle* of this fall became a *nuit éternelle* in which all are punished forever:

> Un Enfant malheureux qui ne sait pas encor
> Que Pyrrhus est son Maître, et qu'il est Fils d'Hector. (271-72)

Reading *Andromaque* in this Augustinian perspective of fall, punishment, and inherited guilt, it would then be possible to view the condemnation arising from Helen's initial act of rebellion as driving the whole plot, from the moment Oreste arrives purportedly to punish the last surviving Trojan male. Andromaque's protest, that an innocent child should bear the weight of a crime committed before his birth, expresses our ordinary human incomprehension at the injustice of inherited suffering:

> Roi barbare, faut-il que mon crime l'entraîne?
> Si je te hais, est-il coupable de ma haine? (1033-34)

Again, those who have decided that "Racinian" rhymes with Augustinian can easily draw a parallel between the defeated Trojans, "dans la flamme étouffés" (1008), and an infernal vision of doomed humanity. Troy, the proud mistress of Asia, is after its fall reduced to "un Enfant dans les fers" (203). In both cases all are guilty. With war, as with the Augustinian doctrine of hereditary guilt through original sin, everyday human ideas of justice and mercy do not apply:

> Tout était juste alors. La Vieillesse et l'Enfance
> En vain sur leur faiblesse appuyaient leur défense. (209-10)

The "endless chain of love," so celebrated in *Andromaque*, is here an endless chain of blood, and thus of guilt, dependence, and shared responsibility: "Du sang qui vous unit je sais l'étroite chaîne" (246). It little matters to Hermione, when Pyrrhus dies, whether Oreste is "Coupable, ou Spectateur" (1480): he is still guilty.

> Men and women thus feel weighed down by the transgressions of which they are guilty, and for which they are accountable, even if they seek to deny responsibility for them. This is the conception of humanity that Racine took from Port-Royal. (Tanquerey 46)

This Augustinian reading will only be confirmed by the final lines of the play, filled with a preacher's lexis of eternal damnation: *épaisse nuit, horreur, ruisseaux de sang, démons, serpents, Enfer, éternelle Nuit, fureurs, déchirer, dévorer*. If *Andromaque* is seen in this light, it is easy to understand the claim that "Racinian tragedy," considered as a unity of experience, replicates what Ronald Tobin calls "the depressing picture painted by Jansenist psychology, representing man as a fallen angel" ("Incomplétude" 132).

In the sense of loss and exile that pervades *Andromaque* some might also wish to see a reflection of St Augustine's insistence (Chenu 34) that human beings are strangers in their own world. In St Paul's famous phrase, "here we have no continuing city" (Heb. 13.14). From the land of lost content Andromaque is quite literally in exile: "Ô cendres d'un Époux! ô Troyens! ô mon Père!" (1049). Oreste, Hermione, and Pyrrhus, though Greek, are still pictured as fundamentally homeless: "Traîner de Mers en Mers ma chaîne et mes ennuis" (44), "Toujours prête à partir, et demeurant toujours" (131), "Épouser ce qu'il hait, et punir ce qu'il aime" (122). Each could pronounce the "Où suis-je?" (1401) that begins Hermione's incandescent final monologue. The image given is of human beings exiled, through the unattainability of their own desires, to an inner landscape of restlessness, insufficiency, and disorientation. A striking example of this loss of bearings is the confusion of love with hate, a sentiment expressed with great frequency in *Andromaque*:

> Errante, et sans dessein, je cours dans ce Palais.
> Ah! ne puis-je savoir si j'aime, ou si je hais! (1403-4)

Here revenge is a kind of homecoming. It is one way of establishing contact, and thus some kind of identity: "une Victime à moi seule adressée" (1194), "Je percerai le Cœur que je n'ai pu toucher" (1248), "Tout me sera Pyrrhus" (1498). In the fallen world of *Andromaque*, which can thus be related to that depicted by St Augustine, desire is desire for what seems good, but only seems. Blindness is thus the natural concomitant of passion. Oreste's "aveuglement funeste" (481), shared with Pyrrhus and Hermione, is reminiscent of that carnal darkness of which the *locus classicus* is certainly Augustinian:

> The single desire that dominated my search for delight was simply to love and to be loved. But no restraint was imposed by the exchange of mind with mind, which marks the brightly lit pathway of friendship. Clouds of muddy carnal concupiscence filled the air. The bubbling impulses of puberty befogged and obscured my heart so that it could not see the difference between love's serenity and lust's darkness. [...] I had become deafened by the clanking chain of my mortal condition. (*Confessions* 24; bk. 2)

Between *Andromaque* and the Augustinian inheritance handed down to Racine by his Jansenist teachers, other parallels could doubtless be found. Things can always be found. Even on the evidence so far adduced, however, it is easy to see how a *prima facie* case can be established in support of Lucien Goldmann's contention that "Racinian tragedy springs from the adaptation of the Jansenist vision of man for non-religious drama" (*Bérénice* 32). In addition, some of the arguments deployed against this interpretation are not themselves completely convincing. An example is the contention that Racinian tragedy cannot correlate with the Augustinian theology of original sin because not all Racine's characters bow to evil:

> If it were once admitted that some human beings, living in a state of fallen nature, were able to escape this corruption, the whole Jansenist edifice would immediately collapse. (Tanquerey 468)

> St Augustine's vision is one of universal corruption, except a handful of the elect, but the tragedies affirm the innocence of all, except a handful of "monsters." (Sellier, "Le Jansénisme" 145)

This viewpoint seems to undervalue Aristotle's contention that tragedy "is essentially an imitation not of persons but of action and life" (ch. 6). The tragic action does not demand an overwhelming number of "evil" characters in order to present a vision of waste, suffering, and helplessness. A powerful sense of evil may be sustained by placing human beings in intolerable situations over which they have no control. It is difficult to quantify this sense of evil by counting goodies and baddies.

## The Jansenism of "Racine": a case against

It is therefore quite possible to identify certain themes in *Andromaque*, such as characters' lack of freedom and control, their common implication in inherited misfortunes, and an ensuing sense of guilt and exile. An obvious question then arises. Is there anything *specifically* "Jansenist" or "Augustinian" here? Even a limited acquaintance with forms of tragedy that preceded those of Racine can convince that these were haunted by similar concerns. A straightforward example is the insistence on human weakness in the face of passion that, as Christian Biet amongst others have reminded us ("Le destin" 109), is less a Jansenist profession of faith than a reminder of Euripides. If people are searching for evidence of an Augustinian influence, they can find it more readily in lines such as these:

> Nul ne se peut empescher
> En ce monde de pecher,
> Tant est notre humaine race,
> Encline à se dévoyer,
> Si Dieu ne vient déployer
> Sur nous sa divine grâce.
> (Garnier, *Les Juives* 103-8)

> [No-one can stop sinning in this world, such is our human race, hell bent on going astray, if God does not come and afford us his divine grace.]

The allusion to the Augustinian theology of grace could not be more direct. It would be comforting to be able to explain it by referring to Jansenism, and the unique socio-political context in which Jansenism and Jansenists flourished. Unfortunately, the lines were penned in 1583.

Where the allusions to Augustinian theology are less direct, it seems therefore obvious that care should be taken before any generalizations are made on such a fragile basis. For example, any desire to demonstrate that the emphasis on human weakness is evidence of an embedded message from Port-Royal should be tempered by the mass of similar evidence that can be taken at will from the literary commonwealth. Maurice Delcroix gives an impressive list of classical and thus "pagan" sources of lines most often adduced in evidence to prove an Augustinian bias (*Le sacré* 353-57). And Jacqueline de Romilly reminds us that the "fatality of love," for example, is to be found not just in the Greek tragedies, such as Euripides's *Hippolytus*, but in what preceded them:

> Well before tragedy came on the scene, poets had insisted on the fact that neither men nor Gods could resist love. [...] This theme was naturally to find a place in tragedy, where the ills caused either by love or by the refusal of love offered a striking illustration of the weakness of man and the sufferings he was destined to face. (*Tragédies grecques* 344)

Nor did an aversion to passion and sexuality in some way distinguish St Augustine himself from the philosophers who preceded him, as Henry Chadwick points out, in his introduction to the *Confessions*:

> Everyone acknowledged that the mating impulse ensures the survival of the human race. But all philosophers with a serious claim to be respected as wise moralists–Plato, Aristotle, the Stoics, the Epicureans–were of one mind in being impressed by its risks and dangers, and by the capacity of sexual desire to disrupt and even destroy the most rational of plans and intentions. None was more negative than the arch-hedonist Epicurus; and his follower, the Latin poet Lucretius, sharply formulated that general distaste for Venus and her works in the most impassioned section of his long poem "On the nature of things." If happiness is understood in terms of the reduction of emotional disturbance to the minimum, then the ancient attitude to sexuality is natural enough. (xvii)

What is true of the portrayal of love also holds for the general picture of humanity that can be constructed from readings of *Andromaque*. It is manifest, for example, that Oreste's picture of man as a plaything of cruel Gods (1658) is an age-old sentiment, so famously expressed by Gloucester in *King Lear*:

> As flies to wanton boys, so are we to the Gods;
> They kill us for their sport. (4.1.35-36)

Similarly, the sense of entrapment that invests the characters of *Andromaque* is a permanent and identifying feature of the tragic genre itself. Characters are cornered through the workings of the tragic plot, like Macbeth "cabined, cribbed, confined" (3.5.24). Thus Raymond Picard can speak of Oreste, Hermione, and Pyrrhus as "crushed by the iron wheels of the plot" (*Parthénon* 61). Characters, though attempting to escape, are compelled by the relentless workings of the plot to face up to the inescapable. There is nothing more or less "Jansenist" about this than for Shakespeare's tragic hero "bound / Upon a wheel of fire" (*King Lear* 4.7.46). In the great tragedies a *machine infernale* seems to acquire its own momentum, and drives forward with awesome anonymity. Paradise is always lost, never to be regained. As Willy says, in *Death of a Salesman*, "How do we get back to all the great times?" (97; act 2). This is tragic theatre, since the beginning. In the unity and intensity of one dramatic action are played out our own typically dispersed and unfocused encounters, as human beings, with what has been called the problem of evil. The tragic genre is older than St Augustine, as is our need to explore the dark side of the human planet.

In Lucien Goldmann's assimilation of Jansenism and the "Racinian tragic vision," a special role is played by "the world," in the religious sense of that phrase: "since the world is *never* everything, it can only be nothing" ("Structure" 254). Following on from this, Jean Rohou explains (*Jean Racine* 130) that Racine became "Racine" through a kind of subconscious ontological transference: the writing of tragedy permitted the expression of an angst created or revealed by a Jansenist education that stressed the vanity of human endeavor and the world's insubstantiality. Why not? Who has the means to disprove such speculations, or to prove them? These hypotheses are not reinforced, however, by any evidence that there is a particularly "Jansenist" cast to the vocabulary of Racine's tragedies. The words he uses reflect a much broader spiritual inheritance. Chateaubriand's *Génie du Christianisme*, with the author's own italics, asserts that "the most moving sentiments of Racine's Andromaque come from a *Christian* poet" (15: 28). As Philippe Sellier points out, "in Racine, almost all the lexical connections made with Augustinianism are unverifiable" ("Le Jansénisme" 146). He later stresses what is a crucial point:

> [...] it is absolutely crucial to distinguish between what is Jansenist and what is simply Christian. As a general rule, seventeenth-century Christianity is predominantly Augustinian, so that nowadays we are too inclined to treat as "Jansenist" statements which can be found in every prayer book and even in the Catholic liturgy of that age. We often misunderstand what it meant to be a Christian in the seventeenth century. (267)

It is clear, as Raymond Picard points out (*Parthénon* 39), that even professional theologians would have problems distinguishing between the "Jansenist" catechism taught to the young Racine and a "non-Jansenist" catechism taught elsewhere. Where, then, is the source of that certainty displayed by those whose profession is literary criticism? For example, a glance at seventeenth-century religious writing will reveal countless examples of injunctions to flee "the world": it is a venerable Christian topos, biblical in inspiration. An illustration comes from the gentle François de Sales, a writer some might imagine to be situated at the furthest remove from the radical "pessimism" of Jansenism. Yet the *Introduction à la vie dévote* constantly returns to the theme of "the world" as a place of perdition:

> O world, abominable regiment: no, you will never see me serving under your flag. I have turned my back forever on your frenzies and your empty promises. (581; pt. 1, ch. 18)

> The only way we can be at home with the world is if we lose our souls along with it. [...] Whatever we do, the world will always be at war with us [...]. We are crucified to the world, and the world must be crucified to us. (290-92; pt. 4, ch. 1)

The readiness to look for "Jansenism" in Racine has caused many to overlook mainstream Christianity. And yet, as Michel Bouvier stresses, the influence of its teaching was omnipresent:

> One must constantly bear in mind that the doctrine of the Church was a source of inspiration for all authors, even for those who only paid lip service to it. They all knew what this doctrine was, even if this only meant that they knew the limits it imposed on their freedom of expression. All writers knew that it was this doctrine that formed the basis of the intellectual consensus shared by their readers, and that the ideas it expressed, even if they were not entirely understood, were the generally fertile soil in which their own discourse would have to take root, in the mind of anyone beginning a dialogue with their work. (148)

Language alone does not therefore allow the theological geographer to trace an isogloss that might clearly distinguish the spiritual territory of Jansenism from that of Catholic orthodoxy. As Philippe Sellier amongst others has tried to point out (*Port-Royal* 2: 253), in what is called "the age of Saint Augustine" the bishop of Hippo's writings were a reference for the whole Western Church. An obvious example is the eagle-eyed Bossuet. Who was more ready to swoop on the tiniest mouse of imagined heresy? Yet this same champion of Catholic orthodoxy has a discourse grained with those same elements that many label as "Jansenist" in Racine's tragedies, and take as identifying features of "Racinian tragedy," as here in his funeral oration for Marie-Thérèse d'Autriche:

> Are we really living, Christians, is what we are living really life? [...] Are not rest and food poor remedies for the illness that continually torments us? As for what we call "the last illness," if we are to understand this phrase properly, is it not just an intensification, and as it were the last episode, of the ill we bring to the world when we come into it? (236)

Those selfsame images of human weakness taken from Racine's tragedies, as evidence of the supposedly Jansenist blood coursing through a single body called "Racinian tragedy," may in reality be found in all those writers who draw from a common Christian inheritance. It is this shared knowledge that enables Jean-Pierre Landry, for example, to assert ("Andromaque" 76) that contemporary audiences saw in *Andromaque* an illustration of St Paul's famous words on the strength of Christ's weakness. He gives no evidence in support, but again, why not? The important point is that the play cannot be tied down to some avatar of Augustinian theology. Even here, however, the abiding influence of stoicism should make critics hesitate to single out Christianity itself as a source. For example, in his contribution to discussion of Philippe Sellier's "Jansénisme des tragedies de Racine" (264), Michel Le Guern explained that a translation of Epictetus, made several decades before Cornelius Jansen came on the scene, contained all the images thought of as being specifically "Jansenist". The idea that humanity toys with the shadows of its transient desires instead of engaging reality, that human beings are caught up in situations not of their own making, and are as though trapped in a world from which they feel alien, is too universal and general a human experience to be simply characterized as "Augustinian" or "Jansenist."

This point cannot be as evident as it seems. It is implicitly repudiated by all those who reach for such terms when they uncover a similar "world-vision" in "Racinian tragedy." Yet Western literature brims over with representations of this "vision." Elements of it can be seen, for example, in what L. C. Knights calls the "insistent and unresolved questioning" that emerges from the Shakespearean tragedies that precede *King Lear*:

> Is there any escape from appearance and illusion? Why do both the public and the world of intense subjective experience seem somewhat flawed and unsatisfactory? What is the status of human values in a world dominated by time and death? On what, in the world as we know it, can man take his stand? (241)

This sentiment expressed in *Macbeth* that "life's but a walking shadow" (5.5.24) is doubtless more neoplatonic than specifically Augustinian. Even here, however, Sophocles preceded Plotinus. It is significant that at the moment of Œdipus's fateful discovery, the great chorus should sing, not of this unfortunate king, but of mankind itself, blind, trapped, and born to suffer:

> Ah, race of mortal men,
> How as a thing of nought
> I count ye, though ye live.
> (*Oedipus Rex* 1186-88)

What "Racinian tragedy" might owe to Jansenism, therefore, is much less obvious than what the Augustinian-Jansenist worldview owes to a common Western tradition. It was Nietzsche who called

Augustinianism "Platonism for the people" (Henry 30). The humanistic tradition of the West nourished Augustine as surely as it nourished Racine. As Jean Giraudoux put it, "Phèdre's so-called Jansenism, if that's what you want to call it, does not possess half the vigor and conviction of Aeschylus's Jansenism" (9).

This same principle holds true for those tempting parallels between the fall of Troy and the fall of man, or between the suffering inflicted on the vanquished Trojans and that visited on lapsed humanity. If the focus can be shifted from what is called "Jansenism" or "Augustinian anthropology" to tragedy and its perennial concerns, Troy then becomes a burning metaphor for that universe of suffering, waste, and evil which is the homeland of the tragic genre. The real continuum is that of the human predicament and of our engagement with it in art, as Marguerite Yourcenar illustrated, poignantly, in 1943:

> One generation witnesses the sack of Rome, as another has witnessed the siege of Paris or Stalingrad, another the looting of the Winter Palace. This series of tragic snapshots is fused into a single image, the capture of Troy, which is the very heart of a fire that has burned throughout history. (440)

It does not take much reading to realize that the representation of guilt in literature long preceded the writings of the bishop of Hippo. A glance at any library catalogue will do the job. What is important, however, is to distinguish between the Augustinian-Jansenist idea of guilt, which is a consequence of the Fall, and the kind of guilt felt by characters such as Oreste or Andromaque. Oreste chooses to follow Hermione's bidding, just as Andromaque initially chooses to sacrifice her son: it is these choices that provoke expressions of guilt (1019-20, 1614-18). This type of guilt, therefore, rather than being some version of original sin, is connected with decisions, taken or to be taken, and the consequences of those decisions. This is a reminder, as seen in the first chapter, that Racine constructs different tragic plots on the basis of characters' choices, often impossible choices that must be made in the fast-evolving situations created by other choices or failures to choose.

In this context it is *Phèdre* especially that is often cited as the textbook case of Jansenist guilt. The following chapter will explore some of the issues raised by questions of freedom and responsibility in this play. For the moment, however, it is worth considering Paul Bénichou's contention that Phèdre's combined sense of guilt and refusal of blame were unique to "Racinian tragedy," and that in consequence this must have been generated by the young Racine's education and upbringing:

> In none of the classical authors will you find, co-existing in the same person, this certainty of transgression and refusal of responsibility. It is not convincing to assert that, for Racine to be a Jansenist, the classical tragedies would have had to be Jansenist too. This is a paradox specific to his play, and Racine does not owe it to Euripides or Seneca rather than to Port-Royal. (*Écrivain* 321)

This answer itself poses many questions, not the least of which is whether this supposedly Jansenist "refusal of responsibility" is something of which the Augustinian catechists of Port-Royal would have approved. Is not a whole narrative strand of St Augustine's *Confessions* based on a growing consciousness of responsibility? There is also the fact that Bénichou, though he is presumably trying to argue from a mindset constructed from what can be retrieved of Racine's childhood, only uses *Phèdre* as evidence. In his long analysis of *Andromaque*, for example (207-32), there is not a single mention of Port-Royal.

The central question therefore remains: that of the nature of this "Racinian" guilt and of its relationship with Jansenism. For example, is it really the case, as Pierre Danger has asserted (87), that "the original sin," for Racine's tragic protagonists, "is quite simply the sin of existence"? A possibly surprising guide here is Aristotle, in his comments on the type of character best suited to tragedy:

> There remains, then, the intermediate kind of personage, a man not pre-eminently virtuous and just, whose misfortune, however, is brought upon him not by vice or depravity but by some error of judgment. (ch. 13)

Phèdre does not feel guilty simply because she exists. She has feelings she cannot suppress, that lead to actions she will regret, in a situation caused by her husband's decision first to bring her to

Trezène and then to leave her there. As Leszek Kolakowski demonstrates, such a structure is hardly in conformity with the Augustinian/Jansenist theology of grace:

> In the Augustinian worldview we are always morally wrong if we act by our own will and always morally right if we are guided by grace. Unlike the tragic situation, this doctrine contradicts our moral intuition about guilt. In this sense, the Augustinian and Jansenist world is not tragic, it is only sad. [...] It may be called "tragic" only in the loose sense in which any irreversible disaster is so called. (190)

There are therefore many reasons that should encourage an endorsement of Philippe Sellier's refusal (*Port-Royal* 2: 225) simply to stick the label "Jansenist" or "Augustinian" on the tragedies of Racine. Indeed, there seems something slightly desperate in Jean Rohou's most recent reiteration of the case for the continuing influence of Racine's Jansenist teachers on the tragedies:

> I am fully aware that at the time he was writing his non-religious tragedies, Racine had turned his back on his schoolmasters and their moral teaching, and was following the path of his own desires. But despite this (or even more because of it!), who can assert that he did not feel haunted by his past [...], in his innermost self, in his imagination, his emotions, his subconscious, all of which which directed the course of literary works that could liberate him from these tensions? ("Pour une étude" 4: 13)

For once, the answer is simple. No-one can possibly "assert" that Racine was not so "haunted." By the same token, no-one can assert that he was. In the meantime, all those who love his plays must wait patiently for access to that "innermost self" to which the biographical details alone do not permit some privileged access.

The caveats entered above have further implications, concerning the obscure relationship between literature, ideology, and society. In this respect Jansenism has often seemed to function as a golden key unlocking the door to a treasure house of glittering socio-cultural generalizations that supposedly characterize "Racinian tragedy." This may be, for example, Marie-Florine Bruneau arguing that her Jansenist reading "has the advantage of reasserting what is the primary role of Racine's work, that of interpreting the age in which he lived" (*Jansénisme* 10), or Christopher Braider claiming that "Racine's tragedies reflect a social response to arbitrary authority for which Jansenism supplies the metaphysical expression" (338). However, in the absence of conclusive evidence, it is clear that Lucien Goldmann's assertion, that there is a necessary link between Jansenist theology and the aspirations of a specific social class, remains just that: an assertion. If, in addition, it proves impossible to isolate specifically "Jansenist" characteristics in Racine's tragedies, this can only increase skepticism about the establishment of a logical chain leading from social class to ideology to literature, and vice versa. Applied to the theology of grace, or to French seventeenth-century history, the term "Jansenist" refers to a particular phenomenon with specific, identifiable characteristics. Applied to literature in general, and to that comfortable entity "Racinian tragedy" in particular, the word becomes so vague as to function only as a synonym for "pessimistic," which itself, as seen in the preceding chapter, is not the most precise of epithets. In the attempt to capture the essence of "Racine," a term such as "Jansenist" or "Augustinian" is less a brushstroke than a pot of paint spilled on the canvas of meaning.

## Imitation and pleasure

There is a final argument against any "Augustinian" reading of Racine's tragedies, though this will be of little consequence to those who emphasize the homiletic function of literature. In past discussions the major roles have fallen to history, ideas, and language. It is perhaps time to introduce an element too often neglected as beneath the debate, though it supports the whole stage: what François Regnault calls "the laws of pleasure" governing the theatre (*Doctrine inouïe* 16). For St Augustine the pleasure derived from a play, especially when it came from the spectacle of suffering, was essentially unnatural and thus by definition immoral:

> I loved to suffer and sought out occasions for such suffering. So when an actor on stage gave a fictional imitation of someone else's misfortunes, I was the more pleased; and the more vehement the attraction for me, the more the actor compelled my tears to flow. There can be no surprise that an unhappy sheep

wandering from your flock and impatient of your protection was infected by a disgusting sore. Hence came my love for sufferings, but not of a kind that pierced me very deeply; for my longing was not to experience myself miseries such as I saw on stage. I wanted only to hear stories and imaginary legends of sufferings which, as it were, scratched me on the surface. Yet like the scratches of fingernails, they produced inflamed spots, pus, and repulsive sores. (*Confessions* 37; bk. 3)

This lead was followed, in the seventeenth century, not just by Jansenists such as Nicole but by many mainstream churchmen, most notably by Bossuet when he gorged on the easy kill of the hapless Fr Caffaro. But paradoxically, as John Lyons has argued (*Kingdom* 73-75), those who opposed the theatre, because of the effect it produced, were for this very reason its strongest advocates. Laurent Thirouin stresses this point in his introduction to Nicole's *Traité de la comédie*:

> The opponents of the theatre saw dramatic art as a very powerful medium. Actors and dramatists were often tempted to play down these arguments, with the reminder that their sole ambition was to provide people with rest and entertainment. But those moralists who condemned them did their utmost to demonstrate the enormous influence a play exerted on its audience. Perversely, the result was not at all what they intended, since their various treatises, however hostile they may be to the theatre, can be viewed as some of the most accomplished meditations ever written on its effectiveness. (10)

Here it is salutary to remember the furious debate with Port-Royal in which Racine was engaged just before composing *Andromaque*. To those who saw the theatre as a poison for the immortal soul, Racine's response was straightforward: "What have novels and plays got to do with Jansenism?" (Picard, Ed. 2: 19). Raymond Picard is one of many to have dismissed the playwright's contribution as a piece of facile polemic, unworthy of such a serious subject: "we could have expected a discussion about the moral, religious, and metaphysical significance of tragedy" (*Racine polémiste* 51). The ground on which Racine chose to fight was not that of transmitting truth but of giving pleasure, leading Picard to remark dismissively that he was "turning theatre into mere entertainment" (Ed. 2: 14).

"Mere entertainment"? For those so easily shocked by such an idea, Racine was certainly provocative. He pointed out teasingly, for example, that the *Lettres provinciales* had only succeeded because of the enjoyment Pascal gave. He added for good measure that the pleasure gained from novels and plays was a constituent part of normal, healthy life in this world: "So let me ask you, what on earth are we to read, if we are not allowed to read books like this?" (Picard Ed. 2: 23). In other words, pleasure is not just a particular sauce, which may or may not be added, but a vital ingredient of the dish itself. This point is hardly superficial or merely polemical. It is implied in the interpretation Racine gives of *mimesis*, in his renderings of Aristotle's *Poetics*. Where the original text states that this should be "in language with pleasurable accessories," Racine's version stresses that "entertainment" (qualified or not by a "mere") is central to the playwright's purpose: "This imitation is accomplished by means of a discourse, a style composed for pleasure" (*Principes* 11). This is the properly aesthetic context in which to consider suggestions that Racine used language, consciously or not, in an "Augustinian" perspective. Few audiences and readers value *Andromaque* primarily because it teaches truths. That is, of course, unless they wish to take hold of imaginative literature and, in Seamus Heaney's words, "barber it down to a stubble of moral and ethical goads" (100).

"The playwright's job," said Pierre Nicole, "is to seek to entertain other people" (36). This was condemnation enough. In Henry Phillips's crisp summary, "Nicole considers that once a Christian has renounced through his baptismal vow the world, its pomp, and its pleasure, he may not seek pleasure or *divertissement* for its own sake" (*Theatre and Critics* 155). In other words, the anti-theatre moralists were not too wide of the mark: pleasure is the name of the game. And pleasure did not play well with churchmen. In some pollution-free parts of Scotland that is still the case: pleasure is too easily associated with the slippery slope to the everlasting bonfire. Back in the seventeenth century, which we have never left, Malebranche, to take one example, did not just take issue with Montaigne on what might be thought of as narrowly philosophical grounds, such as the role of reason or the status of truth. He also objected that the pleasure of reading the *Essays* made the arguments for skepticism attractive, and that this pleasure in itself was something to be avoided:

> It is not just dangerous to read Montaigne for entertainment, and because the pleasure he gives makes you begin to share his point of view without realizing it. But it is also dangerous because this pleasure is more culpable than is commonly imagined. For it is certain that this pleasure comes from carnal desire, and that it fuels this desire [...] We like the way this author writes only because his style moves us and arouses our emotions imperceptibly. (1: 360)

Pleasure was therefore the target. This was never more so than when this pleasure was deliberately and artificially generated for a group of people who assembled for their own enjoyment. A play is by its very nature what Marc Fumaroli calls "a complicity of concupiscence between the audience and the stage" ("Melpomène" 194). In other words, there is something essentially anti-Augustinian in the notion that playwrights might devote all the resources of their craft to give pleasure to their fellow human beings. Worse still, the theatre was denounced not only because it was seen to encourage moral depravity, but because through what St Augustine in the *Confessions* called "fictitious and theatrical invention" (36; bk. 3) it could tempt men and women to value worldly pleasure, that vanity of vanities. This was a danger clearly signaled by Bossuet in a letter to Fr. Caffaro: "It is the world, with all its allurements, pomps, and vanities, that is represented on stage. [...] People are made to love all these things, since the only aim is to show how pleasurable they are" (Urbain and Levesque 137). In Nicole's objections, there is more than a trace of Augustine's "Platonism for the people":

> If all things temporal are mere representations, shadows without substance, it is legitimate to say that actors are the shadows of shadows and the representation of representations, since they are only empty images of things temporal, and often of things that are false. (108)

The pleasure associated with participation in the mimetic action is inherently subversive of any system of ideas which denies intrinsic dignity and worth to a world viewed at best as a place of temporary exile: "The more appealing a play is, the more dangerous it is," opined the severe Fr Senault (Urbain and Levesque 20). For it is impossible to separate the "significance" of a play such as *Andromaque* (however this word might be interpreted) from its aesthetic beauty, or separate that beauty from the emotions aroused by the tragic action. This tragedy is a seamless web or it is nothing: that is the most important "unity."

Beckoning here is the eternal paradox of tragic mimesis. The pleasure given by the representation of suffering was, for St Augustine, an "amazing folly," implicating the person who enjoyed the play: "if he feels pain, he stays riveted in his seat enjoying himself" (*Confessions* 35, 37; bk. 3). A tragedy represents blind unreason, frailty, and disorder. Yet to engage an audience's attention it demands a clarity of insight, a strength of creative purpose, and a rational ordering of material. These qualities *Andromaque* displays in joyful abundance:

> Hé bien, Filles d'Enfer, vos mains sont-elles prêtes?
> Pour qui sont ces Serpents qui sifflent sur vos têtes?
> A qui destinez-vous l'appareil qui vous suit?
> Venez-vous m'enlever dans l'éternelle Nuit? (1681-84)

The daughters of hell crown a heavenly moment of human creative endeavor: the ordering of the material to arouse emotion, the use of metaphor and allusion, the exploitation of rhythm and rhyme in a harmonious correspondence of sound and sense. Emotion and idea, form, image and sound, subtly interfuse in a powerful exploration of our vulnerability as human beings to the acid of unconsoled desire and to the ever-tightening grip of the irreparable act.

The word "human" is not used lightly in this context. The sheer human triumph represented by this dramatic experience is a vibrant reaffirmation, if not of the values, then of the value of the world. The tragedies of Racine were written for pleasure. Three centuries later they continue to provide it, and would have little interest unless they did. Here at least exists some kind of continuing city. This hardly represents an Augustinian vision of a common human inheritance.

## God at work? *Athalie*

The temptation to see an Augustinian subtext in some of Racine's tragedies is stimulated by the notion that "Racinian tragedy" as a whole has one clear marker: a sense of dispossession. Characters are viewed as being at the mercy of a power that operates beyond the narrow circumference of their will and reason. Depending on the play, this power can be identified as passion, fatality, or the Gods, but in terms of control the outcome is similar. For many, the God of *Athalie* is a final and spectacular metamorphosis of this agency exterior to the will. This *deus absconditus* is seen as the real moving force of the play, with characters left to carry out the divine will, knowingly or not. This idea of a hidden God who pulls all the strings was given a certain authority in the nineteenth century by Sainte-Beuve, who proclaimed that "*Athalie* is as beautiful as Oedipus Rex, but with the one true God as well," and that "the main character in *Athalie*, or rather the only one, from the first line to the last, is God" (3: 591, 589).

In a sense, this interpretation is surprising, given what has already been noted of the central importance, in Racine's plays, of a plot constructed on human decisions that only after the event seem inevitable. On this point, however, there is a near consensus: in *Athalie* God does it all. Disagreements tend to turn, not on God's action in the play, but on the type of God it manifests. And yet, at least in the theatre, action and identity are inseparable: here there are no essences. To ask therefore what God does in this play, or whether in fact he does anything, is also to challenge the different identities he has been given. This challenge commands the questions asked here. Is *Athalie* some superior kind of puppet show? If not, what kind of play is it, and what is the identity of this God who is at the play's very heart? Is it possible to see something other than an interventionist God, a God made synonymous with power over body and mind? If so, how does this change of identity change perceptions of a "Racinian tragedy" in which human beings are viewed as dispossessed by an overwhelming power?

Two contradictory images of this God have largely determined interpretations of the play. He is portrayed either as a cynical and heedless manipulator of human designs, or else as a liberator who preserves his people from evil. Voltaires's celebrated ambivalence, well documented by Paul Mesnard (Ed. 3: 579-85) and analyzed by Ronald Ridgway, seems to have set the tone: "*Athalie*, masterpiece of beautiful poetry though it be, is still a masterpiece of fanaticism" (Besterman 107: 214). Following in this Enlightenment tradition, many see what Claude Abraham calls "this gory, unpleasant play" (152) as representing all that is worst in religion. Roger Planchon declares it to be "an apology for a totalitarian spiritual power" (Battesti and Chauvet 252), Renée Saurel views it not so much a play as a work of propaganda, "an engine of war for Catholic triumphalism" (2054), while for Erich Auerbach it is simply "a primitive tribal struggle" (*Passions* 45). In his edition of the play, Peter France is moved to conclude that this tragedy "with its fanaticism, its apparent approval of trickery and cruelty [...] must shock the rational and humane reader" (30).

Since God's party triumphs in a way judged to be contemptible, a common reaction, voiced for example by Marcel Gutwirth ("Jehu") or Paul Ginestier ("Athalie") has been one of pity for the deposed queen Athalie and scorn for the High Priest Joad. This generally accompanies contempt for the values supposedly reaffirmed by a God who, in any case, restores a king destined to be as brutal and sacrilegious as the deposed queen. Thus Michel Butor denounces "the immoral and unjust nature" of the God of *Athalie*, "a God who appears throughout the play as singularly bloodthirsty and perverse" (59). "Barbarity with a divine face": the title of Jean-Jacques Lépine's study could be given to many others. Some take to its logical conclusion what they see as the cruel absurdity of divine providence in *Athalie*. They speak of a work that is anti-Christian or anti-religious, or see it as a drama whose significance is basically political in character.[1]

It goes without saying that an equally robust critical tradition views *Athalie* as a play where God is goodness and love. This tradition is very much alive. "The divine order is restored, and God's plan is accomplished," declares François-Xavier Cuche (186), while for Jean Emelina Racine "delivers a message that is simple, clear, and reassuring [...]: everything is in the hands of God" ("*D'Esther à Athalie*" 217). On this side of the interpretative fence, the emphasis tends to be on the promise of salvation and the coming of the messiah. This approach, reinforced by the rhetoric of Racine's own Preface, has been buttressed by learned exegeses, such as those of Athanase Coquerel or Gabriel Spillebout, that seek to place *Athalie* in what is seen as its proper biblical perspective. These readings are sometimes accompanied by the complaint, as from Fr. Odoric

---

[1] See in particular Salomon, "Athalie" and Bruneau, *Jansénisme* 123. For political readings, see for example Népote-Desmarres, "*Esther* and *Athalie*," and Zysberg. For a Jacobite reading, see Charlier, Goulemot, and Orcibal. Caldicott, "Racine's 'Jacobite' Plays" 100, traces this interpretation back to Michelet. Picard, *Carrière* 417-21, and Forestier Ed. 1715, dismiss it as futile.

Bouffard (388), that adverse reactions to the triumph of Joad and Joas come from incomplete knowledge of the Scriptures. Thus Robert Hill has no doubt as to what has been lacking in commentaries on the play: "a criticism taking as its point of departure the scripture and scriptural commentary which were Racine's point of departure" ("*Athalie*" 47). Seen in this light, the murder of a queen is a manifestation of divine providence.

These two interpretations seem to be polar opposites. Closer inspection suggests another metaphor, that of parallel lines. Both interpretations follow the same track, and fittingly converge in infinity, that is, in their common approach to the God of *Athalie*. Both see the play as an expression of God at work, with individual actions as merely part of the Grand Plan, and characters only what Edwin Williams calls "instruments of the divine Will" (41). Here is a selection from the past few decades:

> In *Athalie*, God is everything, and the different moments in the dramatic action amount to nothing more than different moments of his thinking. (Maulnier, *Racine* 277)
>
> God's omnipotence dominates the play. (Brisson 239)
>
> On stage all the characters rush about doing things, but they are empty shadows; only one of them acts–and the audience only sees the person acting on his behalf–and that is God. (Picard, Ed. 1: 867)
>
> [God] keeps an eye on His puppets while they are going about the accomplishment of His will. [...] God hold the threads of the action, and the characters' words come from him. (Zimmerman 135, 144)
>
> As everyone knows, and has always known, it is God who strikes. (Delcroix, "Athalie" 30.)
>
> God is everywhere at work in righteous vengeance. (Miles 86)
>
> God directs everything. (Rohou, Ed. 1108)
>
> Everything that happens follows God's will. (Jaouën, "*Esther/Athalie*" 125)

Whether this God of *Athalie* is taken to be a tyrant or a savior, therefore, the accepted basis for most critical discussion is the idea that the dramatic action follows the iron rails laid down by the divine will. This idea, however, begs as many questions as it appears to answer. If "this is a God whose influence is unbounded" (O'Donohoe 404), and if characters are merely "God's puppets" (Picard Ed. 1: 869), where does this leave human dignity? What interest can individual characters' actions then have? Is there, as in plays examined earlier, a plot that offers suspense, surprise, uncertainty, and reversal? Does the idea of an omnipresent, manipulative God, as Ingrid Heyndels suggests (130), not corrode the basis of a tragic action that in other plays relies for its structure on a series of choices made by characters?

Whatever the questions or contradictions involved, the vision of the God of *Athalie* as a kind of puppeteer, whether cynical or paternal, holds center stage. There is, however, another way of proceeding. Just as the next chapter will attempt to distinguish between Phèdre the character and *Phèdre* the play, so the following pages will ask whether that the image of God possessed by individual characters is consistent with the reality of God's presence in the play as a whole. This will mean asking whether the freedom of action these characters seem to enjoy is real or illusory. "Impitoyable Dieu, toi seul as tout conduit," cries Athalie (1774). But is the God of Athalie necessarily the God of *Athalie*? And if not, what implications does this have for ideas of "Racinian tragedy" that see human beings cowed by forces beyond their control, a "fatality" this time expressed through the Old Testament God?

### *The implications of plot*

In other tragedies Racine devoted considerable attention, as the first chapter attempted to show, to the creation of a plot, "the life and soul of tragedy," as his primary vehicle for arousing emotion. The plot-construction of *Athalie* is generally admired (e.g. Loukovitch 431; Knight, "Meditations" 190). There are good reasons for this. The playwright built a dramatic machine that would generate suspense and surprise, and give his characters real, if difficult choices that influence the course of events. Here as in the other tragedies, this primacy of the plot has implications for determinist interpretations of "Racinian tragedy."

Consider for example the manner in which, in the opening scenes, the questions asked by Abner and Josabeth, and the response given by the High Priest Joad, create two different types of uncertainty connected with questions of identity. The first kind concerns the identity of the threat to the Temple, of the treasure hidden there, and of Joad's plan of action. Answers to these questions are revealed, gradually, in the working-out of the plot. But from the beginning another type of uncertainty is created, connected with the identity of God. This provokes more far-reaching questions. What defense has weakness against strength? Where is the promised king of the Jews, the universal king? Is it possible to believe divine providence? Here most readers of the play have tended to conclude with great certainty, on one side or the other. This paradoxically suggests that by the end of the play uncertainty still reigns.

In response to determinist theses, it is important not to underestimate the attention Racine devoted to fostering the first level of uncertainty, concerning what is actually going to happen in the play. For example, suspense and surprise are created by our ignorance as an audience of Athalie's real motives: do we believe her rhetoric, the self-portrait of the strong ruler who has done no more than follow the call of duty (467), and do we then accept as sincere her offer to treat Joas as her son (698)? These questions remain open until the final Act. It certainly seems difficult to accept Yves Le Bozec's assertion that "none of the characters in *Athalie* shows any real hesitation" (248). We can dismiss Mathan's description of the queen as male arrogance: "Elle flotte, elle hésite, en un mot elle est femme" (876). But these words indicate with what little confidence we can predict the ending, and recall similar plot markers in other plays:

> Il peut, Seigneur, il peut dans ce désordre extrême,
> Épouser ce qu'il hait, et perdre ce qu'il aime.
> (*Andromaque*, 121-22)

The first chapter has already alluded to the tension that is maintained between our knowledge of the ending, as an audience, and a plot structured, as William Stewart points out ("Mise en scène" 249), to nourish our willing suspension of disbelief. We wonder how the situation will unravel, and how characters will react. The final Act, with its rapidly mounting tension and sense of urgency, is a fitting climax to a plot that at every turn allows for different potential outcomes. This is a far cry from any idea of predetermination, whether the play be seen in Sainte-Beuve's terms (3: 589) as a demonstration of God's glory, or else as some pre-Romantic Promethean fable (Venesoen, "*Athalie*"). Thierry Maulnier is representative of many critics for whom "*Athalie* substitutes divine action for human action" (*Racine* 278). And it is true that characters may see themselves as having no control over events, just as Oreste, Agamemnon, or Phèdre, for example, feel that fate or the Gods have it in for them. But a character's perception or rhetoric should not be confused with the dramatic action as a whole. In the case of *Athalie*, as in other tragedies by Racine, this action advances through decisions taken by characters, and by reactions to those decisions.

Consider the overthrow of Athalie. The plans for this revolution do not descend gift-wrapped from the sky. The High Priest proclaims that things are in the hands of God (226), but everyone turns out to be in the hands of Joad. He presents himself as the instrument of God's vengeance: "Livre en mes faibles mains ses puissants ennemis" (290). But he makes scant distinction between divine Providence and his own plot to rout Athalie, as is clear from the show he promises Abner in the Temple at the third hour:

> Dieu pourra vous montrer par d'importants bienfaits
> Que sa parole est stable, et ne trompe jamais. (157-58)

Joad's rhetoric suggests that only God, not outside help, can save both Temple and child from Athalie: "Non, non, c'est à Dieu seul qu'il nous faut attacher" (1093). In practical terms this reliance on God means relying on Joad. It is Joad who carefully plans every detail of the ambush. He chooses the right moment to strike, personally hands out weapons from his arms cache, gives precise orders for every stage of the final trap, tells the child king exactly when to appear, and then instructs his warriors when to come out of hiding and when to take Athalie away for slaughter. For Joad, God's time has come. But it is Joad who decides when this is to be, witness the exact timing he demands of the Levites set to trap Athalie, in phrases such as "à son entrée," "dès que...," "Prenez soin qu'à l'instant la trompette..." (1675-92). He even tells the participants what expressions they should wear on their faces (1676). If this theatrical production is meant to show the power of God, the play is written and produced by the High Priest, and actively stage-managed by him. Nothing is left to chance, or mere providence:

"Suivez de point en point ces ordres importants" (1674). This Godlike role casts an ironic light on claims that it is God himself who directs the action, and that Joad merely submits to the divine will. To paraphrase Cervantes, it is not a miracle but a stratagem (3: 210; pt. 2, ch. 21).

This is not the image that the High Priest's rhetoric seeks to project. He paints a picture of Athalie's army ranged against the weak and innocent, whose only hope is in God. In practice, this tranquil confidence means having Athalie ambushed by a band of armed men ready for holy murder. Joad's sense of security may well come from his belief that God is on his side, but it is happily buttressed by his meticulously planned scheme to trap Athalie. An example is his reaction to the news that the queen cannot escape:

> Je vois, que du saint Temple on referme la porte.
> Tout est en sûreté. (1704-5)

The action of the play uncovers a wily, ruthless leader who single-mindedly and single-handedly plots victory for his own side. In other words, he uses his image of God as a weapon of war. Joad justifies his military planning in the phrase with which the rebukes Abner's passivity: "La foi qui n'agit pas, est-ce une foi sincère?" (71). And he does not doubt for an instant that he is the Vicar of Jehovah on earth: "Voici comme ce Dieu vous répond par ma bouche" (84). But the reality of what he actually does is significantly different from the rhetoric he uses, which projects the image of someone who is simply a medium for the divine will. In Terence Cave's words, "He is the organizer of the whole charade, representing a sinister but successful conspiracy between arbitrary power and theatrical contrivance" (386). At least from the point of view of plot-construction, therefore, *Athalie* does not present the appearance of an action predetermined by a Higher Power.

Is this only an appearance? Two episodes are often adduced to prove predetermination: Athalie's "dream sent by Providence" (E. Blanc 24), and Joad's vision. Athalie's dream (487-514), with its vision of her mother's downfall and of her own death at the hand of a child, has often been interpreted as clear evidence of God's barely hidden hand. The dream as such, however, can hardly be seen as a special marker put down on this occasion by Racine to show the distinctively divine nature of his play. It was a common dramatic technique: Jacques Morel (*Agréables mensonges* 43) cites 73 examples of the dream in seventeenth-century tragedy. Dreams were often used to create a sense of impending doom: such is their properly tragic function. The dream in *Athalie*–no more than its counterpart in Corneille's *Horace* or the witches' words in *Macbeth*–does not remove characters' freedom to act, or stun them into submission to the supernatural. It is first and foremost as an energizing force in the plot that Racine exploits this dream, which was entirely of his invention. It brings together for Athalie, in a terrifying vision, the different elements that seem to justify her struggle against "le cruel Dieu des Juifs" (498). The dream leads her to enter the Temple, and to recognize the child she sees there. In the economy of the plot it has a determining role to play.

This does not mean, however, that it proves the determining role of God. For example, Athalie does not accept the homicidal message of the dream unquestioningly (516-18). Nor does it spur her to take immediate action. She does not know whether the threat posed by the child in the Temple is real or imaginary, and asks for counsel (542). When Abner seeks to persuade her not to act against the child merely on the basis of what is dismissed as a mere dream (556), Mathan speaks quite differently:

> Le Ciel nous le fait voir un poignard à la main:
> Le Ciel est juste et sage et ne fait rien en vain. (557-58)

This is an impressive declaration of faith in Providence. Only later does it become clear with what cynicism Mathan plays the God card (919-44). His witness is hardly the strongest argument for divine intervention in Athalie's life. In addition, it is not the queen's dream that determines her future behavior, but Mathan's fabrication of the story that the Jews see the child Joas as a future leader (888-92). The effect on Athalie is immediate and direct:

> Ces mots ont fait monter la rougeur sur son front.
> Jamais mensonge heureux n'eut un effet si prompt. (893-94)

In other words, the queen's actions are not motivated by the dream. It is this lie that determines Athalie to take action to neutralize the child, and leads her to the final ambush. Ironically, this lie turns out to be true, and the dream is shown to be an inaccurate representation of reality: Athalie is not killed by the child. Florence Dumora complains that this is too literal an interpretation of the dream, which for her is "true," because the queen is "really" killed by the child, to the extent that the presence of the child leads her to the temple (21). In this sense, perhaps, the point might be taken. At a murder trial, however, this conflation of occasion and agent might wilt under cross-examination. At the very least, therefore, the dream provides shaky evidence for any argument that sees *Athalie*, and Athalie, as the visible expression of God at work. The dream's importance is elsewhere. It is used not just to amplify a sense of foreboding, but to increase the uncertainty into which characters and audience are thrown. It says less about a *deus ex machina* than about how Racine constructs the mechanism of his plays.

The second episode used in evidence to demonstrate the reality of God's controlling hand is Joad's prophecy of the destruction of the Temple and the coming of the New Jerusalem (1139-74). Here it is useful to remember that the High Priest's words, taken from prophetic verses of the Bible, are uttered in a trance-like state, and that he has no later memory of them. As Annie Barnes puts it, "Racine says that Joad *sees*, not that he understands or remembers" ("Prophétie" 107). In his Preface Racine speaks of "holy emotions," and reminds his readers that the words Joad speaks are not his own. A telling point is the abrupt passage from heavenly invocation (1173-74) to material preparations for the *coup d'état* (1177-86). As with the dream, the vision does not influence the course of events, a point stressed by Lucien Benguigui (92). This prophetic scene is at one remove from the action, as Racine seems to suggest in his Preface by calling it "a kind of Episode, that leads naturally to the music." He insists that its prime function is to arouse emotion, "to increase turmoil in the play."

It therefore seems odd to assert that, for Joad to be a truly tragic character, he must be fully self-aware during his vision, as though this were the moment that determined all that followed (Forman, "Lyrisme" 311). On the contrary, it is at every other moment that Joad shows absolute awareness. When he does act, it is with cold rationality and finely tuned stealth. As a simple matter of fact, it is before this vision scene that all his crucial decisions are made (1094-97). Many seem to take at face value his belief that he is "identified with the will of Providence" (Cornud 94), and is the mere executor of God's wishes, a man ready to leave his fate in

God's hands, a mere spectator (Chédozeau, "*Athalie*" 500). This belief is hardly consistent with the complex and continuous activity of the High Priest, involving scheming, spying, and organizing. Inspection of the plot, therefore, invites some degree of distinction between Joad and God. The distinction is capital for any attempt to identify what this God represents, for a general interpretation of *Athalie*, and for what this play in turn is seen to represent in terms of some supposedly coherent entity called "Racinian tragedy."

*Identities and tragedy*

To see the dramatic action of *Athalie* as evolving from choices made by characters is necessarily to challenge the idea of a divine puppeteer. This is not, however, to seek to remove God from the play, still less to see it, with Jean-Marie Goulemot (128), as an exclusively political drama in which the religious references are so much window dressing, serving to provide an aesthetic acceptable to Racine's contemporaries. Jean Cahen (154) has shown that *Athalie*, despite its multitude of proper names, contains relatively little "local color." There is, on the other hand, a good case for arguing that very heart of *Athalie* is religious. Not only is the use of religious language constant, deliberate, and unambiguous. The presence and identity of God, and the possibility of God's salvation of mankind, are questions that concern the play from the sumptuous first line, when we as an audience are placed before *l'Éternel*. To choose to overlook this massively reiterated theme is, as Raymond Picard argues (Ed. 1: 866), to choose not to explore an essential dimension of the tragic action. Even if this point be accepted, however, there are other questions to answer. What kind of *Éternel* is represented in the play? And how does this religious dimension, if it exist, coexist with the reality of human action within it, and the reality of a human suffering that seems to mock any benign idea of the divinity?

The phrase *Athalie, tragédie* is a good place to start, since it is sometimes stated (e.g. Gans, "Tragédie" 66) that its God cannot coexist with tragedy. Visibly, however, as Roy Knight has shown (*Racine et la Grèce* 384-92), Racine paid scrupulous respect to the commonly acknowledged demands of the tragic genre, and consciously integrated elements of Greek tragedy into his own play.

Indeed, for no less an authority than Henri Gouhier, as Thérèse Malachy reminds us (595), the theology of *Athalie* owes much to Greek tragedy and philosophy. One could also point to the pattern of initial error, reversal, and discovery identified by Aristotle as a fundamental of the tragic plot. John Stone for his part (109) has noted the similarities between the moment of revelation in *Athalie* and the Sophoclean revelation-scene. The subject is, after all, "the recognition and coronation of Joas," as Racine explains in the Preface. The queen's reversal is clearly caused by the mistaken desire to seize Joas, whose identity is recognized at the end. And discovery of identity is without doubt an important element in the play: Jean Rohou (Ed. 1128) points out that terms such as *révéler* and *dévoiler* occur more here than elsewhere in Racine.

This said, the question remains: what *kind* of identity or discovery is involved here? Jean Mesnard suggests that the characters in *Athalie* "are only dimly aware of what they are involved in" (9). Are there grounds for accepting this point of view? For Aristotle, a reversal is much more dramatically compelling when it brings about a recognition of identity. But is this "drama of identity" simply limited to Athalie's recognition of Joas, or of God? The play is written and performed for us as an audience to see. Identity is for us to seek. We do not follow the dramatic action as a whole within the mind-set of a particular character. If we allow ourselves to do so, for example in plays such as *Phèdre* or *Hamlet*, this presents its own problems, as we shall see in the following chapter. "Recognition" involves the active participation of the audience, a point well made by Paul Ricœur:

> The pleasure of finding out is thus the pleasure of recognition. That is what the audience does when, in *Oedipus Rex,* it recognizes universals that the plot has engendered through its very construction. And so the pleasure of recognition is both built into the work and experienced by the audience. (*Temps et Récit* 1: 81)

After her downfall Athalie cries out her discovery of another identity, that of God: "Dieu des Juifs, tu l'emportes!" (1768). For her this God is a God of power and vengeance. But is this the identity that we the audience necessarily uncover in the play as a whole?

From the exposition, the series of questions first asked by Abner and Josabeth, and then amplified by Athalie, prepares a traditional denouement of revelation, connected with the identity of Joas. But from the opening scenes another series of questions is asked. To some degree they are questions posed in other tragedies. Is there an order in the universe? May men do as they wish with their fellow human beings? Does everything depend on blind chance? As Prosser Frye has put it, "if such things can be, what becomes of the law of eternal righteousness as given in the heart of man?" (99). These may be dismissed as the type of "metaphysical," unanswerable, and therefore empty questions against which *Candide* was later to seek to inoculate sensible people. If so, the felony is compounded in *Athalie*. Here these questions are placed in an essentially mystical perspective, and concern the identity of God.

Abner touches on these questions in the first scene. He paints a picture of popular unbelief and blasphemy amongst the Chosen People, and of an unspeaking, absent God. Joad's response is to portray a God described in terms of *éclat, pouvoir, puissance, gloire*. And for many (e.g. Gauthier 233), this man of God is God's man on stage. That interpretation, however, poses a problem. If the God of *Athalie* were to be no other than the God of Joad, if *Athalie* were destined to be no more than a display of divine fireworks, it would be difficult not to see the tragic action as being seriously flawed. For with the opening equation "God equals power," how could any "reversal" be any more than superficial? In other words, is the God who is uncovered, in the playing-out of the tragic action, merely a copy of the image of God held high by Joad in the opening scenes, the inscrutable guardian of immutable rules, "Un Dieu, tel aujourd'hui qu'il fut dans tous les temps" (126)? Is this the only identity of God on offer?

This is not, however, the whole story. The exposition, which in Corneille's phrase "must contain the seeds of everything that is to happen" (*Writings* 21), sows other seeds. The first is the fatalistic idea that evil will triumph. This coincides, as seen in the last chapter, with the widely-held view that "Racinian tragedy" is "pessimistic" if it is truly "Racinian" or really "tragic." Pessimism is expressed in Joasbeth's fear that the young child Joas is irredeemably stained by the sins of his Fathers:

> Qui sait si cet Enfant par leur crime entraîné
> Avec eux en naissant ne fut pas condamné? (237-38)

The High Priest prays that Joas be given the kingship only if he is to be a God-fearing king (287-89). But if Joas is to turn out as Josabeth fears, where does this leave the God who restored him? The exposition, therefore, does more than just present Joad's God of power. It also suggests that this God will be put to the test, and might be found wanting. The opening scenes, concurrently, introduce the messianic theme, expressed in the many references to David's line, and in Abner's hope for a king who will rule the world (131-36). As noted in Chapter 1, these two seeds that are planted, one of hope and one of despair, both project the tragic action beyond the one day chosen for its accomplishment. In other words, the tragic action develops not only within the confines of the Temple, and the day, in the struggle between Joad and Athalie, but in the dimension suggestion by the opening line, that of the eternal.

At the level of the material Temple, the exposition presents a situation familiar in tragedy: a ruler has disrupted the order of the law, here expressed by Abner as the Law given by Moses on Mount Sinai (1-14). This state of disorder, which is given a figurative statement in Athalie's dream (507), is expressed in the queen's attempt to go into the Temple beyond where she should. The phrase used is highly evocative in the context of tragedy: "passer les limites" (399). This *hybris*, "having energy or power and misusing it self-indulgently" (Macdowell 21), is a crux of the tragic genre from its beginnings.[2] But Athalie, "Cette Femme superbe," "cette superbe Reine" (398, 739), with that overweening pride proper to the tragic genre, does not recognize such limits.

This view of Athalie's activities is not universally held. A mass of critics, rather than speaking of *hybris*, present the queen as a good ruler, intelligent, tolerant, and human, an enlightened despot who falls victim to Joad's fanaticism, a woman who opposes the tyranny of patriarchal monotheism, and who is ennobled by her sense of duty.[3] "In the tragic pattern," asserts Odette de Mourgues, "God appears cruel, unfair, and moved by an arbitrary wish to destroy Athalie" (125). It may be the case that, in a biblical perspective, the

---

[2] See Barnwell, *The Tragic Drama* 240-44; O'Dohohoe, p. 407; Phillips, "The Divine Sentence" 112; Webster 53.

[3] See for example Adam 5: 56; Bruneau, "*Athalie*" 382; Denain, "Jézabel" 201; Grégoire 332; Henein 104; Stewart, "Le Tragique" 152; Sweetser, "Les femmes" 209; Vossler 94.

queen is guilty of having broken the First Commandment, and thus the covenant with the one true God. *Athalie*, however, is not a sermon, nor a biblical commentary, but a tragic drama that exploits a biblical subject. In this fusion of subject and form it offers its own tragic perspective, in which Athalie's wish to control the Temple might be compared to Néron's desire to possess Junie. This wish is an apt expression of the desire to control everything, since only the Temple is now left to express the spiritual freedom of a few dissidents (15). Mathan too, like Athalie, is presented from the outset as one who seeks to overstep the limits (849-50), and as false counsellor recalls Narcisse in *Britannicus*. Like Néron and Narcisse, both Athalie and Mathan through their actions ask the question "why not?" It is a question that challenges the very existence of any values that could transcend their own desires.

This refusal to recognize limits is one expression of another traditional theme from tragedy, that of blindness. Both Athalie and Mathan desire to find the treasure that David has put in the Temple, but they cannot see beyond discovery of a material kind. Similarly, Athalie wishes to find out everything about the child in the Temple, but searches only for a narrow political truth. This she presents as "la simple Vérité" (630), with an unconscious irony that should of itself create a certain wariness about accepting only a political reading of the play. Athalie congratulates Mathan on opening her eyes to the truth (609-10), but she is blinded to any truth beyond the purely temporal world of her own desires and fears. Mathan, for his part, sees himself as a realist, not one to be duped by appearances (919-22). As with the queen, the "reality" he embraces is a world governed by one law, the satisfaction of his rulers' desires: "Près de leur passions rien ne me fut sacré" (937). For both Athalie and Mathan, then, in a real and threatening sense, nothing is sacred. It is apposite that in *Athalie* Racine should quote a phrase, "Monstre naissant" (603), already used in his Preface to *Britannicus*. The world of Athalie and Mathan, as that of Néron and Narcisse, is its own absolute. Beyond this world of their own desires, there is no sense: within it, there are no limits. This is a genuinely monstrous theme, represented in other tragedies.

The suggestion that there is a moral dimension to the tragic action, as the last chapter attempted to show, can provide one response to the common conflation of "Racine," "tragedy," and "pessimism." This suggestion is reinforced by the discussion of the meaning of the Law, the "règle éternelle" (1381). At the heart of this Law is the belief that God is one, and that there is no other God. This implies that man is not God, and that man's decrees can never be the final word. The child Joas cannot yet appreciate the possibility that he might one day be tempted to play God: "De l'absolu pouvoir vous ignorez l'ivresse" (1389). But the High Priest warns the future ruler that he will not lack counselors to flatter his desires:

> Bientôt ils vous diront, que les plus saintes Lois,
> Maîtresses du vil peuple, obéissant aux Rois;
> Qu'un Roi n'a d'autre frein que sa volonté même;
> Qu'il doit immoler tout à sa grandeur suprême; (1391-94)

These words place the tragic action of *Athalie* in a traditional tragic perspective. The queen's invitation to Joas–'Venez dans mon Palais, vous y verrez ma gloire" (679)–is essentially the same as that given by Néron to the captive victim of his desire: "C'est à vous de passer du côté de l'Empire" (*Britannicus*, 588). A sense of human dignity, a knowledge that there are limits beyond which no person can go: these are foreign entities in a perspective bounded only by the desire for power. It is the queen's blindness to these limits, not the hand of God, which leads her to make the mistake that precipitates her downfall, and brings the final recognition scene.

*What recognition?*

The question remains as to who recognizes what. Both Athalie and Joad impute her downfall to God. Joad has asked for the queen to be blinded by pride into committing an error (292-94), and she in turn finds a scheming God responsible for her own failure to act decisively (1775-76). Many consider Athalie primarily to be the victim of a vengeful God and his spiteful minister. There is also the view, expressed by Dervil Conroy, that she perishes "because she is, in reality, a woman in power, a threat to the patriarchy which must be removed" (72). It is, however, worth looking at the evidence that Athalie herself is at least partly responsible for what happens to her. As Lucien Benguigui expresses it: "we must not overlook, as too many critics do, Athalie's crime. She dies through her own fault, not through the vengeance of God. Her wrongdoing has an internal logic that leads her to her death" (87).

Since Athalie realizes that she has been manipulated and trapped, nothing is more natural than her "Impitoyable Dieu, toi seul as tout conduit." But we the audience, we who see all that happens, are not restricted to this single viewpoint. We can follow the different stages of the *coup d'état* that Joad prepares and executes. We can identify the tragic pattern of the action as it unfolds, and see the reversal springing directly from Athalie's initial error in failing to recognize that there are certain human boundaries one cannot cross without consequences. The resulting reversal appropriately occurs when the queen, heedless of such limits, crosses the threshold of the Temple. Once she takes the decision to seize Joas, there is no turning back, and she is caught up in a mechanism over which she has no control:

> Vous dès que cette Reine ivre d'un fol orgueil
> Da la porte du Temple aura passé le seuil,
> Qu'elle ne pourra plus retourner en arrière; (1681-83)

The revelation of the hidden Joas, together with the dramatic appearance of the armed Levites, produces the most theatrical recognition-scene in all of Racine's theatre. Athalie's "Où suis-je?" (1731) is the classic cry of tragic discovery, the very words uttered by Hermione (*Andromaque,* 1401), as one world is reversed, and identity is revealed. Athalie's error lay in believing that there existed no authority transcending her own power and desires. The error rebounds on her, and brings her to ruin. In her downfall she discovers that she must reckon with a reality beyond her own desires.

While it is therefore not necessary to insert God into this archetypical tragic machine, the identity of the reality discovered by Athalie remains an open question. Put simply, is the God she identifies the same God whose image shines clear from the play? The queen's phrase, "Impitoyable Dieu," reflects her own image of a God existing only in displays of power. This explains her jibes about a God who seems impotent (1710), and her own strategy of suppressing any sign of weakness or emotion:

> Où serais-je aujourd'hui, si domptant ma faiblesse
> Je n'eusse d'une Mère étouffé la tendresse,

> Si de mon propre sang ma main versant des flots
> N'eût par ce coup hardi réprimé vos complots? (723-26)

Ironically, this discourse of power has elements that parallel the High Priest's own image of God. Many (e.g. Yashinksky 69) have underlined the importance of vengeance in this play. Either Athalie or Joad could have spoken of God's "fureur vengeresse" (1378), since for both, vengeance is the clearest expression of divine power. The words Joad associates with the divinity are not just abstract terms such as *pouvoir, puissance,* and *gloire,* but very concrete representations of what this divine power means: *poursuivre, combattre, confondre, frapper, détruire, immoler, exterminer.* Jean Rohou, who sees Joad as the expression of God, considers the High Priest's energetic intervention to be a heroic devotion to duty, and adds for good measure that "any analysis that respects the text cannot see it in any other way" ("Pour une étude" 4: 11).

There is, however, another way of considering Joad's role in the play. Some, like Jean Rohou, might find this "heroic", but that must depend on what is meant by "heroism." Joad certainly presents no shrinking violet of a *deus absconditus,* but a "Dieu qui combat pour nous" (226), manifesting himself in acts of strength and majesty, a God of wrath ready to annihilate those who oppose him (229-34). The role that Joad asks this God to play is a straightforward one:

> Du milieu de mon peuple exterminez les crimes,
> Et vous viendrez alors m'immoler vos victimes. (91-92)

Thus the High Priest sees God expressing himself in the blood-soaked field of the defeated Achab, in Jezabel's body torn apart by thirsty dogs that lick her blood (109-20). His instructions to the Levites reflect his image of an ever-wrathful, ruthless, and even bloodthirsty God: "Dans l'infidèle sang baignez-vous sans horreur" (1360). This God is above all a "Dieu vengeur" (1343), a heavy hand always ready to strike:

> Dieu, dont le bras vengeur, pour un temps suspendu,
> Sur cette race impie est toujours étendu. (233-34)

The fact that it is Joad who is planning and executing the revenge does not change his rhetoric, since he sees himself merely as an instrument: "Dieu sur ses ennemis répandra sa terreur," "L'Ange exterminateur est debout avec nous" (1359, 1698). His final prayer thus represents the culmination of this chilling assimilation of his own hand and that of God: "Grand Dieu, voici ton heure, on t'amène ta proie" (1668).

Athalie and Joad have obviously different roles to play. The queen has a temporal power she wishes to be absolute: for the assault on the Temple she is presented holding a dagger at the ready, and breathing fire and blood (1537-40). But Joad's idea of God seems inextricably linked with hers. At the moment of reversal, this God is evoked by both characters, as before, in terms of power, victory, and revenge. Athalie's "Dieu des Juifs, tu l'emportes!" (1768) is no confession of faith, but the admission that Jehovah is momentarily the victor. Far from recognizing divine omnipotence, her final predictions indicate only that a battle has been lost, but not the war (1784-90). What Athalie "discovers" of the identity of God is therefore to a large extent a reaffirmation of an image of God that both she and Joad have in different ways projected from the outset. In this sense, one can agree with Harriet Stone that "Athalie and Joad have no certainty of knowing because they exist only as a reflection of each other" (*Royal DisClosure* 96). The reality of this God is quite simply proportionate to his power. And paradoxically, of course, this image of God is the least transcendental of all, since it is the reflection of a very human desire for power and revenge. Nor is there any great difference between this God and the harsh Gods apostrophized by Agamemnon and Phèdre, or the fatality Oreste feels weighing on his life, or the unyielding force that condemns Britannicus or Bajazet. Indeed, it is this that prompted Eric Gans to assert that "in the Christian tragedy he was attempting to write, it is the absence of Christ that Racine reveals" (66). This is a longstanding idea, and one that cannot simply be brushed aside: that "God," "the Gods," or "fate," all imply violation and alienation.

## Despair?

This image of a harsh, unbending God fits neatly into that post-Romantic picture of "Racinian tragedy" established with the help of nineteenth-century German philosophy and twentieth-century existentialism, with a dash of Jansenism added. In this sense the God of Joad and Athalie is the perfect topping for that big cake called "Racinian tragedy." Before accepting this comfortable integration, however, some questions do need to be asked. Is *Athalie* merely a display of divine firepower? Is the God of power the only image of God an audience is allowed to glimpse? To ask these questions is to reply to an invitation given by the tragic action as a whole. That means trying to make some sense of the seeds both of despair and of hope sown in the exposition.

The despair is difficult to overlook. Athalie's last words are not her admission of defeat, but her prediction that the new king will, like his ancestors, turn against God's law:

> On verra de David l'héritier détestable
> Abolir tes honneurs, profaner ton Autel,
> Et venger Athalie, Achab et Jézabel. (1788-90)

This future outcome cannot be limited to some political lesson on the impossibility of putting power into practice (e.g. Népote-Desmarres 369). The audience knows that Joas will betray the God in whose name he has been restored to the throne, and then outdo Athalie, by murdering the High Priest, Joad's son. And yet Joas has been presented to the people by Joad as "votre Roi, votre unique espérance" (1326). The child king begins the final scene with a prayer:

> Dieu, qui voyez mon trouble et mon affliction,
> Détournez loin de moi sa malédiction,
> Et ne souffrez jamais qu'elle soit accomplie. (1797-99)

This prayer will not be answered. Athalie's final prediction comes true. Her defeat has not taken mankind beyond the cycle of outrage and revenge in which it seems trapped. For the idea of God as power, still less as goodness, this seems to be a reversal on an infinite scale.

This apparent shipwreck of divine providence seems only to confirm the view that "Racinian tragedy" is closely bound up with a near-Aeschylean sense of fatality, and that human beings, do what they want, can in the end do nothing:

> When shall the ancestral curse relent,
> And seek to rest, its fury spent?
>> (Aeschylus, *The Choephori*, final chorus)

In other words, is *Athalie* based on this ancient idea of a tragic cycle, as John Lapp has put it, "ever renewing itself in time" (62)? Will the promise be fulfilled, or will the cycle of revenge continue? Paul Ricœur has spoken of "this endless chain of cruelty, where crime engenders crime [...], and which steeps us in the kind of fundamental wickedness that is how things are" ("Culpabilité tragique" 290). Does *Athalie* not give an image of humanity still trapped within such a cycle of revenge? At the very least, one might doubt André Blanc's assertion that one of the identifying marks of "Racinian tragedy" is that "good always triumphs over evil" (230). As Thérèse Malachy expresses it (596), at the end of *Athalie* there is not much cathartic peace of mind on offer.

For what has been the point of restoring Joas to the throne? Not all will find it as easy as Bernard Chédozeau ("Dimension religieuse" 175) to adopt a "Providentialist reading" which alone is supposed to make sense of the whole business. Ann Delehanty asserts that "all of Racine's viewers would have known that despite Joas' malevolent acts, the telos of Old Testament history was successfully fulfilled in the advent of Christ" (163). This may well be the case. But "Racine's viewers" also knew, and know, that the advent of Christ did not put a stop to the massacres of history, which were not infrequently even initiated in his name. There might also be some skepticism about George Steiner's contention that "the entire drama turns on a dialectic of light and darkness" (100), or Judd Hubert's statement that "*Athalie* dramatizes the struggle between two forces: God's timelessness and man's temporal, corrupt nature" (142). Quite simply, as Charles Mazouer has put it, "how can we possibly understand this suffering?" (131).

This question is integral to the tragic action. The Chorus chants what is the eternal taunt for the believer, one that resurfaces in the narratives of Christ's crucifixion: "Votre Dieu ne fait rien pour vous" (819). Is there any evidence that *Athalie* provides a comfortable answer to this question? Darkness is visible, but the light? If God is power, and the power supply fails, is there anything left but what Erica Harth calls "the hopelessness of a world without alternatives" (395)? It is a world in which God is a fiction, and from which he is absent or aloof, whichever is worse. The opening lines of this tragedy, as so many others since *Oedipus Rex*, tell of an order disrupted. Here the order is the Law, given by God to his people. But what restoration is it, for Joas to be a murderous idolater? Joas promises solemnly to obey God, and is anointed with the holy oil, but to what end? How can the plaintive cry of the chorus be answered?

> Combien de temps, Seigneur, combien de temps encore
> Verrons-nous contre toi les Méchants s'élever? (810-11)

What then of that mighty design, which for Joad justifies trickery and assassination: "Il faut finir des Juifs le honteux esclavage" (1334)? For as surely as we the audience know, in *Iphigénie*, that Troy will fall, here we know here that the Temple will be destroyed. Joad has placed his faith in a God who wins battles for his people, and intervenes on earth to show his mighty power. In the reversal of this idea we discover that God does not answer to this name.

Harriet Stone, perhaps in the spirit of Voltaire's conclusion to *Candide*, suggests that, to understand this play, "we ought to avoid the pitfall of seeking its meaning in its theological context" ("Marking Time" 101). Given the theological labyrinth from which it seems there is no escape, many will sympathize with what seems a prudent critical option. Paradoxically, perhaps, this option might seem to be reinforced by the view, recently reiterated by Jean Emelina ("D'*Esther à Athalie*" 217, 220), that even theologically Racine is adopting a perfectly banal, orthodox, and thus unproblematic stance. These points of view, however, hardly address the questions posed by the play, or account for the reactions it has aroused over three centuries. For many *Athalie* is not just a religious tragedy, but a tragedy of religion. Implicit in the playing-out of its dramatic action are questions which, for some at least, are of a fundamental nature. Is "God" no more than a name given to the inscrutable interaction of chance and necessity? Are human beings condemned to powerlessness, dispossession, and alienation, in a universe where justice itself is only a name? If "here we have no continuing city," does this reposition "Racinian tragedy" within some neo-Augustinian fold, but in a Jansenism without God? There are no easy answers to these questions. Whatever different views may be held, *Athalie* does offer an experience of darkness which recalls Pascal's vision of a world without God: "Considering the blindness of mankind, and gazing out at a whole universe that is silent, with mankind deprived of light, alone and forsaken" (fr. 192). In a post-twentieth-century universe, is it in such bleak terms that *Athalie* can most plausibly be read? If that be the case, does *Athalie* not then conform with the commonest ideas of "Racinian tragedy"?

## *A sense of God?*

Any attempt to respond must be prefaced by the reminder that imaginative literature has always grappled with such issues. Humphrey Kitto sees a similar interrogation emerging from the works of Sophocles: "Is the human universe governed by chance, in which case morality and religion have no status, or does it obey law?" (60). Inevitably, questions such as this provoke contrasting responses. Terence Cave, for example, warns against the idea that any tragedy contains "some moral 'truth' smugly carried off by the spectator after the curtain falls" (342). On the other hand, for Arthur Miller, not the most smug of playwrights, "the discovery of the moral law [...] is what the enlightenment of tragedy consists of" (*Theatre Essays* 5). These opposing reactions mirror the paradox represented in the playing-out of the tragic action of *Athalie*. For the apparent triumph of the unjust and the irrational runs parallel, as has been seen, with the suggestion of a starkly contrasting reality: a world in which human actions meet restraints that, if ignored, lead to catastrophe. Northrop Frye expresses this idea of hidden restraints in robust fashion: "Whether the context is Greek, Christian, or undefined, tragedy seems to lead up to an epiphany of law, of that which is and must be" (*Anatomy of Criticism* 208). Is there such an epiphany in *Athalie*?

There is certainly explicit reference to the law, that is, to the Law:

> Ô divine, ô charmante Loi!
> Ô justice, ô bonté suprême!
> Que de raisons, quelle douceur extrême
> D'engager à ce Dieu son amour et sa foi! (347-50)

The idea that there are limits, and that there is thus more to the world than fate, or chance, or power, leads in *Athalie, tragédie tirée de l'Écriture sainte*, to something that necessarily transcends the human condition. This "something" is as difficult to define as it is to ignore. Might it be called "a sense of God"? Many do not have much time for such mysteries. Neither do Athalie nor, paradoxically, Joad. Athalie refuses to countenance any authority beyond her own exercise of it. But no less totalitarian is Joad's God, seeming to justify any inquisitions, witch-hunts, and crusades undertaken in the name of a Higher Truth. In Pascal's words, "we make an idol of the truth itself, because truth without charity is not God" (fr. 926). Michel Cournot, in his account of Alain Zaeppfel's 2003 production of *Esther* at the Comédie-Française, remarked that it was impossible to watch it "without having in mind, at every turn, Auschwitz" (30).[4] A similar point could be made about *Athalie*. How many can now hear the word *holocauste*, even used in its narrow liturgical sense (1259), without a feeling of horror and shame?

For many this "sense of God" is above all a sense of outrage. An example is Alain Niderst: "God is present in the evil that reigns on earth. The subject of *Athalie* is the incarnation of God" (*Les Tragédies* 159). Is the God-thing then just a grim absurdity? In the words of Shakespeare's battered, half-demented King Lear, "Is man no more than this?" (3.4.101). The preceding chapter, with *Iphigénie*, touched on some of the complexities that surround what has been called the problem of evil. The affirmation of faith in a loving God, which in *Athalie* is chanted in every chorus, has always come up against what seems to make a mockery of any such faith: the persistence of injustice and suffering. In Paul Ricœur's phrase, "the problem of the evil God springs from the very heart of faith in God" ("Culpabilité tragique" 306). At the same time, that very sense of justice and human dignity that are outraged seem themselves to point to something beyond the purely human. This paradox is at the very heart of Pascal's riddling words: "It is incomprehensible that God could exist, and incomprehensible that he could not" (fr. 809).

---

[4] Is *Athalie* is "a kind of anti-Semitic polemic," in the hypothesis advanced by Ronzeaud, in Delcroix, "*Athalie*" 45, or were the wartime Occupation authorities justified in seeing it as "Jewish propaganda" (Paraf 91)? On this subject, see Benguigui (141-47), who also quotes O. Ullmann's contention that Racine is "one of the Just" (19).

This is not an area where convincing explanations grow on trees. And *Athalie* is a play, not a treatise of metaphysics. In the very bankruptcy of the idea of a God of power, the play does, however, provide one chink of light. This is that we perhaps worship or reject a false image of God, because as human beings we tend to create God in our own image. The same suggestion was made in *Iphigénie*. In other words, do we, like Joad no less than Athalie, forge a weapon called "God," to fight with or against, in the workshop of our own emotional, psychic, and intellectual needs? This question is implicit in the paradoxical critical reactions provoked by the tragic action of *Athalie*. If the best reversals are accompanied by scenes of recognition, then in the reversal of the image of God as power, are we not being invited to consider a different identity? It is no more than an invitation, through a narrow door, that many will not have the least desire to open. But the exposition has planted a second seed, one of hope, expressed in the messianic belief that God would deliver his people. Mathan and Athalie, Abner and Joad, ironically or with belief, all speak of this messiah as a powerful ruler and king of kings (136, 734, 996). And yet, in the reversal of Joad's God, is any hope to be placed in a God of vengeance and victories? Within the tragic action in its totality, would this make sense? On the other hand, if God is not the God of power, what else is left?

The very beginnings of one tentative suggestion of a response come in the first chorus. This places God's promise to his people in a strange new dimension, that of love:

> Il nous donne ses lois, il se donne lui-même.
> Pour tant de biens, il commande qu'on l'aime. (358-59)

Joad's God, on the other hand, is a "Juge sévère" (1815), one whose existence is confirmed through fire and destruction (1021-24). The chorus asks for a different kind of faith, whose object is a God of love:

> L'esclave craint le tyran qui l'outrage;
> Mais des enfants l'amour est le partage. (367-68)

The mere suggestion of a "loving God" begs the question that the chorus itself asks, at the end of Act III: how can this possibly be

(1214-15)? How can the promises of a God of love coexist with evil and the threat of its permanence? These contradictory elements run parallel in the High Priest's vision, which Racine presents in the language of discovery:

> Mes yeux s'ouvrent,
> Et les siècles obscurs devant moi se découvrent. (1131-32)

Joad's lack of awareness, after the event, of the words he has uttered, together with their prophetic nature, the music which arises to accompany them, all combine, as has been noted, to make this moment a kind of accessory to the main action. But it is this very singularity that makes it also a privileged moment of vision in the tragedy. This vision is an invitation to seek God not in the material and the temporal, witness the fall of Jerusalem and the destruction of the Temple (1149-61), but in the spiritual and eternal, seen in a quite different expression of the messianic promise:

> Quelle Jérusalem nouvelle
> Sort du fond du désert brillante de clartés,
> Et porte sur le front une marque immortelle? (1159-61)

This allusion to the New Jerusalem is an indication of one direction in which some see the play leaning, towards the New Testament, in which the Temple is spiritual, and is figured in the Christ who is destroyed and is risen again. Here H. P. Salomon protests that "Racine's play contains not a single reference to the Christian religion" (14). For Annie Barnes, however, references to the liturgy of Advent and Christmas "immerse us in a Christian atmosphere" ("Littérature et liturgie" 22), a point developed by Philippe Sellier amongst others (*Port-Royal* 2: 242). Both see this New Testament orientation underlined in the many references to the liturgy of Advent and the Epiphany. As always, interpretation will depend here on each person's different ideas and perception.

The words that have been recurring here are promise, invitation, allusion, gleam. None implies the security of truth or certainty. In other words, it is not just a question of "seeing God" in *Athalie* if we have faith, as François-Xavier Cuche seems to suggest, in a phrase which seems to make light of many centuries of religious experience: "God is only absent for those who cannot see him"

(186). Racine hardly sets out with the agenda of his near contemporary John Milton, in *Paradise Lost*:

> That, to the height of this great argument,
> I may assert Eternal Providence,
> And justify the ways of God to men. (1.24-27)

Whatever the playwright's intentions in *Athalie*, the tragic action in performance seems far from being the confident "statement of faith" that Georges Montgrédien (142) and so many others have been able to see in it. As Racine's term *entrevoir* implies in his Preface, the fulfillment of the messianic promise is something that some may be able less to see than to glimpse.

Here is a personal glimpse, based on the evidence so far advanced. It is of a God who, to be the God of love, cannot be the God of Athalie and Joad, the God who avenges and destroys, the God we human beings make in our own image, the truth we ourselves so confidently possess. Is it conceivable that this God can only therefore be simultaneously God and victim, or, as René Girard has expressed it, "the God of victims" (215), one that cannot impose his will on others without ceasing to be himself? Is this subversive new order, to which some might allow themselves to be guided in *Athalie* as by a distant star, related to what Pascal calls "that moral universe which has at its head a crucified God" (fr. 963)? The icon of the God of power lies shattered on the hard ground of history. The messianic promise remains. For René Girard, "the God of victims" may be uncovered only in the Gospels (225). What if the crux of *Athalie* were Calvary? For some at least, at the end of the play, in the discovery that the God of power is absent, this is a visionary gleam that remains: "O promesse! ô menace! ô ténébreux mystère!" (1212).

Here reason falters, and Peter France's "rational reader" apologetically, or maybe apoplectically, makes for the door. Beyond the claims of reason, however, there might still be something here. *Athalie* might also be interpreted as pointing to the possibility of a God who must pass human understanding to make any sense. In Pascal's phrase, "If there is a God, he is infinitely beyond our comprehension" (fr. 418). Some will very properly refuse to venture beyond the bounds of the rational, and most of all in a context such as this. But let us imagine, for example, that some who approach this play lean somewhat towards the age-old idea so insistently developed by Montaigne, and energetically transmitted by Pascal, that not everything in human experience can be circumscribed by reason. Let us also imagine that, instead of wishing to wrap "Racinian tragedy" into a series of neat intellectual packages, they are open to the idea of tragedy outlined by Gilbert Murray:

> The tragic conflict has in it an element of mystery derived ultimately from the ancient religious conceptions of *katharsis* and atonement. The contest takes place on a deeper level of reality. It is not to be estimated in terms of ordinary success or failure, ordinary justice or injustice, but in terms of some profounder scheme of values in which suffering is not the worst of things nor happiness the best. (66)

In that case, they might, as audience and readers, be more sympathetic to the idea that it is to a mysterious God of love that the whole tragic action seems to move, as to the only possible light in a dark sky of vengeance, in a dimension of time which is, from the first line, that of *l'Éternel*. In the unraveling of the tragic action, some at least will thus find it possible to see what Théophile Spoerri has called "a glimmer of eternity" (182). This is a gleam of that distant epiphany to which Racine alludes in his Preface:

> Scripture categorically states that God will not wipe out all the family of Joram, and desires to keep for David the Lamp he promised him. Now what is that Lamp but the light that one day was to be revealed to the nations?

It is, of course, difficult neatly to fit any of this into received ideas of "Racinian tragedy" viewed as an ideologically coherent unit. In one way, as has been seen, *Athalie* does follow a traditional pattern of tragic action of error, reversal, and recognition. In this process, in a no less traditional way, it is possible to recognize the limits placed on human power: those with power overreach themselves, and their designs are overturned. Yet in another way, it could be argued that in *Athalie* any purely rationalistic concept of recognition, and thus of the truth, is itself overturned and placed in another dimension. For Aristotle, "A Discovery is, as the very word implies, a change from ignorance to knowledge" (ch. 11). In so far as the tragic action brings the audience to question the identity of God, this process in *Athalie* can only be a passage from knowledge to ignorance.

Like *Phèdre*, to which the next chapter will turn, *Athalie* can become a labyrinth. It is certainly an intricate pattern of complexities and ambiguities, paradoxes and ironies. This is a dramatically subtle as well as being a theologically appropriate way of approaching the hidden God. It is perhaps the ultimate triumph of *Athalie*, written after all when its author had returned to the narrow Jansenist fold, that it has provoked so many contrasting and opposing insights and emotions. Once again, "Racine" proves an elusive prey.

Chapter 5

THE PROBLEM WITH *PHÈDRE*

Is it possible to treat *Phèdre* as an ordinary play? More than any other of Racine's works it represents "Racine" and supposed features of "Racinian tragedy" already encountered, such as "pessimism," "fate," "the Gods," "Jansenism," and "poetry." It has also become emblematic of the world of Louis XIV, and the real and supposed values of that age. It is easy to understand Montherlant's exasperation with the mantra that "Racine embodies the genius of France" (4). There is a well-documented cultural and critical tradition that was given the authority of Voltaire, and then amplified by Gustave Lanson and the Third Republic's New Model Army of conscientious pedagogues. This gradual construction of the national canon transformed the literature of the *Grand Siècle* into the crown jewels of French civilization, a glittering moment for which the preceding centuries were evolution and preparation. If "Racine" was often viewed as the crown in that collection of brilliant pieces, *Phèdre* was undoubtedly the jewel in the crown. That tradition persists. In universities worldwide, as in French schools, when one play by Racine is to be studied, it is almost invariably *Phèdre*, "his crowning masterpiece" (Gérard 108), the work "that more or less encapsulates all the others" (Venesoen, *Complexe* 83), the play in which "all the key themes of Racinian sensibility seem to have come together" (Ubersfeld, "Auteur tragique" 57).

In other words, if we as cultural consumers are looking for the finished article of that cultural production line called "French classicism," then here it is, packaged to perfection, emblem and incarnation. "In making an end, *Phèdre* makes *history*," asserts Christopher Braider, "closing out the classical era in such a way as to nominate itself as constituting its in every sense ultimate embodiment" (326). There is a seemingly inexhaustible supply of variants on this theme, only some examples of which can be given here. Hyperbole sometimes comes from unexpected quarters. Thus Alain Lipietz, erstwhile head of the Green Party in France, declares *Phèdre* to be "the culmination of the gradual development of Western culture" (10). Concerning this tragedy perhaps more than any other, the terms "classic" and "classical" are used freely, and synonymously. Since that supposedly homogeneous product called "Racine" is taken to be "that classic amongst classics" (Schmitt 281), "the most classical of all" (Dumur 52), *Phèdre* is perceived to be "the purest of French tragedies" (Sellier Ed. 1: 582), "the keystone in French tragic drama" (Steiner 84), "the most scrutinized tragedy in the entire Classical canon" (Goodkin, Birth Marks 231), "the model masterpiece of the classical mind" (A. Blanc 251). Indeed, *Phèdre* is the only one of Racine's plays in which Bernard Weinberg does not find the "flaws" he so easily unearths in the others. It effortlessly attracts descriptors such as "perfection," "culmination," or "summit," and seems to be the work of French literature for which the term *chef d'œuvre* was created. Boris Donné provides a fair representation of the language commonly used: "There is an absolute quality about *Phèdre*: on its very own it represents an ideal of literary perfection, and acts as a symbol for the *Grand Siècle*, the seventeenth century, and French Classicism" (Ed. 23). Thierry Maulnier is not alone in considering this play as at the same time essentially "Racinian" and completely exceptional: "*Phèdre* stands alone amongst Racine's works just as Racine's works stand alone in the century" (*Phèdre* 8).

Exceptional, and yet totally "Racinian." This context begs two simple questions. Is it still possible to look at the "ordinary" things within *Phèdre*, such as the plot? And if so, might this modify reactions to some of the bigger issues that this play has always raised? Responding to these questions inevitably leads to other, more fundamental ones. Is it easy to maintain a single, unified reading of *Phèdre*, and thus to present this one play as the quintessential embodiment of "Racine" and the "Racinian tragic vision"?

*An ordinary play?*

To suggest that critics should first look for the ordinary in *Phèdre* is guaranteed to court derision. The interpretation of this play is extraordinarily complicated by the extraordinary status it has achieved, within the corpus of Racine's tragedies as in the canon of French literature. To this must be added the extraordinary attention granted its heroine, and the extraordinary weight of erudition, commentary, and hypotheses borne both by the work and by this one character. *Phèdre* bears such a burden of critical comment that it is reasonable to feel that there remains nothing more of substance to be said about it. Indeed, to make this very point is a natural opening gambit for the critic. Already in 1964 Roy Knight ("Dieux païens" 422) bemoaned the fact that the amount of criticism devoted to *Phèdre* had made the play difficult simply to read, a point later echoed by Michel Butor (28). Thirty years of criticism further on, Jean-Pierre Landry ("Phèdre" 407) followed the safe route of using La Bruyère's lament that "everything has already been said" as the opening shot in his own contribution. No more than here, perhaps, are critics conscious of adding gloss to gloss.

There is another problem. Considering *Phèdre* as *the* masterpiece of French "classical" literature also tends to place the emphasis on the perfection and coherence of the work, treated as some Mallarmean *calme bloc ici-bas chu*. It is as though the play had undergone a reverse ageing process: the passage of time has smoothed out the wrinkles. Here there are no surprises, as at the theatre, but a set of patterns waiting to be uncovered by the vigilant critic. This is home territory for universal explicatory structures of all sorts, whether these be sexual archetypes or the "tragic vision" and "Augustinian anthropology" so tirelessly expounded by Jean Rohou:

> Racine's *Phèdre* is a masterpiece not just in the sense that its many borrowings are perfectly integrated into a vision of humanity: they also fit perfectly into the evolution of his dramatic work and the poetic harmony which are the expression of this vision. […] The human problems it raises come across as an expression of an antagonism that structures the whole world in which we live. (Ed. 1052, 1070)

The extraordinary status that *Phèdre* has achieved also seems linked with a feeling, articulated most notably by Paul Valéry and Henri Brémond, that it is more poem than play. The implied suggestion is that by moving to pure poetry the solitary reader can somehow be elevated to a higher plane of human consciousness and expression than any mere drama could provide for an audience. For many there is certainly the sense that *Phèdre*, composed in some of the most sublime words written in French, has an incantatory quality not found in Racine's other tragedies. Thierry Maulnier, for example (*Phèdre* 42), venerates it as a beautiful song of despair in which eternal truths about the forces that possess humankind are uttered by a dominant character riven by an all-consuming passion.

To describe the role of Phèdre as "dominant" is perhaps to understate the case. For Marc Fumaroli "the soul of Phèdre is the soul of the tragic art" ("Melpomène" 191). And Jean Rohou (Ed. 1054) sees this one character as expressing not just the whole tragic action of the play, but a synthesis of the whole *tragique racinien*, if not of humanity itself, riven by primal, antagonistic impulses. In such a perspective such as this, the play seems to exist to project the drama being enacted within the heroine. This is Thierry Maulnier's central thesis, but many others who do not share his general approach share something of this point of view. Thus, for example, while no-one in recent times has stressed the importance of plot construction more than Georges Forestier, even he seems to nod vigorously in Maulnier's direction, despite a prudent and repeated "appears":

> [...] Racine created a character who, on the psychological and moral level, appears to be a genuine allegory of the human condition, and, on the dramatic level, plays a role that is a microcosm of tragedy as a whole. [...] the personal drama that is played out within the heroine provokes and intensifies the drama as a whole, which appears to be subordinated to it. (Ed. 1630-31)

At an elementary stage, as I have tried to show elsewhere ("Enseigner" 254) it is perhaps inevitable, given curricular constraints and present distastes, that "Racine" should be assimilated to *Phèdre*, and then to Phèdre, and interpreted via some extracts from some of her famous speeches in some famous scenes. A few words spoken by one character, usually about what she sees happening to herself, are thus presented as a key to "Racinian tragedy." But it is not just at an "elementary" stage that this happens. The same approach, in what is doubtless a more sophisticated version, is common throughout the Academy. Many critical works, and recent ones, are largely devoted to what happens to Phèdre. Thus Lionel Acher's summary of the play, for example (86-88), is essentially a description of Phèdre's role in it, while Patrick Dandrey's *Phèdre* focuses on Phèdre. This is a character whose personal crisis can thus appear to stand above the messy business of the play. Phèdre talks for *Phèdre*, and has come to represent the ideal "Racine." As Marie-Louise Coudert expressed it, "Phèdre *is* Jean Racine" (115). She is the perfect *homme racinien*.

From the very beginning, there has always been a fascination with the personal character of the protagonist. Longepierre spoke of "the admirable character of Phèdre, that masterpiece of the human mind" (58). And in 1677, the year of the first performance, Saint-Évremond (4: 431) asserted that Racine in his plays gave priority to character over plot. In his comments on this statement Georges Forestier adds that with *Phèdre*, "French tragedy seemed to have brilliantly completed its transformation from a tragedy based on plot to one based on character" (Ed. 1615). In other words, there is certainly support for the view that *Phèdre* is best approached via Phèdre. And yet, from the evidence of Racine's plotting techniques in those plays already examined, Saint-Évremond's assertion seems surprising. It would be even odder if his claim were true only in respect of *Phèdre*. It should be added that elsewhere in his edition (xxxvii-ix), Forestier has qualified Saint-Évremond's remarks with the salutary reminder of the importance Racine attached to the tragic subject, and to the way in which it is structured through a plot to generate the tragic emotions.

The exceptional socio-cultural position now occupied by this one work, and the no less exceptional status granted its heroine, make it important to remember a very ordinary detail. It was composed as a play, to be performed on stage. *Phèdre*, no less than *Andromaque* or *Mithridate*, was created for an audience, as a dramatic action driven by a plot in which characters, in Aristotle's terms, exist for the sake of that action. In this respect it can be shown that *Phèdre* follows the Aristotelian principles on which Saint-Évremond insists:

> It has been my contention that to make a fine play you must choose a fine subject, set it out and develop it well, and bring it naturally to its conclusion; and that the characters must be made to accord with the dramatic subject, rather than letting them determine how that subject is treated. (qtd. in Forestier, *Passions* 193)

In other words, before we as critics start treating *Phèdre* as an exhibit for anthropological examination, we might consider the dramatic machine at work. For *Phèdre* works, in every sense of the phrase, as the abbé de Bellegarde was one of the first to point out:

> Nothing sustains the audience's interest quite so well as the way in which the events of a play are interconnected: they should be so closely linked with each other that each one proceeds naturally from the one before. This logical sequence of events and passions creates suspense, and allows us to feel what the actors themselves feel. In his *Phèdre* Racine has organized this connection between events very skillfully. (qtd. in Picard, *Nouveau Corpus racinianum* 353)

An emphasis on plot, it is true, might chafe with interpretations which, sitting comfortably in their bespoke paradigms, leave little room for surprise or uncertainty. But it is worth persisting, if only to keep Jacques Scherer's words in mind:

> The notion that a solution has already been found for the problem posed by a play is in total contradiction with the status accorded the character by the new dramatic theory of the seventeenth century, which is based on the free and active exercise of the will by characters. (*Cérémonie* 28)

An attempt to see *Phèdre* first and foremost as a play, and thus to examine the workings of the plot, involves challenging common views relating to the emblematic singularity of the role of Phèdre. Both Georges Forestier (Ed. 1630) and Jean Rohou (*Avez vous lu Racine?* 305), whose interpretations differ in almost all other respects, insist that the play possesses a "contradictory coherence," a point already developed by Thierry Maulnier (*Phèdre* 38). The success and status of the work would indeed seem to bear witness to a high degree of aesthetic coherence. But does such coherence imply a set of interpretative certainties? Does it necessarily suggest that a single philosophical vision can be identified that underpins the whole?

## *Phèdre* and Phèdre

In the search for a totally coherent and comprehensive system to explain "Racine" and thus *Phèdre,* or vice versa, the royal road is a circular one. The spotlight falls on one character, Phèdre, who expresses a deterministic world-vision, in what then becomes essentially an elegy in which only what concerns Phèdre is important. Similarly, a concentration on the "poetic" or incantatory passages, spoken by Phèdre, necessarily focuses the attention on this one character, and on the character of this character, just as any focus on this character leads to a concentration on these same "poetic" passages. As Maurice Descotes (*Grands rôles* 148) and Karl Maurer (329) have shown, this concentration on the character of Phèdre was established in the nineteenth century. The twentieth fully reaffirmed it. Paul Valéry, famously (1: 499-501), speaks of "Phèdre the woman," the "incandescent Queen" who transforms a play into a lyrical monologue. For Thierry Maulnier, expressing with some color a point regularly made before and since, the other characters in the play "serve humbly at the altar on which she offers her immortal death-throes to the universe" (*Phèdre* 37). At first sight such interpretations might seem supported by the important place occupied by Phèdre's monologues, and by the other moments when she is in dialogue with herself. Does any other character really count?

This exceptional concentration on one character is the mirror image of Phèdre's own exceptional self-projection. The other characters, when they first come on stage, want to know what others have done or will do, and attempt to work out their plans in consequence. When Phèdre enters, it is herself, with physical directness, that she puts on stage, *Ma force, mes yeux, mes genoux, mon front, mes cheveux*: "Tout m'afflige, et me nuit, et conspire à me nuire" (154-61). Jean Rohou interprets what he calls this "auto-idolatry" in an Augustinian perspective, as "self-love, the source of concupiscence" (Ed. 1058-59). And Michel Bouvier sees Racine's plays, as the title of his article suggests, as a dramatization of self-love. This interpretation, however, does not explain why other characters, in other supposedly "Augustinian" plays, do not express themselves in a fashion similar to Phèdre. For in Racine's theater this character is the undoubted champion of self-reference: "Connais donc Phèdre, et toute sa fureur" (672). This particular declaration to Hippolyte leads to her regret that "je ne t'ai pu parler que de toi-même" (698), a statement shot through with unconscious irony, since to Hippolyte she has here only spoken of herself. When she relates to Œnone her discovery of Hippolyte's love for Aricie, it is in terms of a *douleur* and *tourment* (1225-26) that only she of all mortals must bear:

> A quel nouveau tourment je me suis réservée!
> Tout ce que j'ai souffert, mes craintes, mes transports,
> La fureur de mes feux, l'horreur de mes remords,
> Et d'un refus cruel l'insupportable injure
> N'était qu'un faible essai du tourment que j'endure. (1226-30)

An evocation of the lovers' happiness brings her back to "moi, triste rebut de la Nature entière," to "mon malheur," "mes pleurs," and "mes larmes" (1241-50).

Another example of this rhetoric of the self is when Phèdre's murderous desire to destroy Aricie (1259) dissolves in a "Que fais-je?" of realization (1264). Here the emphasis is not on the danger she has caused Hippolyte by her inaction, for even now she does not try to save him. It is on her own state of mind, on her own guilty feelings, and on her own unfortunate fate (1273-94), in a lament that gradually isolates her from Œnone. Jean-Pierre Landry ("Phèdre" 411) asserts that after this "Que fais-je?," the heroine ceases to display self-pity. This hardly concurs with the evidence:

> Du crime affreux dont la honte me suit,
> Jamais mon triste cœur n'a recueilli le fruit. (1291-92)

In this long passage, there is a remarkable absence of any reference to the man with whom she is in love. Only later does she allude to the fact that, if he dies, it will be due to others (1313-16). This self-containment is hardly typical in Racine's tragedies. For example, even at Hermione's moment of paroxysm, the image of Pyrrhus is obsessively present: "Il m'aimerait peut-être, il le feindrait du moins" (*Andromaque*, 1600). For Phèdre, the obsessive presence is

Phèdre. In Bernard Dort's words, "She speaks neither for Hippolyte, nor Œnone, nor Thésée [...]: She speaks for herself. [...] She wants to make her passion become her destiny" (15). This is Phèdre's world, but is it the world of *Phèdre*? Is Phèdre alone in it?

Critical preoccupation with the character of Phèdre is therefore understandable, especially given the predominant place she holds in the play. "Phèdre is an exceptional character, but too much so," muses Jean Vilar, "and the result is that she takes over the whole play" (19). But if it is a *one-woman-show*, what of the other characters, and what of the play itself? Is the part somehow greater than the whole? There is doubtless a parallel to be drawn with Hamlet, viewed as the tortured soul of early modern consciousness. But Hamlet is not *Hamlet*. The celebrated passages of existential self-doubt do not simply blot out the Jacobean revenge drama in which Hamlet is one player amongst many. "The play's the thing," as that character famously says (2.2.600). Similarly, Phèdre is far from being *Phèdre*. Jean-Louis Barrault makes the point forcefully, with an explicit rebuttal of Paul Valery's Phèdre-centered interpretation:

> Care must be taken that the performance does not resemble a concerto for solo instrument, and that everyone's attention is not focused on Phèdre at the expense of the other characters. [...] Put a work of art on stage, and not an "incandescent Queen." [...] "Phèdre, the woman," must once again become part of "*Phèdre*, the tragedy." [...] Phèdre is not a concerto for solo woman: it is a symphony for an orchestra of actors. (*Mise en scène* 16)

The play's original title, *Phèdre et Hippolyte*, is a small indication that the heroine's fate is bound up with that of others. Indeed Jean Rohou, perhaps paradoxically, points out (Ed. 1052) that Phèdre has fewer lines, proportionately, than Titus or Mithridate. Not everyone will go so far as Christian Rist, who in his 2002 production made Hippolyte and Aricie the moving forces of the play. It seems difficult to deny that Phèdre occupies a central role in the dramatic action. But as far as that dramatic action is concerned, it is not the only important role. Frederich Hegel (326) dismissed Hippolyte's love for Aricie as an "absurdity" that impaired the tragic quality of the play, but against the great philosopher one might argue, with appropriate meekness, that this guilty love proves as damaging as that of Phèdre, since in both cases revelation and non-revelation provoke disproportionate consequences. The play opens with Hippolyte, and his relationship with his father. The exposition as a whole outlines a whole nexus of relationships and concerns. These are political and dynastic as well as passionate: there is no dialogue here between Phèdre and the Gods. Indeed, it was precisely what he saw as Racine's failure to concentrate on Phèdre that Fénelon chose to criticize in his "Lettre à l'Académie":

> He created two plays in one, by adding to the passion-torn Phèdre a Hippolyte who is in love, and thus not in character. Phèdre should have been left all alone with her passion [...]. There would only have been one dramatic action, and it would have been quick and lively. (2: 1169)

With Thésée's return in Act III–an event that occurs in the dead center of the play–the father-son relationship becomes as crucial as any in which Phèdre is involved. It is thus difficult to agree with Patrick Dandrey, who in this follows so many others, that "what governs each stage of the plot until the end is the adventure of Phèdre" (64). One measure of the place occupied by the relationship between Hippolyte and Thésée is the physical presence of the king. For Thierry Maulnier, Phèdre "is at the forefront for the five acts of the play" (*Phèdre* 124). In fact, she is actually present in only three of the last fifteen scenes, while Thésée appears in all but four of them As befits a king, it is he who directs the action from his return, and he whose decisions are responsible for the outcome. By any standards, the character not named in any version of the play's title has a significant role in the plot.

This is not a point of view that enjoys wide acceptance. It is common to take the part for the whole, and, consequently, to see patterns in that one part that express the whole. For Jean Rohou, as for so many, Phèdre contains the necessary paradigms, and the paradigms provide the answers: "an analysis of the play demonstrates that all the problems it raises are contained within its main character" (Ed. 1057). And Lionel Acher sees the opposition between the two strands of Phèdre's ancestry, expressed in the famous line "La fille de Minos et de Pasiphaé," as being "the very source of the dramatic movement as a whole" (79). Such analyses have clearly proved attractive. The attempt to consider *Phèdre* as a whole, however, makes the identification of a single such pattern more problematic. Plays are not essays, as Terence Cave stresses:

> Knowledge is fragmented and dispersed between the characters in such a way as to give more prominence to the pattern of uncertainty than to the state of affairs, to any single character's apprehension of it [...]. The epistemology of Racine's plays [...] is not anchored in the consciousness of a particular subject. (342)

## Plot, after all

Jacques Morel and Alain Viala, in refuting the idea that *Phèdre* is more poem than play, insist on its identity as "a strongly plotted family drama" (Ed. 174). Previous chapters have attempted to outline the central role played by the plot in other tragedies by Racine. These plays were crafted as dramatic machines geared to arouse emotion, and thus engage hearts and minds, reminding us of Boileau's advice to budding dramatists in his *Art Poétique* III: "Seek out the heart, fire it, stir it." Eugène Vinaver denied there could be a link between the audience's emotional engagement in a play and something so banal as the "combination of incidents" that Aristotle defined as the plot, and even suggested that in *Phèdre* "the emotional intensity increases the fewer incidents there are to disturb it" (Racine, *Principes* 45). Yet again, this point of view would be more convincing if it were supported by evidence. Just as in a more immediately obvious example such as *Andromaque,* it can be shown that in *Phèdre* the arousal of emotion involves suspense, surprise, melodrama, and the creation of uncertainty. It is easy to transform this emblematic tragedy into a closed set, a *jardin à la française* of formal patterns. Such patterns mirror theories, and project certainty. To look at the play as a dramatic machine is to uncover a much more open-ended and thus uncertain process. Jacques Scherer speaks of "unexpected developments, at the beginning of each tragedy, that come gradually to be caused by actions and reactions that in every case could have been different" (*Cérémonie* 27). It is for this reason that the question arises, as it did with *Britannicus, Iphigénie,* and *Athalie,* as to whether at the very end closure is achieved, and the uncertainties are resolved.

In *Phèdre* uncertainty is cultivated from the outset. This is hardly strange. Racine was not a metaphysician, but a practicing and practiced dramatist. Uncertainty was his trade. One of the pleasures of coming to *Phèdre* with some other of his plays in mind is to see the extent to which similar expositional techniques are used to create doubt, curiosity, and thus emotional and mental involvement. The same techniques have been seen employed in *Athalie*, which like *Phèdre* is so often seen as running on rails laid down by a force external to characters' wills. In *Phèdre*, as in other tragedies by Racine, the opening scene turns on a series of questions, involving a series of terms such as *ignorer, doute, mystère*. Where is Hippolyte's father? Why is he absent? What is his real identity? Where is he to be found? What is Phèdre's mysterious illness? Why is Hippolyte running away? Where will his love for Aricie lead? Many of these liminal questions do not concern Phèdre, and not all receive a quick or easy answer. There is poignancy in Hippolyte's ignorance of his father's whereabouts (7), a poignancy only increased by the "faits moins glorieux" (83) that point to the dark underside of Thésée's heroism. For one might ask whether the son ever finds the father he is seeking. It is because of this open-ended nature of the dramatic action that Racine can arouse emotion by the use of irony, by inviting the recall of some of the statements made in this opening scene, such as "Phèdre depuis longtemps ne craint plus de Rivale" (26), or the reference to Hippolyte neglecting his horsemanship, "l'art par Neptune inventé" (131). A similar example comes with Aricie's entrance in Act II. At the outset she only asks questions, including the equally poignant "Je cesse d'être esclave, et n'ai plus d'Ennemi?" (375). In other words, the playwright, whatever his other designs, is also seeking to craft a plot built on the unresolved, the swiftly changing, and the surprising.

This technique cannot be dismissed as "mere plotting," as though the conduct of the plot was an end in itself, with no consequences for the way the play as a whole generates emotion and holds an audience. An example is the way in which Racine exploits reports of Thésée's death and subsequent reappearance. The initial surprise at the first news is extreme (325), but the death is soon accepted as a fact, despite Aricie's questions (392). In Act II this "fact" permits Hippolyte to confess his forbidden love to Aricie, and Phèdre her love to Hippolyte. It is only once characters cannot go back that the truth is revealed to be false, and the dead man returns to a changed world of guilt and darkness. Another example of Racine's careful plotting is his use of suspense and surprise. Two illustrations are the revelation, first, of Hippolyte's love to Phèdre, and then of his death. The first is a "coup de foudre" (1195), and the jealousy it ignites in Phèdre seals his fate. But with that part of ourselves that is caught up in the dramatic action, we the audience do not know any more than the protagonists what is going to happen: Aricie, in Act V, tells Hippolyte there is still time to convince his father (1337). Indeed, William Schlegel (107) was surprised and disappointed by the bloody outcome: how much more appropriate, he thought, that Hippolyte should return safe and sound for a final reconciliation scene with his father. Thus his death, however much it may be anticipated, still comes as a shock, especially to the father who had so actively sought it: "Quel coup me l'a ravi? Quelle foudre soudaine?" (1497). The repeated use of *foudre* is an apposite reminder of the role played in Racine's plotting techniques by the sudden intrusion of what only afterwards seems inevitable. In other words, the dramatic action does not move to the drumbeat of some irresistible fatalism. It is advanced by a dramatist's plotting craft. *Phèdre* is too often viewed as a kind of Rolls Royce of world literature. And it is true that it has generated its own myth, and comes freighted with ideals and expectations. But it is first and foremost a vehicle that moves, and was designed to move. And its engine is a well-crafted plot.

Even leaving aside d'Aubignac's celebrated "To speak is to act" (407), it is thus difficult to accept Jean Rohou's opinion that *Phèdre* "is not a tragedy of action" (Ed. 1070). In this play, as the "Unity of Time" intrinsically demands, the dramatic action opens as close to the denouement as possible. A sense of urgency is instilled from the beginning, with Hippolyte's decision to leave and Phèdre's wish to die. Thésée's return, and his desire to exact summary justice, only increase the pressure. This is no incantation. That is, of course, unless the tragic action be viewed as a kind of abstraction, in some way removed from a world in which things are done and choices are made. Thus for Lucien Goldmann, "Racine's problem was to fill five acts with a timeless dramatic action that only lasted a moment" ("Structure" 258). There is, however, much evidence to support Philippe Sellier's contention that "Racine makes the race against time an essential agent of his tragedies" (Ed. 1: 29). In *Phèdre* increasingly, as the knot of the dramatic conflict unwinds, a number of different actions takes place in a very short space of time, as Jacques Scherer points out:

> The fifth Act of *Phèdre* pushes this rapidity to the very limit: Hippolyte leaves the palace, crosses the town, goes through the town gates of Trézène, encounters the sea-monster, tries in vain to hold back his horses, and dies; Aricie arrives on the scene, comes across Hippolyte's lifeless body, and faints; her confidant Ismène brings her back to Trézène and consoles her; Théramène, who has witnessed the events that have taken place, since he gives an account of them, comes back to the royal palace; and we are expected to believe that all of this has only lasted the time it takes to speak seventy-six lines! (*Cérémonie* 219)

It is sequences such as this that enable Christian Delmas to point out "the breathless pace of the dramatic action, made up of sudden decisions and abrupt about-turns," and to conclude that "nothing is decided in advance" (*Mythologie* 259). Characters live in a world full of twists and turns, where events do not happen but strike, like lightning, and where the outcome is uncertain until the very end. The workings of the plot are a strong argument against any variant of the "incantation" thesis, and the related suggestion of a Phèdre-centered universe.

*What truth?*

A further element creating uncertainty in *Phèdre* is the doubt that attaches to all attempts to know the truth. This traditional tragic motif serves as a powerful plotting tool. Aricie's question to Thésée, "Discernez-vous si mal le crime et innocence?" (1430), could also be asked of Lear or Othello. It is difficult to exaggerate the emphasis placed on ideas of secrecy, suppression of the truth, and flight. Marc Fumaroli, for example ("Dieux païens" 181), alludes to the frequency of the terms *croire* and *voir* in *Phèdre,* and to the tragic import of their near synonymy. Does one character, Phèdre, alone escape from this epistemological labyrinth? One might think so, to judge by the frequency with which the epithet "lucid" is used to describe her. In the twentieth century this image was reinforced by critics such as Lucien Goldmann, who relayed

György Lukacs's idea of a necessary link between "lucidity" and the concept of "the tragic": "it is precisely this lucidity that makes the *homme tragique* aware of his perpetual transgression, one made all the more serious by its involuntary nature" ("Structure" 257). The underlying thesis is straightforward: even if Phèdre can do nothing against her possession by love, she still knows her own inner state, her motivations, and the consequences of her actions. Few ideas about the play are more common. Two examples: "Phèdre is unable to crush her sinful longings despite her fundamental innocence and the clarity of her moral judgment" (Gérard 109); "Phèdre always know what is happening to her" (Prost 76).

The "lucidity" idea certainly accepts at face value the rhetoric Phèdre herself uses:

> J'aime. Ne pense pas qu'au moment que je t'aime,
> Innocente à mes yeux je m'approuve moi-même,
> Ni que du fol amour qui trouble ma raison
> Ma lâche complaisance ait nourri le poison. (673-76)

This is the image *Phèdre* presents, and it is one that has been largely taken on board. It is, however, an image that deserves some scrutiny. Some accept that it is somewhat clouded. For example, Lionel Acher points out (90) that Phèdre can deny reality at some crucial moments, and be perfectly lucid at others. Paradoxically, within the same few pages of his edition Raymond Picard maintains that Phèdre "can put enough distance between herself and her self to know, judge, and condemn herself" (737), while also saying that she blinds herself, and that "her sincerity is only a form of guilty hypocrisy towards herself" (742).

To find a way through the confusion here, all that can be done is to set Phèdre's rhetoric against the evidence of the play as a whole. She undoubtedly claims self-knowledge, and is often taken at her word: "Je sais mes perfidies" (849). But both her denunciation of Œnone and her self-justification show a certain half-willed refusal to face the truth, recalling Œnone's opening diagnosis: "Vous haïssez le jour que vous veniez chercher?" (168). This lack of transparency extends to the motives that cause her to beg Thésée to show clemency to Hippolyte. Ruth Calder suggests that Phèdre is "a heroine who makes noble efforts to live up to a lofty moral standard" (113). That must remain a matter of judgment. However, there is a troubling similarity between her account of the act—"Je volais toute entière au secours de son fils" (1196)—and her famous description of love's thrall, "C'est Vénus tout entière à sa proie attachée" (306). This suggests that in her desire to save Hippolyte, contrition is inseparable from passion. What she presents as a mission of mercy is aborted by a fit of jealousy. When this jealousy turns to remorse, even then she says only that she *might* have spoken out (1198-1201). Phèdre desires, but in that desire is there a desire to know? Her half-willed desire to flee the light gives all its savor to the final couplet from her declaration of love:

> Et Phèdre au Labyrinthe avec vous descendue,
> Se serait avec vous retrouvée, ou perdue. (661-62)

In this ballet of falsehood and self-deception the participation of Thésée and Hippolyte is equally important. Little "transparency" is implied in Théramène's description of Hippolyte: "Chargés d'un feu secret, vos yeux s'appesantissent" (134). Yet, like Phèdre, this character has often been interpreted on the basis of his own rhetoric, in this case as "the symbol of daylight" (Zimmermann 117). Thus for Odette de Mourgues, quite simply, "Hippolyte *is* innocence and *is* daylight" (158), and for Jean Rohou "Hippolyte is the embodiment of purity" (*Avez-vous* lu *Racine?* 312). In the same vein Marc Fumaroli suggests that "a single alexandrine, possibly the most transparent line of poetry in French, can be Hippolyte's motto: 'Le jour n'est pas plus pur que le fond de mon cœur' (1112)" ("Dieux païens" 173). But to this point of view one could oppose Hippolyte's self-description to Aricie: "Maintenant je me cherche, et ne me trouve plus" (548). Rather than take these different lines from their context, as a description of the "essence" of this character, whatever that might mean, could one not simply say that each of these statements fits into Hippolyte's rhetoric of persuasion at a given moment, whether to convince Thésée of his probity, or Aricie of her power to transform him?

Between the imagined interior worlds of Hippolyte and Phèdre, therefore, there is no easy opposition of light and dark. When Théramène tells his friend that "Vous périssez d'un mal que vous dissimulez" (136), this is a direct reminder of his picture of the dying Phèdre, "atteinte d'un mal qu'elle s'obstine à taire" (45). It is true that Hippolyte's relationship with Aricie is described in Apol-

Ionian terms: "Tous les jours se levaient clairs et sereins pour eux" (1240). But these words are spoken by Phèdre, and reflect her own image of this relationship. What they reveal is the mix of guilt, frustration, envy, and self-pity with which she imagines a purity to which she is denied access. Similarly, Hippolyte's self-attribution of the transparency of daylight–"Examinez ma vie, et songez qui je suis" (1092)–is no confessional interlude. It is a statement made to convince his father of his transparent honesty, ironically at a moment when he is concealing the true state of his relationship with both Aricie and Phèdre. Heroism this may be. But it is hardly "le jour le plus clair." And if Hippolyte does admit his true feelings about Aricie to Thésée, this is only in order to refute his father's idea that his son's sexual "froideurs" explain, and are explained by, an unnatural love (1114-18). This belated confession of a partial truth, made as a last resort and in self-justification, in some way justifies his father's riddling reply: "Tu te feins criminal pour te justifier" (1128).

Thésée in his turn leaps to false conclusions about his son's life, as others have earlier about his own death. This rush to judgment is symptomatic of the ironic world of appearances created by the dramatic action. The truth cries out, but cannot easily be found, especially when it is actively sought. When Thésée sees his apparently criminal son arrive, he wonders how appearances can be so far from reality:

À ce noble maintien
Quel œil ne serait pas trompé comme le mien? (1035-36)

Ironically, the image has not this time been deceptive. But how can Thésée know? The truth is deformed by the desire to suppress it, or is refracted by the curving mirror of desire. Thus Thésée constantly uses the word "traître" of Hippolyte, making assumptions about his son's character that seem to spring from his own adulterous practice, alluded to in the exposition, "Sa foi partout offerte, et reçu en cent lieux" (84). Characters are caught in the very nets of falsehood and unreality they have helped to create. Phèdre and Hippolyte could also say, with Thésée, "Je ne sais où je vais, je ne sais où je suis" (1004).

From this maze of uncertainty and ambiguity, it is not just characters but we ourselves, as audience and readers, who must stumble in the creative penumbra for realities incompletely grasped. Some fortunate critics have access to Phèdre's "nature" or "deeper self." Jean Rohou's position here seems to waver. In his edition he finds that "the cause of Phèdre's torments is to be found in her very nature" (1054). Yet in *Avez-vous lu Racine?* he reminds his readers that "in plays, the character of characters is not the real cause of their behavior, feelings, and passions," and calls up in support Saint-Évremond who, following Aristotle, declared that "the theatre should not be about explaining human nature, but rather representing the human condition" (68-69). This poses the question as to whether such an entity as Phèdre's "nature" really exists. Edward Forman has opined that "all Racine's greatest tragic creations agonize above all about their sense of identity" ("Spirit" 275). But in a play the players participate in a dramatic action: they do not explore their own personalities, using the play as a psychiatrist's couch. As Terence Cave points out, "self knowledge [...] is both spasmodic and problematic; the locus of the self is saturated with uncertainty" (345). Perhaps all those who approach this play should take to heart Phèdre's statement: "Dans le fond de mon cœur vous ne pouviez pas lire" (598). Eric Gans (*Paradoxe* 79) stresses the importance Racine gives to the image of the labyrinth in this play. This leads to a more general question: in the labyrinth created within and between characters, is there a single clear "truth" that some heroic critic can identify and claim as a prize?

*Fatalism, dependency, responsibility*

Ideas of uncertainty and unpredictability sit uneasily with the deterministic way in which *Phèdre* is often viewed. As Maurice Delcroix shows (*Le sacré* 384-86), this critical perspective often involves terms such as "necessity," "destiny," and "fatality." Racine, claims Thierry Maulnier, "gives the play from the outset the stamp of irreversible necessity" (*Phèdre* 14). These words are echoed by countless other critics who, like Jacques Mercanton, see the play as "a funeral ceremony in which, from the beginning, the victim has been condemned without appeal" (61). This view is commonly linked with what are taken to be Augustinian ideas of determinism or predestination, ideas that themselves are often conflated with fatalism. "Behind the tremendous force of the play seems to be a cruel Jansenist conjecture," asserts George Steiner (86). Thus for Jean Rohou, if Phèdre makes extensive use of the language of possession and dependency (for example, 269-316), it is because she is "a child of original sin" (Ed. 1054). And Pierre Moreau, as though crossing Saint Augustine's *City of God* with some of Zola's rhetoric in *Germinal,* views Phèdre as embodying "the determinism within us, that of the flesh, of Original Sin, of that fire lit in the blood of the whole human race" (150).

These questions are, literally speaking, infinitely difficult. It is worth recalling, however, that for a seventeenth-century theologian it would have seemed an aberration, as Michel Bouvier and others have pointed out, to separate the Augustinian doctrine of the passions from that of the Church as a whole:

> [...] this doctrine, developed over the years by the Fathers and Doctors of the Church, nourished by carefully filtered contributions from Classical antiquity [...] is the fruit of sixteen centuries of reflection, during which time scholars of dazzling genius, from all sides, examined the ideas behind it in great detail, while remaining faithful to Holy Scripture and obedient to the teaching authority of the Church. St Augustine saw himself as the interpreter of the Apostles, St Thomas Aquinas drew his authority from that of St Augustine, and St François de Sales wanted to draw all his knowledge from both St Augustine and St Thomas Aquinas [...]. (148)

On might also note in passing the evidence advanced by Susan James (114) that St Augustine held emotions to be essentially acts of the will. Literary commentators, however, tend to have more robust ideas than theologians about what "Augustinian" means, and how it influenced works such as *Phèdre*:

> There is no doubt that the eponymous heroine was created in the light of Augustinian thought, relayed and hardened by Jansenism. First and foremost came the fundamental idea of predestination. [...] It is this that explains Phèdre's inability to resist a passion that she condemns [...]. Nowadays we would say that she was genetically programmed. (Dosmond 31)

In this vision of the play, characters whose fate is sealed struggle vainly in a universe deaf to their pleas for help, a world that is by definition unjust. From this comes the idea of characters as mere instruments, or passive receptacles, as in David Maskell's observation about characters in Racine "acting like puppets under the influence of obsessions they cannot control" (233). Phèdre especially is seen in this light, leading Raymond Picard to say (Ed. 1:741) that the question of her responsibility is the fundamental problem in the play. There is an obvious parallel here between the many references to forces that mock the apparent freedom to act, such as Phèdre's "Implacable Vénus" (814), and the defeated Athalie's "Impitoyable Dieu, toi seul as tout conduit" (*Athalie*, 1774). All that is needed is to extrapolate a series of similar phrases from *Phèdre* to be able to present what might appear to be rock-solid evidence for the determinist view.

The language of dependency certainly exists. The real question is what it signifies in context, and whether it only concerns Phèdre. Here a measure of prudence is necessary. The previous chapter alluded to the fact that this language belongs to a well-worn wardrobe used extensively in European literature. Its arch-exponent, Petrarch, had himself drawn from classical authors who were in turn used by Racine, via the novels and love-poetry of the earlier part of the century. In other words, as Peter France has pointed out, there is a long-standing relationship between "vehement emotion and decorative rhetoric" (*Racine's Rhetoric* 242). "Does the metaphor of love as a flame," asks Philippe Sellier, "come from the poetry of Racine's time, from St Augustine, Seneca, Virgil, Theocritus, Euripides, or Sappho?" (*Port-Royal* 2: 233).

To take just one example of this cultural heritage, a glance at Sir Philip Sidney's "Astrophel and Stella," composed a century earlier than *Phèdre*, will turn up an abundance of such metaphors, and all "poor Petrarch's long-deceased woes" (sonnet 15). This language typically involves metaphors of combat and defeat such as the siege, or the wound of love's arrow, together with such images as shackles and slavery, or storms and shipwrecks. This same vocabulary is used, not just by Phèdre, but also by Hippolyte and Aricie (e.g. 524-52), as it had been used, generally if unevenly, in Racine's previous plays, much to the discomfort of those who, like Saint-Évremond and Mme de Sévigné, felt that tragedy merited nobler things. Thus Phèdre stresses the sense of irrational possession ("Un trouble s'éleva dans mon âme éperdue," 274), but so does Hippolyte ("Par quel trouble me vois-je emporté loin de moi!" 536). Phèdre finds

Hippolyte everywhere, and cannot control her feelings, but Hippolyte expresses the same idea:

> Contre vous, contre moi vainement je m'éprouve.
> Présente je vous fuis, absente je vous trouve. (541-42)

"O Absent presence," cries Sidney's Astrophel (sonnet 106). It is hardly the *idea* that is original here.

Equally, it would be blinkered to focus on terms relating only to the "enslavement" of Phèdre. Hippolyte, in his declaration of love to Aricie, twice uses the term "captif" to describe his state, just as Aricie herself has affirmed her desire to "Enchaîner un Captif de ses fers étonné" (451). As Jean Emelina remarks, "the 'malady' of love—its 'fires,' 'shackles,' 'ill-fated flame' in which the will surrenders—is the most admirable and enviable of ills" ("Le mal" 106). This splendidly polemical observation doubtless needs qualification, since only the context permits some appreciation of the scale of real suffering. But there are even more reasons to qualify Roland Barthes's assertion that "the Racinian Eros is all about alienation" (*Sur Racine* 26). When Aricie greets "l'amour, et ses folles douleurs" as the very opposite of the unhappiness she has hitherto suffered (420), an audience can recognize that this vocabulary is part of a ceremony, like imposed figures in ballet. Phèdre's self-dramatization is more striking, with greater emphasis on the sense of love as wound and disease, but the main features of her love rhetoric necessarily participate in that same ceremony.

While admitting that a common language is shared, Jean-Michel Pelous (76) seeks clearly to distinguish between its deterministic resonance, when used by Phèdre, and its superficiality, when used by the young lovers. This is quite a brutal distinction, unless Phèdre can be in some way isolated from the dramatic action: neither stance argues for aesthetic coherence. It is generally admitted that Racine uses a traditional love-vocabulary in situations and in a manner that restores something of its literal vigor: the wound of love *is* mortal. One could also argue that Aricie and Hippolyte use a language whose triviality is only superficial, since both will face dire consequences for their love. Equally, however, it might be said that, in using this vocabulary, Phèdre is employing a rhetoric of love whose ceremonial character attenuates its literally deterministic meaning. The phrases uttered by Phèdre cannot totally be isolated, as they so often are, from what actually happens, and from the context of the whole play. Nor can they be isolated, as Jacques Scherer remarks, from a European tradition of which *galanterie* is one flamboyant manifestation: "The power granted to love comes from accepting a set of aesthetic principles, not (as the fatalist critics would have it) from some metaphysical doctrine that sees this as an inherent part of the human condition" (*Cérémonie* 116).

The question that constantly returns, therefore, is whether *Phèdre* as a whole dramatic experience projects a sense of repression, inevitability, and lack of choice for all its characters. Here again, uncertainty rules. The play is built on a series of tensions between the language of determinism and characters' choices, choices that in turn impact on other situations and decisions. How could it be otherwise? If the central role of the plot in generating emotion is admitted, what interest would a play have as a dramatic action, and how credible would it be found, if the action ran predictably on rails to its destination, with the characters like helpless passengers, again *à la Zola*, in a train hauled by some monstrous locomotive impervious to their cries of distress? Here Bénédicte Louvat issues a useful reminder:

> [...] fatality as a way of explaining human conduct is incompatible with plays whose key principles are plausibility and necessity: for how is it possible to construct a plausible dramatic action if at any moment characters can point to the burden of fatality that weighs on them, and so are able to declare that they are not guilty of the acts they commit? In French classical tragedy the protagonists are not only free, but are responsible for their actions: indeed, that is one of the prerequisites for the construction of any dramatic action. (*Poétique* 18)

The frequency in *Phèdre* of verbs such as *faire, pouvoir,* and *vouloir* already points to a degree of freedom in the exercise of the will. There is an element of contradiction here between this freedom and the type of common deterministic thesis articulated by Jean Rohou, according to which "all the characters in this play [...] are at the mercy of deep-rooted desires that their conscious minds cannot curb" (Ed. 1047). Aricie, for example, describes herself as "le triste jouet d'un sort impitoyable" (418), yet she makes it clear that her love for Hippolyte is the result of admiration for his moral qualities, and makes a conscious decision to ensnare him (437-53). Thésée for his part, with his repeated use of the word *crimes* (1182, 1184), reacts to Hippolyte's supposed designs on Phèdre in terms of human responsibility. Another example of the characters' will to act is the use of the term *dessein*. The very first words of the play, "Mon dessein est pris," express Hippolyte's intention to search for his father, flee his stepmother, and escape the threat posed by his love for Aricie. Théramène might well opine that, in the matter of love, there is no choice: "Si votre heure est une fois marquée..." (114). This does not prevent both characters then returning to discussion of the initial plan of action (141). In his dialogue with Aricie, in the following Act, on the politics of Thésée's succession, Hippolyte speaks already with the authority and decisiveness of a king:

> Je puis vous affranchir d'une austère tutelle.
> Je révoque des lois dont j'ai plaint la rigueur.
> Vous pouvez disposer de vous, de votre cœur. (474-76)

As Jacques Scherer remarks, "the rational activity of characters, even when this is hidden by their words, implies a freedom which is perhaps the most formidable argument against any fatalistic interpretation of the tragic" (*Cérémonie* 219). And Peter France stresses the importance of hope in the dialectic of Racine's tragedies: "The action of the plays depends crucially on the search for solutions; though we may know that their efforts are vain, the protagonists [...] are not so willing to accept a tragic fate" ("War" 150). For example, Phèdre's often-expressed sentiment that heart, mind, and will are no longer her own–"Les Dieux m'en ont ravi l'usage" (181)–does not prevent her having her own "affreux dessein" (195). Is this tantamount to "enslavement"? Or is there an element of what Basil Donné in his edition calls "voluntary enslavement" (49)? The contradiction between what Phèdre says and what she does makes the question permissible.

This contradiction also poses the question as to whether Phèdre's deterministic rhetoric should be taken at face value. Raymond Picard sees her using predetermination as a conscious weapon: "Phèdre, by a kind of naive cunning, makes fatality one of the elements of her love strategy. [...] she seems to use the image of fatality either as a means of action, or else as an excuse or disguise for her own weaknesses" (Ed. 1: 742). It is Phèdre, after all, who decides to speak, even though she presents this choice as that of Œnone (246). And it is Phèdre who talks unambiguously of Hippolyte, even though it is Œnone who is blamed for actually naming him (264). Similarly, there is something of a conflict between Phèdre's presentation of an "incurable amour" sent by Venus (283), and the decision she takes to force Hippolyte's exile:

> Contre moi-même enfin j'osai me révolter.
> J'excitai mon courage à le persécuter. (291-92)

As in the case of Hippolyte, the fact that such decisions are overturned by events underlines, not any predetermined outcome, but the unpredictability of situations evolving beyond the control of any single character. A sense of pressure is created by the working of the plot, in conjunction with the restriction of time and constriction of place. It is this unrelenting pressure more than anything else that creates a sense of inexorability. Phèdre does not confront Hippolyte again in Trézène through the agency of a scheming Aphrodite: it is her husband who decides to send her there. Irony is not determinism.

In Act V Hippolyte finally carries out "Un plus noble dessein" (1387), involving escape and marriage, and so speeds to his doom. Does this make a mockery of his freedom to act? It would be idle to deny the force of this properly tragic irony: characters rush to the fate they seek to escape. But the irony is the more poignant in that the characters themselves decide. They do not know what will happen, and make decisions that it was possible for them not to have made, however much they might feel they are the "Objet infortuné des vengeances célestes" (677). It is these decisions, once taken, that advance the action. Thus Œdipus kills his father and marries his mother, in ignorance. Only in retrospect does there seem to be any inevitability. In these plays, as Jacques Scherer has remarked, God is replaced by "the event" (*Cérémonie* 132). The event might seem portentous in retrospect: but before the event, potential is open to human choice and design. In the tragic mimesis, the inevitable and necessary are expressed through the contingencies of choice, hesitation, and error, in a continuing present yet to reveal what the future holds. This tension between what is uncertain before, and only seems inevitable after, is expressed thus by Paul Ricœur:

> [...] the dramatic action introduces a hesitation, that is both acceleration and delay, a hesitation that invests the inevitable with the uncertainty that is proper to the contingent. The inevitable must be played out within a framework of uncertainty as to the outcome, and what is essentially implacable must be expressed for us through the contingent. ("Culpabilité tragique" 292)

The active role played by characters is nowhere clearer than in the scene where Phèdre confesses her love to Hippolyte. Phèdre constructs the image of a passive victim:

> Cet aveu que je te viens de faire,
> Cet aveu si honteux, le crois-tu volontaire? (693-94)

This image is accepted by most commentators, and most famously by Hegel, for whom Phèdre's absolute dependency diminishes the tragic dimension of the play:

> The mind of Phèdre is depicted as entirely motivated by the words of Œnone. A character of real distinction acts out of its own initiative [...]. Only when action is the direct result of its own reflections do we get that clear relation between personal initiative and the consequent result which carries us with the full weight of guilt or responsibility. (159)

However, there is no reason why Phèdre's confession, at this particular moment, should be seen as any more or less "voluntary" than her previous refusal to confess, a point well made by Raymond Picard: "Is it not evident that Phèdre, at the outset of this tragic day, could have once again resisted the entreaties of Œnone?" (Ed. 1: 741). If the confession is a necessity, the necessity is primarily dramatic. It is this act, together with Hippolyte's confession of his love to Aricie, that sets the tragic machine in motion. As Jacques Scherer stresses (*Cérémonie* 72), this error gives an interpersonal reality to what had only existed in the mind, and precipitates reversal and catastrophe.

Phèdre, it is true, often portrays herself as not being in control. This is overwhelmingly so in the *labyrinthe* sequence of the confession to Hippolyte (645-62), where she presents herself as speaking in a trance-like state. Since her words come from one as though possessed, is her declaration of love not involuntary? This is certainly the idea that critics, overwhelmingly, have chosen to embroider: "she is not responsible for what she says, and is as though sleepwalking" (Maulnier, *Phèdre* 55); "beyond herself, half-crazed" (Bénichou, *l'Écrivain* 315); "her words are dictated to her in a dream" (Vinaver, *Entretiens* 18); "used and controlled by her language" (Dandrey 98); "the character drifts away from semantic logic" (Viala, *Lectures* 233); "Phèdre's visions are hallucinatory, without rational control" (Barnwell, "Drama and Poetry" 132). Indeed, this is one point that has united critics who are habitually in opposition. Thus for example Georges Forestier speaks of Phèdre's dream-like state (Ed. 1635), and Jean Rohou of hallucination (Ed. 1058). But even here it is at least worth asking, as Gilles Declercq has done, to what extent these words of Phèdre are woven with conscious art into a discourse of seduction, requiring what he calls "the conscious application of her rhetorical skill" ("Poéticité" 45).

In the image Phèdre constructs, throughout the play, there is no uncertainty: her life is decided by the Gods, or Œnone, or by any force or character that allows her to retain this passive role. As Roger Pons points out, she expresses guilt in general, but for no action in particular: "she maintains two contradictory convictions: that she is the most criminal of all creatures, and that she is responsible for nothing" (173). If then we, as spectators or readers, become obsessed with this one character, and if we accept her own image of what happens, this one character's world necessarily becomes our own. It is obvious that this is not the only interpretation possible. It might be asked, for example, how Phèdre could denounce Œnone's "conseils flatteurs" (771) if not herself possessing a certain degree of freedom? Indeed, she speaks these words when she has rejected her nurse's advice to run away (763), and continues with an even more determined rebuff:

> Je ne me verrai point préférer de Rivale.
> Enfin tous tes conseils ne sont plus de saison.
> Sers ma fureur, Œnone, et non point ma raison. (790-92)

Phèdre might therefore choose to present an image of passivity. Seen through the glass of rhetorical analysis, as Michael Hawcroft demonstrates, we can see a different picture:

> Mistress and confidant can engage in persuasion and counter-persuasion, but when the mistress gives a command, the persuasion ceases, and the confidant has to obey. Phèdre wins the debate by social rank rather than by argument. She simply refuses to listen to Œnone's reasons. (181)

This is the heroine supposedly gulled by a flatterer, or directed by forces external to her own will, "whose only weakness," in Alain Niderst's words, "is to have spoken, and to have thought it possible to live and be happy" (*Les Tragédies* 134). Not for nothing did Kenneth Tynan see her as "an active collaborator" (210). As Jacques Scherer stresses (*Cérémonie* 34), at any point in that fateful day Phèdre could have refused to listen to Œnone, and in the end she did.

This context gives an more objective reality against which to set Phèdre's final self-justification:

> Le Ciel mit dans mon sein une flamme funeste.
> La détestable Œnone a conduit tout le reste. (1625-26)

It is of course Phèdre who makes a conscious decision to have Œnone bribe Hippolyte with political power: "Fais briller la couronne à ses yeux" (800). Indeed, she not only tells Œnone what to do, but gives her careful instructions on how to act the part, as any good producer would:

> Presse, pleure, gémis, peins-lui Phèdre mourante.
> Ne rougis point de prendre une voix suppliante. (809-10)

In Phèdre's self-projection, as a merely passive object of forces external to her will, there is a parallel to be drawn with Hamlet's image as a delayer. It has been pointed out that the evidence to support this latter image subsists only in Hamlet's own words, some of which are spoken after he has stabbed the man he takes to be his father's killer. It might therefore be appropriate, following J. C. Maxwell on the prince of Denmark (211), to speak of "double vision" in the case of Phèdre, as Paul Bénichou in fact does (*L'Écrivain* 321). In both cases this involves going beyond what the character says, and asking what in reality happens. That reality springs from a tragic plot based, not on any "fatality," but on what

Georges Forestier calls "reversibility," actions that could have been other than what they are: "an alternating sequence of rational decisions, passion-filled hesitations, and irrational changes of mind, leading to a downward spiral of incomprehension and misunderstandings that a single word would be enough to halt" (*Passions tragiques* 222).

Phèdre is thus so far from being a passive figure that she delivers injunctions even in her monologues, which are sometimes dialogues with the Venus she perceives to be an outside force: "Déesse, venge-toi," "Qu'il l'aime" (822-23). When Œnone suggests, in the most morally explicit terms, that Hippolyte should be sacrificed to safeguard their own honour–"Il faut immoler tout, et même la Vertu" (908)–Phèdre gives her free rein (911). Even now, it is not Œnone but Phèdre who, Iago-like, with devastating suggestiveness, plants the seed of jealous fury in her husband's soul:

> Vous êtes offensé. La fortune jalouse
> N'a pas en votre absence épargné votre Épouse, (917-18)

Conversely, and paradoxically, it is not Phèdre but Œnone who pronounces those words that encapsulate, and might seem to justify, so many interpretations of the play:

> On ne peut vaincre sa destinée.
> Par un charme fatal vous fûtes entraînée. (1297-98)

It should not be forgotten, however, that this apology for determinism leads to Phèdre expelling Œnone for poisoning her mind. This irony is an apposite commentary on the determinist thesis. For the evidence of the play itself shows characters making choices, constructing strategies, that in turn influence other choices and strategies.

Sets of phrases, such as "Avec quelle rigueur, Destin, tu me poursuis!" (1003), taken in isolation to support a determinist hypothesis, do not therefore reflect what happens, and what the characters make happen. The characters act. Even their inaction can have portentous consequences, as in Phèdre's failure to stop Œnone, or Hippolyte's silence. In addition, as already noted, an important part of that action is in characters' rhetoric: Phèdre is no exception. In this context it is useful to remember the "threefold freedom" that Jacques Scherer discerns in the characters in Racine's tragedies:

> [...] their freedom, which implies responsibility [...], not to persevere in an error committed out of love, their freedom to overcome or refuse an obstacle or dilemma, which is the quintessential dramatic freedom, and their freedom to leave a place that is dangerous for their moral integrity, if necessary through a voluntary choice of death. [...] It will also be noted that these are only negative freedoms. They are the freedom not to do something. This is because characters, who in the last analysis are only given the freedom to refuse or to transcend, are defined first of all by the unbearable situation in which they are placed: but within that situation they are free. Has human freedom ever had a meaning except within a given situation? ("Liberté du personnage" 269)

## The Gods

What then, it might be asked, of "the Gods"? The anonymous author of "Sur les tragédies de Phèdre et d'Hippolyte" (qtd in Forestier Ed. 880), in a tract that appeared five days before the publication of Racine's play, expressed skepticism about "the anger of Venus" and "the omnipotence of these imaginary Gods." Most modern critics have gone in the opposite direction. If Venus and Neptune are protagonists in the action, the obvious conclusion seems to be that characters have no freedom: in Simone Dosmond's words, "the relationship between human beings and the Gods can only be one of dependence" (29). "Racine's is the last Phaedra who can persuade us of the reality of the Gods whom she holds responsible for her plight," assert Edward James and Gillian Jondorf (109), who also claim that "the crime is the doing of a goddess" (117).

Critics have painted this divine presence in various guises: pagan and Christian, Old and New Testament, with "the Jansenist God" a popular favorite.[1] While Phèdre has often been presented

---

[1] See Bénichou, L'Écrivain 321; Calder 120; Jasinski 2: 474; Kaufman 62; Maulnier, Lecture 31; Moreau 144; Revaz 172; Woshinsky, Signs of Certainty 84. On Phèdre's place between myth and psychological drama, see France, "Myth and Modernity" 241. For a synthesis, see Battesti and Chauvet 503-07.

as a play about human beings facing human dilemmas, it thus seems excessive to see it qualified as "a tragedy without Gods" (Méron 48). The very emphasis on mortality could be seen as a metaphysical statement, as in Œnone's "Mortelle subissez le sort d'une Mortelle" (1302). Jean Rohou indeed remarks (Ed. 1079) that the term *mortel* occurs 14 times in *Phèdre*, as against an average of twice in the previous tragedies. Jacques Scherer (*Cérémonie* 25, 137), while refusing any determinist thesis, still points to what he calls "the theatralization of the Gods," and signals the uniqueness of *Phèdre* in this respect. Of one thing at least there is no doubt: that the Gods are present as realities to the characters.

But what then is their reality within the dramatic action? There is no shortage of moments in the play when Phèdre accuses the Gods' vindictive desire to make her suffer torments ever more refined. Many accept at face value the rhetoric of this one character, and thus project it onto the play as a whole. *Phèdre* can then be viewed as a metaphor for a human condition in which characters, doomed from the outset, struggle against impersonal forces that crush them. In this context terms such as "alienation" crop up regularly. This explains to a large extent the reaction of Erich Auerbach that "the general effect is not Christian at all" (*Mimesis* 303) Despite this point of view, however, it is relatively common to see variations of the central idea that through Phèdre, and thus in *Phèdre,* Racine was replicating an image of a bleak post-lapsarian universe firmly planted in his consciousness by an Augustinian upbringing and environment. Christian Delmas gives his own skeptical summary of this approach:

> The problem is generally conceived of in terms of fatality, grace, and predestination, as though Racine had been trained as a philosopher or theologian; or else it is seen in terms of one character, Phèdre, as though Racine had the ambition merely to portray character, and so wrote his plays around one or two characters rather than creating his characters in function of his plays. (*Mythologie et mythe* 241)

To this one might object that dramatists do not have to be theologians or philosophers to share the same attitude or concerns as their contemporaries. The second point made by Delmas, however, is crucial, and has been reiterated in this chapter: Phèdre is not alone on stage, however dominating her presence. It is from the play as a whole that "meaning" or "vision" may be inferred, however such terms might be interpreted.

To take this play as a whole, a first point concerns the way in which Racine treats the supernatural. He had made clear, in the Preface to *Iphigénie*, his refusal to resort to a *deus ex machina*, something common in the opera of the time, to resolve the tragic dilemma. In the Preface to *Phèdre* he also states that, while the "embellishment provided by mythology" adds greatly to the poetic impact, the play itself must be humanly credible. These declarations are consistent with his practice. In *Iphigénie* only the credulous see the intervention of Diana (1785-88). Similarly, in *Phèdre*, the audience is made aware that Thésée may not have killed all the monsters that plagued the shores (948), a possibility used metaphorically by Aricie (1445). In the desire to provide "natural" explanations in order to defend the play from any charge of implausibility, Basil Donné (Ed. *Phèdre* 190) has also suggested that the appearance of the sea-monster is some wonder of nature that only those on the scene attribute to Neptune. Such an explanation, however, would leave the audience with another implausibility: the extreme coincidence of Thésée's prayer to Neptune and the monster's appearance. There is no easy solution.

What is certain, however, is that the idea that some God spurs on Hippolyte's crazed horses is only given the status of a rumor, qualified by the same "On dit" (1539) that was used to characterize the "incroyables discours" that surrounded the death of Thésée (380-88). Ismène is ready to believe the story of Thésée's visit to Hades, but it is Aricie's skepticism that turns out to reflect reality:

> Croirai-je qu'un Mortel avant sa dernière heure
> Peut pénétrer des morts la profonde demeure? (389-90)

One might wish to see some cruel trick of the Gods in the answer given to Phèdre's prayer that Hippolyte should know love. The real irony, however, comes from the working of the plot: this love is established before the prayer is made. Racine's creation of characters for whom the Gods are part of the everyday world is therefore perfectly consistent with his refusal to allow events to be impelled by forces from beyond these characters and their passions. Thus Théramène goes to the region "Où l'on voit l'Achéron se perdre chez les Morts" (12), and Phèdre imagines the "Nuit infernale" (1277) where her father judges the dead. This is the "merveilleux vraisemblable" advocated by Rapin (84).

In attempts to set references to "the Gods" in their aesthetic context, it also seems prudent not to underestimate the aesthetic purpose implicit in the use of mythology. Marc Fumaroli's "Abeilles et araignées" already provides a brilliant analysis of the controversies surrounding the literary exploitation of mythology, or "la Fable," in the second half of the seventeenth century. Suffice to say here that recourse to it was a matter of convention rather than of metaphysics. In addition, as Georges Forestier stresses, "in the Christian era whatever glory still invests the pagan Gods is purely literary and symbolic" (Ed. 1578).

All this of course does not prevent these mythological figures from being used to project human motive and desire in a form that fuses intensity and beauty. Thus Marc Fumaroli remarks that the Gods "give the full measure of the fever that takes hold of the imagination and passions," and that "Venus is a universal structure of the imagination, combining love, suffering, and death" ("Dieux païens" 43, 49. Though Racine never presents the Gods as having any objective basis, their presence is real for the characters, and above all for Phèdre. And it is this presence that allows him powerfully to present an experience of dispossession and injustice with which these characters struggle to come to terms. What he calls "the embellishment provided by mythology," apart from its aesthetic role, thus simultaneously permits sympathy and distance. His use of mythology allows his audience to be in this supernatural world, but not of it. At least as far as *Phèdre* and *Iphigénie* are concerned, there is therefore a metaphorical sense in which one can engage with Michel Butor's sweeping statement that tragedy for Racine can be summed up as a clash between man and the Gods (49). In Georges Forestier's words, "the Gods have no other reality–but it is a terrifying one, springing from repressed passion–than in the consciousness of characters, who bring them to life in the words they speak" (Ed. 1638).

The role of the Gods is thus hedged around with ambiguity. They are perceived as real by characters. Yet this use of a mythological dimension coincides with the demands of a dramatic action that advances through the choices these characters make. Phèdre makes many references to Venus and the Gods, usually to suggest that she has no choice—"Puisque Vénus le veut..." (257)—and that she is part of a family doomed from birth (277-78). There is no doubting the role Venus plays in Phèdre's mind. But, as already noted, Phèdre does not simply submit to some preordained fate. She makes several decisions, some of which involve abandoning the power of decision to Œnone (363, 911). There is a distance between characters' representation of reality and the audience's experience of the dramatic action as a whole. A sense of being trapped and helpless does not prevent characters from making choices that determine the course of the dramatic action.

This dichotomy goes some way to explaining the strange impression produced by the expulsion of Œnone. It is strange not just because Phèdre charges Œnone with a responsibility that in reality is her own, but also because, in terms that recall Thésée's invocation of Neptune, she calls down divine retribution on her nurse: "Puisse le juste Ciel dignement te payer" (1319). This is the same Phèdre who has just referred to the vengeance of a "Dieu cruel" (1289-90), and who will restate that charge in the last scene of the play. In other words, "the Gods" can be not only a mental construct but an alibi. The same process has been seen at work in *Athalie*. It is the oldest story in the world, as Montaigne points out (*Essais* 1: 592). At least to some extent, Phèdre's Gods are created in response to the conflicts she has to face.

Thésée provides another clear example of the ambiguity surrounding the divine in *Phèdre*. Simone Dosmond, for example, claims that the king is merely a passive vehicle, and that "an irresistible force leads him to meet his destiny" (32). This victim status is undoubtedly as much claimed by Thésée as by Phèdre, and so merits the same question: does the rhetoric accord with what actually happens? For example, Thésée asks the Gods why they allowed him to escape from his prison (956), but later explains that the escape was down to his own cunning (968). Similarly, he abandons his wife for yet another amorous expedition, this time his friend's, yet blames cruel destiny for what happens in his absence (959, 1003). And he can decry "les Dieux impatients" and their "faveurs meutrières" (1496, 1613), while having earlier sought from the same murderous Gods an exemplary punishment that could not come quickly enough (1190-92). Indeed, the first, awesome punishment meted out to Hippolyte, exile from the known world, is delivered directly by father to son, without any divine intervention

(1051-52). In the circumstances, therefore, Jean Rohou's assertion that the Gods are "principally responsible for the death of a just man" (Ed. 1069) may not totally convince. It is only natural for Thésée to cry "Inexorables Dieux, qui m'avaient trop servi!" (1572), but the rhetoric cannot hide the simple fact that he has sprung a trap of his own making. This direct responsibility has led Christian Delmas to ask whether Neptune, the supposedly avenging God, has any existence outside Thésée's own desire for revenge (*Mythologie* 245).

In the attempt to counter the massive critical tendency to remove choice and thus responsibility from characters, and to displace the locus of decision onto some divine agency or malevolent fate, related points might be made in the case of Hippolyte. For example, he places his trust in divine justice, while refusing Aricie's plea to tell the truth to the judge (1349-52). Equally, he wishes to make his vow of undying love in a sacred temple where perjury is punished (1394-98), but has omitted to mention this lie detector to a father who is openly accusing him of perjury (1134). In addition, he is killed, not by the monster, but by the horses he can no longer control: "Ils ne connaissent plus ni le frein ni la voix" (1536). One reason for his death is therefore invested with a purely human irony: to pursue his love for Aricie he has neglected Neptune's art, horsemanship (550). His sense of injustice is real, as his dying words testify: "Le Ciel, dit-il, m'arrache une innocente vie" (1561). But the question remains: to what extent has any force contributed to his misfortune that does not radiate from the network of decisions made by all the characters, himself included?

*The problem of evil*

Despite the evidence that can be advanced to support ideas of human choice and responsibility, characters still live in a world peopled by divinities whom they feel exert influence, and to whom appeal may be made. As far as "Racinian tragedy" is concerned, this is once again "exceptional," leading again to the question as to whether it fits into any neatly constructed "Racinian tragic vision." Philip Butler says, uncontroversially, that *Phèdre* "is suffused with an atmosphere of legend that is unique in Racine's plays" (260). The Gods are everywhere present, and for everything can be blamed, especially their absence. As Hamm puts it, in Beckett's *Endgame,* "The bastard! He doesn't exist!" (29).

Many critical reactions to *Phèdre* recall Paul Ricœur's contention that "the secret of tragedy is theological," and that "the core of that theology is the problem of the 'evil God'" ("Culpabilité" 288). It is therefore unsurprising that the God of *Phèdre* should be described as "a cruel spectator of the circus-games on earth" (Rouquier 25). Anne Ubersfeld considers this indifference to suffering as characteristic of the "Jansenist God whose incomprehensible justice answers to no-one" ("Auteur tragique" 56). Pierre Moreau sees the characters as "crushed, and even possessed by the Gods, of whom they appear to be simultaneously the playthings and a kind of inferior extension" (137), while Antoine Adam (4: 372) speaks of a theology of cruelty that anticipates the marquis de Sade.

In the circumstances, confidence in the Gods, and appeals for their protection, are all the more poignant, as in the prayer Hippolyte declares he will make in the temple:

> Nous prendrons à témoin le Dieu qu'on y révère.
> Nous le prierons tous deux de nous servir de Père.
> Des Dieux les plus sacrés j'attesterai le nom. (1401-3)

Minutes later he will be torn to pieces, justifying the mute protest of Aricie: "Par un triste regard elle accuse les Dieux" (1584). Unsurprisingly, therefore, both characters and critics blame the Gods with some insistence. The accusation is that the Gods cause the misfortunes of humanity, seeking arbitrarily to extinguish every small candle of hope. On the other hand, there is the other picture: a plot at work in which characters act, making choices that have cascading and disproportionate consequences. What then? Is the audience being invited to go ever deeper into what resembles a metaphysical maze?

One point at least might be made. While the sense of injustice felt by characters does not prove the reality of divine intervention or non-intervention, it does at the same time express the real sense of helplessness, and therefore of injustice, that clings to the human condition, and that has always nourished the tragic genre. The words spoken by Phèdre and Hippolyte, at the outset, cannot be unsaid: they set the murder-machine rolling. And once Thésée makes his initial error of rushing to judgment, reversal follows, a reversal the more ironic in that it gives the king exactly what he has asked for. What is inexorable in *Phèdre*, just as in the other tragedies, is the *machine infernale* of a tragic plot.

This very sense of the inexorable, however, gives rise to other questions, for which there are no ready answers. The actions of characters may well set in motion a cycle of violence and injustice. But how can the momentum be halted? And what caused those actions in the first place? It is easy to understand why Raymond Picard calls *Phèdre* "a drama of freedom" (1: 741), why for Paul Bénichou "Racine's *Phèdre* poses the question of freedom with an insistence and in a manner quite foreign to its classical sources" (*L'Écrivain* 321), and why others such as Jean Rohou (Ed. 1056) see the fundamental problem raised by the play to be that of human responsibility. Once all of this is said, it is less easy to identify a pattern, or single out a cause. Indeed, one of the sources of the play's interest and dynamism is the fact that responsibility is, in Christian Biet's words, "shared and diffracted" ("Le destin" 114).

In the end, therefore, is what is being said quite simply–but nothing here is simple–that *Phèdre* re-enacts passion, that is, a suffering that works on the audience's emotions? In the emotions so created there is a sense of waste, in David Hall's phrase "the intuition of loss" (217). These emotions are haunted by what has been called the problem of evil, which also surfaced in the previous chapter. As Philippe Seller points out (*Port-Royal* 2: 225), this "problem" is painfully expressed in the oppression of innocence. How could God create the light of day, for darkness to cover the face of the earth? What brake is put on the powerful to prevent them doing what they wish? Where is justice to be found? Is all that exists and happens a matter of blind chance? Some of the incomprehension surrounding these fundamental problems was given expression in Racine's first attempt at the tragic genre:

> Ô toi, qui que tu sois qui rends le jour au monde,
> Que ne l'as-tu laissé dans une nuit profonde?
> (*La Thébaïde*, 23-24)

These same questions are implicit in the phrase uttered by Théramène after his description of Hippolyte's death: "Et moi, je suis venu détestant la lumière" (1589). In such a context it is not quite so easy to accept what Albert Gérard presents as a "general consensus," that images of sun and light describe "the perfection of the moral order" (117), or Odette de Mourgues's assertion that "the serenity of the pure light of day [...] symbolizes the triumph of moral order" (130). In Théramène's words there is a disturbing suggestion: it is not labyrinths or caves that conceal the monstrous, but the ordinary light of day. Similarly, it is not the accumulation of references to the indifference or cruelty of the Gods that provide a metaphysical challenge in *Phèdre*, but the dramatic action as a whole.

In other words, "the Gods" may not play any role as independent entities, but a sense of the transcendent, or a rejection of it, hovers always somewhere near. *Phèdre*, like many other great tragic dramas, represents a moment of violation, a violation of something essential to humanity that many will feel sacred. Need it even be said that these questions have never received any resolution? This is true in particular of the questions raised by issues of free will, determinism, causation, and responsibility. We critics might, of course, wish to spend our days like that select group of Milton's fallen angels, university professors before their time:

> Others apart sat on a hill retired,
> In thoughts more elevate, and reasoned high
> Of Providence, Foreknowledge, Will, and Fate—
> fixed fate, free will, foreknowledge absolute—
> And found no end, in wandering mazes lost.
> (*Paradise Lost* 2.557-61)

The evidence of *Phèdre* offers no easy way out of the maze. Jacques Scherer again goes to the heart of the matter: "The sense of the tragic [...] only blossoms in the shade. Something has perhaps been at work behind the scenes. But it is impossible to say what it is. The fact that we cannot know is in itself tragic" (*Cérémonie* 39).

## Final clarity?

"The action of a play," declared Marmontel, "can be considered as a sort of problem for which the denouement provides the solution" (12: 105). And indeed, one element in *Phèdre* seems to have escaped this uncertainty that envelops it: the supposed restoration of purity, harmony, and clarity in the denouement. A typical formulation is that of Robert Nelson: "The day at last triumphs over night in a Racinian tragedy" (105). The basis for this consensus is usually Thésée's reconciliation with Aricie, and, perhaps even more so, Phèdre's celebrated final couplet:

> Et la Mort à mes yeux dérobant la clarté
> Rend au jour, qu'ils souillaient, toute sa pureté. (1643-44)

In critical accounts across the whole range, the same terms recur to describe the state in which the heroine dies: purity, purification, clarity, and even divine grace (which in the case of someone calmly committing suicide seems bizarrely at odds with traditional Christian catechetics). Thus for Ivan Barko "the heroine's suicide prefigures Christian redemption: Phèdre dies to save the world" (372), and Jean-Pierre Landry is on the same wavelength: "She sacrifices herself to restore order and justice to the world. [...] She comes back to life, real life, a life of purity and clarity" ("Phèdre" 414-16). Equally, for Edward James and Gillian Jondorf, "Phèdre is resolved to tell the truth and restore the purity of a daylight which has been sullied by her criminal passion" (83). Such comments are commonplace.[2]

Purity? Clarity? Truth? Do those who follow this line of argument wish their readers to forget that Phèdre dies still blaming Hippolyte's death on the Gods and "La détestable Œnone" (1625-26)? The heroine's voluntary blindness towards her own role leads Henry Phillips to ask whether her remorse at the moment of death "is endowed with any real content" ("Bien mourir" 161), and Olive Classe goes further: "Phèdre remains untransfigured by remorse and death; even as she pays homage to the truth, she performs a flawed good deed, adding to the tinge of malice in her motive distortions of the facts" (55). Evidence such as this should temper Jean-Pierre Landry's suggestion ("Phèdre" 412) that with her "Pardonne" at the end of Act IV, Phèdre discovers the real face of God, that of a father capable of love and pity. Thésée, it is true, recognizes the mistake he has made in condemning his son. Yet the recognition is hardly complete: he does not question his own past

---

[2] For example, Coudert 119; Fumaroli, "Melpomène" 195; Ogel 314; Pineau 47; J. Pommier, *Racine* 220; Stewart, p. 273; Regnault, "Le nœud" 16.

as a serial adulterer, as though this fact was exterior to the events that have taken place, and in particular, to his summary judgment of his son. He has earlier expressed the desire to find the truth–"Connaissons à la fois le crime et le criminel" (986)–but even at the end there is little evidence that he seeks to look reality in the face. His acceptance of Aricie, in what is the last line of the play, might be viewed as a spontaneous act of reconciliation, except that he is doing no more than grant the last wish of his dying son (1566).

Does *Phèdre* end like Milton's *Samson Agonistes*, with "Calm of mind, all passion spent"? Timothy Reiss speaks of a "negation of the past" (*Tragedy and Truth* 264), and Pierre Giuliani of the restoration of "a lost harmony" (175). But Thésée grants Hippolye's last wish, in what is the penultimate line, with the grudge factor still high, "Malgré les complots d'une injuste Famille" (1653). Well does Harriet Stone say that this play "offers no final release from these reciprocal acts of violence" (*Royal DisClosure* 72). And Phèdre goes to her death denouncing Œnone for having falsely accused Hippolyte, "La Perfide abusant de ma faiblesse extrême" (1629). It is paradoxical that, in what seems a *locus classicus* of recognition following error and reversal (1647), the degree of self-recognition should be so low, and passions so high.

Since earliest times the passions are held to fill human minds with darkness: Malebranche himself embroidered on this truism in his *Recherche de la vérité* (1: 67). It is not certain that either Phèdre and Thésée have completely thrown off the dark restraints so well described by Karl Reinhardt in relation to Œdipus: "What we have had to consider is illusion and truth as the opposing forces between which man is bound, in which he is entangled, and in whose shackles, as he strives towards the highest he can hope for, he is worn down and destroyed" (134). In the circumstances, it seems difficult to challenge Ronald Tobin's sober judgment that the ending of *Phèdre* "is not entirely conclusive" (*Racine Revisited* 140).

*Uncertainties*

One conclusion at least is possible, however: the ordinary things do matter, even in *Phèdre*, perhaps especially in *Phèdre*. It is our choice, as readers and critics. We might turn from excessive concentration on the sole character of Phèdre. We might instead start looking at the play as a whole, no longer as a seamless web of the purest classicism, but first of all as a dramatic machine that is, in Christian Biet's phrase, "put together with scattered and contradictory materials" ("Le destin" 113). We might therefore accept the central role of the plot, with the uncertainties it creates and the choices on which it is built. We might see that some difficulty surrounds terms such as "truth," "knowledge," and "lucidity," in a work marked by ideas of flight, concealment, and self-concealment. We might admit the irresolvable nature of issues involving freedom, responsibility, and determinism. We might concede the intractable and eternal problems surrounding the coexistence of evil and God. If so, it becomes easier to view a play that is a network of complexities in which all the characters are caught, and from which audiences and readers caught up in the dramatic action cannot completely avoid entanglement. The least that can be said is that the uncertainties and complexities of *Phèdre* have consequences for those interpretations that so easily uncover patterns and paradigms, or a "tragic vision," shared with the other plays.

*Phèdre* may of course offer a sense of completeness, as an aesthetic experience. This sense of completeness might seem to be justified by the epithets suggesting that something definitive has been achieved, in the tragic genre as in Racine's own work. But even here, as David Hall reminds us, a degree of caution is perhaps advisable: "In the aesthetic experience, there is always an element of the mysterious in the sense of the inexhaustible, the unfathomable, or the paradoxical (and therefore irresolvable) character of things". (169). The maze remains a powerful metaphor for this most alluring of uncertainties.

## CONCLUSION

It has been difficult to find a fixed star by which to sail the good ship "Racine." By looking pragmatically at some of the evidence provided by some important questions in the major tragedies, this work set out to explore an entity often called "Racinian tragedy" or *le tragique racinien*. Terms such as these imply recognizable and reasonably consistent criteria, commanding general agreement. They imply the unity and coherence of a single work, whatever means is chosen to interpret it. The evidence examined in the preceding pages hardly supports this implicit premise.

This underlying notion of a single, living body of tragic work reflects a historical construction called "Racine," one initiated by Racine himself in his collected editions and sanctioned by his son's biography, or hagiography. The foundations of this imposing monument were constructed in the eighteenth century with the cult of the *Grand Siècle*, and it was given its title deeds by the literary nationalism of the Third Republic. The various literary theories of the last century only accentuated this impression of organic unity. The search for coherence found, and still finds, much reward in those theories that see the plays first and foremost as expressions of tensions and struggles within Racine's life and the society in which he lived.

This book has suggested throughout that this nexus of related approaches leaves some grounds for skepticism. The main reason is the existence of significant differences between the tragedies of Racine, each considered as the individual plays they were created to be, and any notion of "Racinian tragedy" as a coherent whole. The major tragedies considered here are structured in different ways, raise different problems, and offer few certainties. This was first seen with Racine's various plotting strategies in *Bérénice, Mithridate,* and *Athalie.* In each of these plays the "tragic" depends less on some general "vision" than on a quality of emotion created first by the plot, and enhanced by the poetic medium. The situation is further complicated by looking at the implications of terms such as "Racinian." The "exceptional" status of *Bajazet* can at the very least provide arguments to challenge the validity, or uncover the fragility, of supposed Racinian "norms," the more so in that no agreement is forthcoming as to what the "exceptional" might be. A look at some of the problems posed by *Britannicus, Iphigénie, Andromaque,* and *Athalie* casts doubt in turn on the reliability or pertinence of elements such as "pessimism," "Jansenism," or different forms of determinism that are so often considered to be unambiguous identifiers of "Racinian tragedy." Equally, as the final chapter attempted to show, it is not necessary to view *Phèdre* as some ode to metaphysical despair chanted by a heroine who alone represents the "tragic." Like the other plays examined here, *Phèdre* too can reasonably be viewed as a tragic action given life and movement by all the characters. The structure of ambiguity and indeterminacy it creates gives no sure evidence to support any particular all-embracing theory about that "Racine" that it is invariably seen to represent.

"The works of Racine are infinitely complex," concluded Phillip Butler (295). The more I have tried to understand these different tragedies, the less I have been tempted to view this judgment as a form of critical defeatism. Given the complexity and uncertainty that distinguish each of these plays, it is difficult to imagine that there is some magic key that might unlock the door marked "Racinian tragedy." There exist, self-evidently, many varied and well-argued interpretations both of the tragedies themselves and of the "tragic" in "Racine." That is one clear indication that a term such as "Racinian" is most securely used with an essentially nominal value.

As with the works, say, of Shakespeare or Corneille, we critics all establish links and patterns when we look at different tragedies. This is a natural and uncontroversial procedure. Seeking points of comparison and contrast, however, is not the same as accepting that there exists an entity such as "Racinian tragedy," if that phrase is used to imply the existence of a *tragique racinien,* some coherent unit of thought and experience, akin to a single, progressive intellectual narrative into which the plays fit snugly, each in its place as part of a unified whole, with the whole tending to explain or even determine the significance of the part. It is one thing to search for coherence: a pattern will always please the inner eye. It is quite another to construct a "Racinian tragic vision" of which the tragedies are the expression, the more so when not all of the tragedies are regarded as sufficiently "Racinian" to be truly "tragic," or sufficiently "tragic" to be truly "Racinian." John Lapp devoted a large chapter of his book to "The Essence of Racinian Tragedy." It is difficult to share his confidence that such a concentrate can be distilled, if only because "Racine" is not a single plant or species ready to yield its secrets to the literary botanist.

The term "Racinian tragedy," with its notion of an underpinning "tragic vision," generates terms such as coherence, structure, and identity. It implies notions of comprehension, resolution, and closure. It invites general statements of a sort that critics such as Serge Doubrovsky could express with a definitive ring: "Sons in conflict with mothers, in the absence of the Father [...]; that, and only that, is the defining pattern of Racinian tragedy" (243). Examination of the individual tragedies, and of the criticism to which they have given rise over the centuries, invites greater caution, and proposes another set of words: difference, difficulty, uncertainty, irresolution, incompleteness. This last word is crucial. David Maskell distinguishes between the written text and "the performance text, which is the potential performance of the written text" (1). Could one not say that each new critical reading has a different performance in mind? Different critics have uncovered or proposed different paradigms that explain "Racine," all equally and impressively coherent. The question remains whether this coherence exists outside the perceived need for it. Leon Chestov (186) expressed the hope that philosophers would obtain the privilege of being able to admit openly that it was not their job to solve problems. Might the same privilege be extended one day to literary critics?

Whatever his contribution to the establishment of the image of a coherent "Racine," Voltaire was resolutely skeptical of anything that would explain everything:

> There are always some difficulties that stand in the way of even the most universally accepted theories. Systems of thought are like rats: they can squeeze through twenty little holes, but always come up against two or three where they do not fit in. (Moland 17: 530)

In this context another image has surfaced naturally in this book, that of Procrustes. For what advantage is gained by taking living, individual plays and tailoring their limbs to fit a particular critical bed? Whatever overarching theory of Racinian tragedy might currently be in vogue, is it outrageous to view Racine's plays in the first instance, and in the last, as individual works? This focus would at least have the advantage of providing a reminder that these plays, so often considered only as parts of a whole, were originally created as unique stage events, to give pleasure to a particular audience on a particular night. As such, each one of them is a representation of conflicting experiences. In the circumstances, as Christian Biet points out, one cannot legitimately extract even from a single play a voice that is authoritatively "Racinian":

> [...] it would be futile to try to find some precise, structured theory in Racine's work, since by their very nature his plays–and indeed, plays in general–represent characters in conflict, characters who are caught up in their own contradictions. One could even go so far as to say that the role of the theatre is to display the complexity of different lives, to represent how difficult it is to find any coherent theory or moral system, and to leave the audience to have the last word, since the last word is theirs by right [...]. ("Le destin" 106)

A related question is the notion that there is a core meaning to "Racine," some golden seam of significance underlying the individual plays, as though the light could be reached by tunneling deeper. To speak confidently of Racine's "tragic vision" is to suggest at the same time that the "meaning" of "Racinian tragedy" has been uncovered. Some (e.g. Revaz 165) are fortunate enough to be able to see this vision clearly, and thus transmit the "sens profond," the underlying meaning of "Racine." But what or where is this "underlying meaning"? May anyone uncover it, or may it only be revealed to and by the erudite, in a discourse that only the erudite can confidently interpret, safe within the Academy? You do not have to be a Wittgenstein to know that the "underlying meaning" of supposedly simple words and phrases can pose problems. So in a work composed of hundreds of such speech acts, combining together, phrases written more than three centuries ago, in a genre, language, and cultural environment which have long ceased to exist, words that in each performance can be given a different emphasis, how can the "real" meaning be attained, if such a thing itself ever existed? That is another way of saying that "the text," like the oracle in *Iphigénie*, will always project different meanings, depending on the way in which it is acted or read: "Toujours avec un sens il en présente un autre" (433).

This leads to what is a further complication for attempts to decipher the code of these literary texts: the small matter of the theatre. The works considered here are not novels, poems, or philosophical tracts. The importance of non-verbal language is one clue, as Harry Barnwell (*Racine's Tragedies* 16) and others have pointed out. Plays are, fundamentally, different. They have difference embedded in their genetic code. It is not only, as has been seen, that each of these tragedies is different from the others. Each one is ready to generate a different interpretation each time it is performed. This is crucial. Michel Bernard reminds us that "a performance is not something that accompanies a play, it completes it" (280). A similar point might be made about the audience, or audiences, for whom the play is performed. Indeed, as Garnett Sedgewick has said, "there can be no play without a spectator; he too is part of the performance" (33). And Racine's tragedies have been performed, on different occasions, by different groups of actors, for different audiences, in different parts of the world, in different centuries. It is true that there is an ambient pessimism about the place of "classical literature" in society or at school, together with a recurring view, expressed for example by Jean Vilar half a century ago, that "Racine is undoubtedly the most difficult French dramatist to perform" (17). To these opinions only hard facts can be opposed. The sell-out success of the productions of *Phèdre* and *Esther* in Paris in 2003 gave no reason to suggest that performances of Racine's tragedies would suddenly cease in a brave new century.

A performance is by definition a renewal. Jacques Morel (*Agréables mensonges* 25) has spoken of the essentially "unfinished" quality of a play, where each performance is a further interpretation. This fundamental point is spelled out by James Knowlson: "Nothing can be said to be definitive in the theatre. A play or a role is constantly open to reinterpretation. A different directorial approach, different actors and actresses, a different stage space and the end result must inevitably differ" (ix). In other words, it seems hazardous to suggest that there exists what Pierre Marcabru (qtd.

in Delft, "Pleasure" 159) has called a "primal innocence" of the theatrical text, our old friend the "underlying meaning" that some producers willfully choose to ignore. Everything is more fluid, dynamic, personal, difficult to keep still, or keep down. A play lives in performance, and as it lives it moves, in every sense of that word. This has implications for some of the problems it presents, as Henry Phillips suggests: "Simply, the characters' problems are actors' problems. That is to say that both characters and actors have to make choices regarding the performance of the words they must speak: they have to convince an audience" (*Language and Theatre* 144). Particular views of a particular play can be influenced by a particular way it is performed. It is in this perspective that Alain Viala emphasizes the necessary dialectic between criticism and performance:

> Producers and actors have their own way of doing things: they are pragmatic, and follow their own feelings and intuition. By so doing they tell us something about Racine's plays: they pose a question for university research, and demand that this question be addressed. Academic criticism–structuralist, post-structuralist but also non-structuralist or anti-structuralist–has strongly tended to envisage Racine's plays as a coherent whole, the permanent features of which must be uncovered. We have had an abundance of interpretative "systems," from Mauron to Goldmann, from Barthes to Rohou. Every one of the tragedies is consequently viewed as an integral part of the particular system. But contemporary productions of Racine perhaps contradict this systematic vision, or at the very least lead us to qualify it. For if some producers have their own system, others do not, so that in any case it is diversity that prevails. ("Tendances" 31)

A similar point might be made about the "Racine" that can be "explained" by some totalizing paradigm, based on what is a selection of the historical evidence now available. Most would now accept (though this is no guarantee of anything) that Racine's theatre does not exist in some timeless polar void, as Bernard Dort seems to suggest: "Racine's is a theatre of refusal: it stands alone, trapped in its own ice, impervious to history, to its space and time" (16). It seems reasonable to suggest that historical, cultural, and linguistic contexts must be taken into account when attempting to assess a series of different works of literature. However, it is going rather further down the road towards that mythical junction of literature and history to imply that those same works can be given a unity, in this case called "Racinian tragedy," because they are supposed to mirror a set of attributes abstracted from a certain image of the society of the author's time and of his projected relationship with it. In other words, if in our sophistication as critics we manage to avoid seeing "Racine" as a national monument created in the eighteenth and nineteenth centuries, another image invites our consent, that of an author and thus of his works that are *only* the reflection of an age.

There is, however, a slight problem here. One might not totally accept the Jenkins thesis that "all history is theoretic, and all theories are positioned and positioning" (70). But it is difficult to disagree that what is called "a history book," however authoritative it might be, is only one of many possible discourses on the period or issue in question. Georges Dupeyron is not the first to argue that an interpretation of an incomplete biography, and of its intricate and unprovable links with the different plays, can have little objective validity:

> We look for Racine and we cannot find him. This is because anyone could have been brought up by the Jansenists, had actresses as mistresses, trembled from fear and love in the presence of Louis XIV, learned by heart the formal rules of dramatic theory inherited from the Greeks; anyone could have had an Oedipus complex, or been both witness and reflection of a particular social class. But for all that, not everyone could have imagined and then composed *Andromaque* and *Phèdre*. (73)

In all of this, can we completely escape from our individual tastes, experience, and expectations as readers or members of an audience? It would be pleasing to imagine it. But here we hardly need Gombrich's reminder, as formulated by Marion Hobson, that we interpret according to what we expect to see, "within a framework of possibilities that is not neutral" (9). "Racinian tragedy" might seem to have a clear identity, like sister terms such as *classique* or *le tragique*. When what constitutes this identity is scrutinized more closely, the image tends to break up. If, as for Hamlet, "the purpose of playing [...] was and is to hold as 'twere the mirror up to nature'" (3.2.25), different audiences and readers will necessarily see a different image, since they look all at the mirror from the angle of their own taste. In this context, it is sad to see René Pommier declare, after 160 pages of painstaking polemic, that "there is absolutely nothing, in Goldmann's interpretation of *Britannicus*, that deserves the attention of students of Racine" (*Britannicus* 160). How can any critic not welcome multiplicity and difference? Who can be "right" or "wrong" here? It seems obvious that the increasing number of viewpoints makes it increasingly less likely that any single one will permit some privileged access to some "deep significance" or "truth" about an "essential Racine" that has somehow escaped the notice of other scholars. In other words, "Racine" can best be apprehended less as an object than as what Amy Wygant calls a "construction zone" (7), a building always in the process of completion, when it is not being torn down. In such debates it is useful to remember the point made with appropriate gentleness by Denis Donoghue:

> It could be argued that literature, which is largely and perhaps entirely fictive, should be prefigured by notions and hypotheses, the work of speculative instruments. If we can't say anything about first-and-last things, and if scientists tell us that the best part of their work is hypothetical and notional, then it would seem reasonable to pursue our theories in a mood hospitable and airy.
> But we soon discover that our discourses are not at all hospitable. On the contrary: we find that the favoured terms of reference and agency are far more likely to threaten than to invite. If the word "theory" denotes a loose federation among scholars of diverse interests, and if many of these share nothing but a prejudice that they have certain enemies in common, then it is strange that the play supposedly of notions and hypotheses, by definition severed from the ultimate questions, is conducted in remarkably insistent terms. I often find myself wondering about the authors: where have they found such conviction, in the declared absence of any ground of ultimacy? (36-37)

In the past century the relationship between the critic and the work of literature sometimes assumed similarities with that between the scientist and the material of his experiments, and was often expressed in a language that for the outsider was equally arcane. We are all, readers and critics, inheritors of an eighteenth-century classification of "Racine" as an eternal, unmoving value, and of a positivist nineteenth century, relayed by a twentieth century always ready to "explain" literature in near-scientific terms. In this context Gaston Bachelard is always a good read. As mentioned in the Introduction, his corrosive critique of scientific determinism could be equally applied to the type of criticism that flourished in the latter decades of the past century, where it seemed important to find categories, and tailor the work to fit:

> The sense of the *determined* is the sense that there is a fundamental, underlying order: it is the peace of mind given by systems, the safety to be found in mathematical connections. [...] the psychology of Determinism is derived from our efforts to rationalize reality. (102)

To these challenges there seems no reasonable response other than the kind of patient, intelligent probing of so many critics, who seek to establish or challenge meanings, sources, influences, and patterns in a multitude of different contexts. Some are doubtless even now working towards the establishment of some critical Grand Design for the twenty-first century, secure in its certainties, encompassing and explaining that construct called "Racine" as though it were an inert object or a set of objective data. May they be granted a favorable wind for their hermeneutic journey. The evidence suggests, however, that the more inclusive the critical system is at the time, the less conclusive it appears over time. It is a fair bet that "questioning Racinian tragedy" will always be on the agenda. There is no last word.

But there is a necessary final one, in what is an attempt to avoid as much as possible the temptation of any flamboyant critical crescendo. It is a warning about the person who has calmly sat in judgment on so many critical minds better equipped than his own, and who even now seeks to hide behind the words used by George Orwell at the end of his *Homage to Catalonia*:

> In case I have not said this somewhere earlier in the book I will say it now: beware of my partisanship, my mistakes of fact and the distortion inevitably caused by my having seen only one corner of events. (313)

# BIBLIOGRAPHY

N. B. Reference will normally be made to a collected volume of an author's articles that have appeared beforehand in different sources, or to a critical work that incorporates previously published material.

1. EDITIONS OF RACINE'S WORKS

*Œuvres*. Ed. Paul Mesnard. 8 vols. Paris: Hachette, 1865-73.
*Œuvres complètes*. Ed. Raymond Picard. 2 vols. Éditions de la Pléiade. Paris: Gallimard, 1950-52.
*Théâtre complet*. Ed. Jacques Morel and Alain Viala. Classiques Garnier. Paris: Dunod, 1980.
*Théâtre complet*. Ed. Jean-Pierre Collinet. 2 vols. Paris: Gallimard, 1982-83.
*Théâtre complet*. Ed. Philippe Sellier. 2 vols. Paris: Imprimerie nationale, 1995.
*Théâtre complet*. Ed. Jean Rohou. Paris: Poche, 1998.
*Théâtre, Poésie*. Ed. Georges Forestier. Éditions de la Pléiade. Paris: Gallimard, 1999.
*Andromaque*. Ed. R. H. Knight and H. T. Barnwell. Geneva: Droz, 1977.
*Athalie*. Ed. Peter France. Oxford: Oxford UP, 1966.
*Bajazet*. Ed. Georges Forestier. Paris: Poche, 1992.
*Bajazet*. Ed. Christian Delmas. Paris: Gallimard, 1995.
*Bérénice*. Ed. Jacques Scherer. Paris: SEDES, 1974.
*Bérénice*. Ed. Georges. Forestier. Paris: Poche, 1987.
*Britannicus*. Ed. Philip Butler Cambridge: Cambridge UP, 1967.
*Iphigénie*. Ed. Daniel Achach. Paris: Larousse, 1965.
*Iphigénie*. Ed. Marc Escola. Paris: Flammarion, 1998.
*Mithridate*. Ed. Gaston Rudler. Oxford: Blackwell, 1943.
*Phèdre*. Ed. Boris Donné. Paris: Flammarion, 2000.
*Principes de la Tragédie en marge de la Poétique d'Aristote*. Ed. Eugène Vinaver. Paris: Nizet, 1951.

2. WORKS FIRST PUBLISHED BEFORE 1900

Aeschylus. *The Orestian Trilogy*. Trans. Philip Vellacott. Harmondsworth: Penguin, 1956.
Aristotle. *The Art of Poetry*. Trans. Ingram Bywater. Oxford: Clarendon, 1967.

Aubignac. François Hédelin, abbé d'. *La Pratique du théâtre.* Ed. Hélène Baby. Paris: Champion, 2001.
Augustine. *Confessions.* Trans. Henry Chadwick. Oxford: Oxford UP, 1991.
———. *The City of God.* Ed. Whitney J. Oates. New York: Random House, 1948. Vol. 2 of *Basic Writings of Saint Augustine.* 2 vols.
Baillet, Adrien. *Jugement des Savans sur les principaux ouvrages des auteurs. Revus, corrigés et augmentés par Mr. de la Monnaye.* 13 vols. Amsterdam, 1725.
Boileau, Nicolas. *Œuvres complètes.* Ed. Françoise Escal. Bibliothèque de la Pléiade. Paris: Gallimard, 1966.
Bossuet, Jacques-Bénigne. *Oraisons funèbres.* Ed. Jacques Truchet. Paris: Garnier, 1961.
Boswell, James. *Life of Johnson.* Ed. R. W. Chapman. London: Oxford UP, 1953.
Cervantes, Miguel de. *The History of Don Quixote of La Mancha.* Ed. John Gibson Lockhart. 4 vols. London: Nimmo and Bain, 1881.
Chapelain, Jean. *Opuscules critiques.* Ed. Alfred C. Hunter. Paris: Droz, 1936.
Chateaubriand, François René de. *Œuvres complètes.* 36 vols. Paris: Pourrat, 1836-40.
Corneille, Pierre. *Œuvres complètes.* Ed. André Stegmann. Paris: Seuil, 1963.
———. *Writings on the Theatre.* Ed. H. T. Barnwell. Oxford: Blackwell, 1965.
Diderot, Denis. *Œuvres complètes.* Ed. Jules Assézat. 20 vols. Paris: Garnier, 1875-77.
Dryden, John. *Essays.* Ed. W. P. Ker. 2 vols. Oxford: Clarendon, 1926.
Du Bos, Jean-Baptiste. *Réflexions critiques sur la poésie et la peinture.* 6th ed. 3 vols. Paris, 1755.
Fénelon, François de Salignac de la Mothe. *Œuvres.* 2 vols. Ed. Jacques Le Brun. Bibliothèque de la Pléiade. Paris: Gallimard, 1983-97.
Fontanier. *Études de la langue française de Racine.* Paris, 1818.
François de Sales. *Introduction à la vie dévote.* Paris: Nelson, 1947.
Garnier, Robert. *Œuvres complètes.* Ed. Raymond. Lebègue. 4 vols. Paris: Belles Lettres, 1949-74.
Gasté, André. *La Querelle du* Cid*: pièces et pamphlets.* 1898. Geneva: Slatkine, 1970.
Granet, François. *Recueil de Dissertations sur plusieurs tragédies de Corneille et de Racine.* 2 vols. Paris, 1739.
Guéret, Gabriel. *Le Parnasse réformé.* Paris, 1668.
Hegel, Georg Wilheim Frederich. *On Tragedy.* Ed. Anne and Henry Paolucci. Westport: Greenwood, 1978.
Heinsius, Daniel. *De Constitutione tragœdiæ. La Constitution de la tragédie, dite La Poétique d'Hensius.* Ed. Anne Duprat. Geneva: Droz, 2001.
Hugo, Victor. *Œuvres complètes: Critique.* Ed. Jean-Pierre Raynaud. Paris: Laffont, 1985.
Johnson, Samuel. *Works.* Vol. 7. New Haven: Yale UP, 1992.
Keats, John. *The Poems.* Ed. H. W. Garrod. London: Oxford UP, 1956.
La Bruyère, Jean de. *Œuvres completes.* Ed. Julien Benda. Bibliothèque de la Pléiade. Paris: Nouvelle Revue Française, 1934.
La Fontaine, Jean de. *Œuvres.* Ed. René Groos, Jacques Schriffrin, and Pierre Clarac. 2 vols. Bibliothèque de la Pléiade. Paris: Gallimard, 1958.
La Harpe, Jean-François de. *Éloge de Racine.* Amsterdam, 1772.
———. *Lycée, ou Cours de Littérature ancienne et moderne.* 10 vols. Paris, 1800.
Longepierre, Hilaire Bernard de. *Parallèle de Monsieur Corneille et de Monsieur Racine.* Paris, 1686. Granet, 1: 47-69.
Malebranche, Nicolas. *Œuvres.* Ed. Geneviève Rodis-Lewis, 2 vols. Bibliothèque de la Pléiade. Paris: Gallimard, 1979-92.

Marmontel, Jean-François. *Œuvres complètes*. 18 vols. Paris, 1819.
Mercier, Louis-Sébastien. *Du Théâtre, ou nouvel essai sur l'art dramatique*. Amsterdam, 1773.
Milton, John. *The English Poems*. Ed. H. C. Beeching. London: Oxford UP, 1960.
Molière, Jean-Baptiste Poquelin. *Œuvres complètes*. Ed. Georges Couton. Bibliothèque de la Pléiade. Paris: Gallimard, 1983.
Montaigne, Michel de. *Essais*. Ed. Maurice Rat. Paris: Garnier, 1962.
———. *The Essays*. Trans. Michael Screech. Harmonsworth: Penguin, 1991.
Montesquieu, Charles de Secondat de. *Œuvres complètes*. 3 vols. Paris: Hachette, 1865.
Nadal, A., abbé. "Dissertation sur la Tragédie de *Mithridate*." Parfaict, XI, 253-74.
Nicole, Pierre. *Traité de la comédie*. Ed. Laurent Thirouin. Paris: Champion, 1998.
Nietzsche, Frederick. *The Birth of Tragedy and Other Writings*. Ed. Raymond Geuss and Ronald Speirs. Cambridge: Cambridge UP, 1999.
Olivet, Pierre-Joseph Thoulier, abbé d'. *Remarques sur la langue française*. Paris, 1767.
Parfaict, François and Claude. *Histoire du théâtre français*. 15 vols. 1734-49. Geneva: Slatkine, 1967.
Pascal, Blaise. *Pensées*. Ed. Louis Lafuma. Paris: Seuil, 1963.
Racine, Louis. *Remarques sur les tragédies de Jean Racine*. 3 vols. Paris, 1752.
Rapin, René. *Réflexions sur la poétique de ce temps et sur les ouvrages des poètes anciens et modernes*. Ed. Elfrieda Dubois Geneva: Droz, 1970.
Sainte-Beuve, Charles Augustin. *Port-Royal*. Ed. Maxime Leroy. 3 vols. Bibliothèque de la Pléiade. Paris: Gallimard, 1953-55.
Saint-Évremond, Charles de Margutel de. *Œuvres en prose*. Ed. Roger Ternois. 4 vols. Paris: Didier, 1963.
Schlegel, August Wilheim von. *Comparaison entre la* Phèdre *de Racine et d'Euripide*. Paris, 1807.
Scudéry, Georges de. "Observations sur *Le Cid*." Gasté 71-111.
Sévigné, Marie de Rabutin-Chantal, marquise de. *Correspondance*. Ed. Roger Duchêne. 3 vols. Bibliothèque de la Pléiade. Paris: Gallimard, 1972-78.
Shakespeare, William. *Complete Works*. Ed. Peter Alexander. London: Collins, 1951.
Sidney, Philip, "Astrophel and Stella." *Silver Poets of the Sixteenth Century*. Ed. Gerard William Bullett. London: Dent, 1947. 173-225.
Sophocles. *The Tragedies*. Trans. E. H. Plumptre. London: Strahan, 1865.
Villars, abbé Montfaucon de. "La Critique de Bérénice." Forestier Ed. 511-19.
Voltaire, François Marie Arouet. *Œuvres complètes*. Ed. Louis Moland. 52 vols. Paris: Garnier, 1877-85.
———. *Œuvres complètes. Correspondance*. Ed. Theodore Besterman. 107 vols. Geneva: Institut et Musée Voltaire, 1953-65.

3. OTHER WORKS

Abraham, Claude. *Racine*. Boston: Twayne, 1977.
Acher, Lionel. *Jean Racine. Phèdre*. Paris: PUF, 1999.
Adam, Antoine. *Histoire littéraire française du XVII$^e$ siècle*. 5 vols. Paris: Domat, 1948-56.
Akerman, Simone. *Le Mythe de Bérénice*. Paris: Nizet, 1978.
———. "*Iphigénie* ou la tragédie du classicisme." Zebouni 97-109.
Albanese, Ralph. *Molière à l'École républicaine. De la critique universitaire aux manuels scolaires (1870-1914)*. Stanford: Anma Libri, 1992.

Albanese, Ralph. *La Fontaine à l'École républicaine. Du poète universel au classique scolaire*. Charlottesville: Rookwood Press, 2003.
Alemany, Véronique. "Racine et Port-Royal: d'un centenaire à l'autre." Declercq and Rosellini 237-55.
Ambroze, Anna. *Racine, poète du sacrifice*. Paris: Nizet, 1970.
Antoine, Gérald. *Vis-à vis ou le double regard critique*. Paris: PUF, 1982.
Apostolidès, Jean-Marie. "La belle aux eaux dormantes." *Poétique* 15 (1984): 139-53.
———. *Le prince sacrifié*. Paris: Minuit, 1985.
Aragon, C-E. "Étude de quelques actes de langage dans *Bajazet*." *Cahiers de littérature du XVIIe siècle* 5 (1983): 75-106.
———. "La figure invisible dans *Bajazet*." *Littératures* 13 (1985): 17-27.
Armstrong, Arthur Hilary. "St Augustine and Christian Platonism." Markus, *Augustine* 3-37.
Audet, Jean R. and Milan Kavacovic. "*Bérénice* à l'endroit." *Romance Notes* 19 (1979): 353-57.
Auerbach, Erich. *Mimesis*. Trans. William R. Trask. Princeton: Princeton UP, 1953.
———. *Le Culte des passions. Essais sur le XVIIᵉ siècle français*. Trad. Diane Meur. Paris: Macula, 1998.
Ault, Harold. "The Tragic Protagonist and the Tragic Subject in *Britannicus*." *French Studies* 9 (1955): 18-29.
Baby, Hélène. "Racine sait-il composer? De l'unité d'action dans la tragédie racinienne." Declercq and Rosellini 81-98.
Bachelard, Gaston. *Le Nouvel Esprit scientifique*. Paris: PUF, 1968.
Backès, Jean-Louis. *Racine*. Paris: Seuil, 1981.
Barko, Yvan. "La Symbolique de Racine: essai d'interprétation des images de lumière et de ténèbres dans la vision tragique de Racine." *Revue des Sciences Humaines* 115 (1964): 353-77.
Barnes, Annie. "La Prophétie de Joad." *The French Mind: Studies in Honour of Gustave Rudler*. Ed. Will Moore, Enid Starkie, and Rhoda Sutherland. Oxford: Clarendon, 1952. 90-108.
———. "Littérature et liturgie au dix-septième siècle." *French Studies* 20 (1966): 15-24.
Barnett, Richard-Laurent, ed. *Re-lectures raciniennes. Nouvelles approches du discours tragique*. Tübingen: Narr, 1986.
———, ed. *Les Épreuves du Labyrinthe. Essais de Poétique et d'Herméneutique raciniennes. Hommage tricentenaire*. Special Issue, *Dalhousie French Studies* 49 (1999).
Barnwell, Harry. *The Tragic Drama of Corneille and Racine. An Old Parallel Revisited*. Oxford: Clarendon, 1982.
———. "Racine's *Andromaque*: new myth for old." *Myth and its making in the French theatre. Studies presented to W. D. Howarth*. Ed. Edward Freeman et al. Cambridge: Cambridge UP, 1989. 57-70.
———. "Drama and Poetry of the Unseen in Racinian Tragedy." *Seventeenth-Century French Studies* 22 (2000): 125-40.
———. *Racine's Tragedies: the Paradox of Passion and Restraint*, Institute for Advanced Research in Arts and Social Sciences, Occasional Papers Second Series, no. 2. Birmingham: University of Birmingham Institute for Advanced Research in Arts and Social Sciences, 2000.
———. "Moins roi que pirate: some remarks on Racine's *Mithridate* as a play of ambiguities." *Seventeenth-Century French Studies* 24 (2002): 179-90.
Barrault, Jean-Louis. *Mise en scène de Phèdre*. Paris: Seuil, 1946.
———. "Connaisance de Racine." *Cahiers de la Compagnie Madeleine Renaud–Jean-Claude Barrault* 40 (1962): 3-105.

Barthes, Roland. *Mythologies*. Paris: Seuil, 1957.
———. *Sur Racine*. Paris: Seuil, 1963.
Batache-Watt, Emy. *Profils des héroïnes raciniennes*. Paris: Klincksieck, 1976.
Battesti, Jean-Pierre, and Jean-Charles Chauvet. *Tout Racine*. Paris: Larousse, 1999.
Bayley, Peter. "Let's dump Classicism." Tobin, *Classicisme* 261-64.
Bayley, Peter, and Dorothy Gabe Coleman, eds. *The Equilibrium of wit*. Lexington: French Forum, 1982.
Beckett, Samuel. *Endgame,* ed. S. Gontarski. London: Faber and Faber, 1992.
Bellos, David. "Introduction." Spitzer i-xxxviii.
Benguigui, Lucien. *Racine et les sources juives d'*Esther *et d'*Athalie. Paris: L'Harmattan, 1995.
Bénichou, Paul. *Morales du grand siècle*. Paris: Gallimard, 1948.
———. *L'Écrivain et ses travaux*. Paris: Corti, 1967.
Bernard, Michel. "Esquisse d'une théorie de la théâtralité d'un texte en vers à partir de l'exemple racinien." *Dramaturgies. Langages dramatiques. Mélanges pour Jacques Scherer*. Paris: Nizet, 1986.
Bernet, Charles. *Le vocabulaire des tragédies de Jean Racine. Analyse stylistique*. Geneva: Slatkine, 1983.
Bertaud, Madeleine. *Le XVIIe siècle. Littérature française*. Nancy: Presses Universitaires de Nancy, 1990.
Bertrand, Dominique. *Lire le théâtre classique*. Paris: Dunod, 1999.
Bessière, Jean. *Théâtre et destin: Sophocle, Shakespeare, Racine, Ibsen*. Paris: Champion, 1997.
Beugnot, Bernard. "Vu du XVIIe siècle: littérature, religion, spiritualité." *Études françaises* 31.2 (1993): 53-61.
Biard, J. D. "Le Ton élégiaque dans *Bérénice*." *French Studies* 19 (1965): 1-15.
Biet, Christian. *Racine ou la passion des larmes*. Paris: Hachette, 1996.
———. "Le destin dans *Phèdre*, ou l'enchaînement des causes." Bessière 91-115.
———. *La Tragédie*. Paris: A. Colin, 1997.
———. "*Mithridate*, ou l'exercice de l'ambiguïté: 'Que pouvait la valeur dans ce trouble funeste?'." Carlin 83-97.
———. "Le mythe du Grand Racine et l'ombre du désir." Battesti and Chauvet v-xxii.
———. "De l'épique au dramatique: la tragédie en France entre politique, Histoire, amour et spectacle (XVIIe et XVIIIe siècles)." Hoogaert 131-57.
Blanc, André. *Racine*. Paris: Fayard, 2003.
Blanc, Emmanuèle. "D'*Esther* à *Athalie*: une forme à la rencontre de son sens." *Information littéraire* 50.2 (1998): 20-25.
Bolduc, Benoît. "*Iphigénie*: de la vaine éloquence à l'artifice efficace." Tobin, *Classicisme* 93-112.
Bonzon, Alfred. *La Nouvelle Critique et Racine*. Paris: Nizet, 1970.
———. *Racine et Heidegger*. Paris: Nizet, 1995.
Bouffard, Odoric. "*Athalie*, tragédie biblique." *Culture* 22 (1961): 387-91.
Bourguy, Victor. "Problématique de la poétique shakespearienne." *Magazine littéraire* 393 (December 2000): 28-32.
Bouvier, Michel. *La Morale classique*. Paris: Champion, 1999.
———. "Une dramaturgie de l'amour-propre: le théâtre de Racine." Declercq and Rosellini 189-210.
Bowra, Maurice. *The Simplicity of Racine*. Oxford: Clarendon, 1956.
Braga, Thomas. "Double vision in Racine's *Phèdre*." *French Review* 64 (1990): 289-98.
Braider, Christopher. *Indiscernible Counterparts. The Invention of the Text in French Classical Drama*. Chapel Hill: U. of North Carolina Press, 2002.

Bray, René. *La formation de la doctrine classique en France.* Paris: Hachette, 1927.
Brémond, Henri. *Racine et Valéry.* Paris: Grasset, 1930.
Brisson, Pierre. *Les deux visages de Racine.* Paris: Gallimard, 1944.
Brodsky, Claudia. "'The Impression of Movement': Jean Racine, *Architecte.*" *Yale French Studies* 76 (1989): 162-81.
Brody, Jules. "'Les yeux de César': le langage visuel dans *Britannicus.*" *Studies in Seventeenth-Century French Literature Presented to Morris Bishop.* Ithica: Cornell UP, 1962. 185-201.
———. "*Bajazet*, or the Tragedy of Roxane." *Romanic Review* 60 (1969): 273-90.
Brown, Peter. "Political Society." Markus, *Augustine* 311-35.
Bruneau, Marie-Florine. "*Athalie*, l'unique tragédie pure de Racine." *Romanic Review* 76 (1985): 374-88.
———. *Racine. Le Jansénisme et la modernité.* Paris: Corti, 1986.
Brunetière, Ferdinand. *Histoire de la littérature française.* Paris: Delgrave, 1912.
Bury, Emmanuel. *Le Classicisme. L'avènement du modèle littéraire français (1660-1680).* Paris: Nathan, 1993.
———. "Les Antiquités de Racine." *Œuvres et Critiques* 24.1 (1999): 29-48.
———. "Racine historiographe: théorie et pratique de l'écriture historique." Tobin, *Classicisme* 151-68.
———. "Mémoire, *doxa* et argumentation: le déliberatif à l'œuvre dans la dramaturgie racinienne." Declercq and Rosellini 381-95.
Bury, Marianne. "Racine et Shakespeare dans la bataille romantique: beaucoup de bruit pour rien." Declercq and Rosellini 645-66.
Butler, Philip. *Classicisme et baroque dans l'œuvre de Racine.* Paris: Nizet, 1959.
Butor, Michel. "Racine et les dieux." *Répertoires I.* Paris: Éditions de Minuit, 1973. 28-60.
Cahen, Jean. *Le Vocabulaire de Racine.* Paris: Droz, 1946.
Calais, Étienne, et al. *Analyses et réflexions sur la tragédie racinienne.* Paris: Ellipses, 1995.
Calder, Ruth. "Contrition, Casuistry and Phèdre's Sense of Sin." *Seventeenth-Century French Studies* 21 (1999): 113-22.
Caldicott, Edric. "For the Non-Classical in Seventeenth-Century French Theatre." Tomlinson 27-38.
———. "Racine's 'Jacobite' Plays: The Politics of the Bible." Caldicott and Conroy 100-20.
Caldicott, Edric, and Derval Conroy. *Racine: The Power and the Pleasure.* Dublin: University College Dublin Press, 2001.
Campbell, John. *Racine:* Britannicus. London: Grant and Cutler, 1989.
———. *Questions of Interpretation in* La Princesse de Clèves. Amsterdam: Rodopi, 1996.
———. "'Enseigner Racine,' *mission impossible*?" Tobin, *Classicisme* 249-60.
———. "La part du classique dans le *classique étranger*: le cas de Shakespeare." *Littératures classiques* 48 (2003): 61-71.
Carlin, Claire, ed. *La Rochefoucauld,* Mithridate, *Frères et sœurs, Les Muses sœurs.* Tübingen: Narr, 1998.
Carlin, Claire, and Katherine Wine, eds. *Theatrum mundi. Studies in Honor of Ronald W. Tobin.* Charlottesville: Rockwood Press, 2003.
Cave, Terence. *Recognitions: A Study in Poetics.* Oxford: Oxford UP, 1987.
Chambrure, Guy de. "Opération survie." *Théâtre populaire* 20 (1956): 37-48.
Charlier, Gustave. "*Athalie* et la Révolution d'Angleterre." *Mercure de France* 1 July 1931: 79-80.
Chatelain, Marie-Claire. "*Bérénice*: élégie ovidienne et tragédie racinienne." Landry and Leplatre 95-107.

Chédozeau, Bernard. "Le Tragique d'*Athalie*." *RHLF* 67 (1967): 494-501.
———. "La dimension religieuse dans quelques tragédies de Racine: 'Où fuir?'." *Œuvres et Critiques* 24.1 (1999): 159-80.
Chenu, Marie-Dominique. "Situation Humaine: Corporalité et Temporalité." *L'Homme et son destin d'après les penseurs du moyen âge. Actes du Premier Congrès International de Philologie Médiévale, 1958*. Louvain: Nauwelaerts, 1960. 23-49.
Chestov, Léon. "Pensées inédites." *Revue d'Histoire et de Philosophie Religieuses* 33 (1953): 181-201.
Chevalley, Sylvie. "Les deux Bérénice." *Revue d'histoire du théâtre* 22 (1970): 91-124.
Cheyns, André. "Racine héritier de la Grèce dans *Iphigénie*: les personnages d'Ériphile et d'Agamemnon." *Lettres Romanes* 50 (1996): 3-35.
Clarac, Pierre. "*Athalie*. La prophétie de Joad." *Information littéraire* 14 (1962): 227-28.
Classe, Olive. "En quelle situation? Some notes on the end of Racine's *Phèdre*." *Newsletter of the Society for Seventeenth-Century French* 4 (1982): 53-59.
Claudel, Paul. *Œuvres complètes*. Vol. 15. Paris: Gallimard, 1950.
Cloonan, William. "Love and *Gloire* in *Bérénice*: a Freudian perspective." *Kentucky Romance Quarterly* 22 (1975): 517-26.
———. "Father and sons in *Mithridate*." *French Review* 44 (1975-76): 514-21.
Collet, Paule. "*Iphigénie en Aulide* ou la tragédie de l'innocence." Calais 71-80.
Collinet, Jean-Pierre. "Racine et ses personnages invisibles: le cas d'*Iphigénie*." Bayley and Coleman 176-92.
Combel, Victor. "L'hypotypose dans la tragédie de Racine." *17ᵉ siècle* 188 (1995): 495-504.
Conesa, Gabriel, and Franck Neveu, eds. *L'agrégation de lettres modernes 2004*. Paris: A. Colin, 2003.
Connon, Derek. "Diderot and Racine." Howe and Waller 243-62.
Conroy, Jean. "Construction of identity." Caldicott and Conroy 75-99.
Cook, Albert. *French Tragedy. The Power of Enactment*. Athens, Ohio: Swallow Press, 1981.
Coquerel, Athanase. *Athalie et Esther de Racine avec un commentaire biblique*. Paris: J. Cherbuliez, 1863.
Cornud, Mireille. "Les Tragédies sacrées: *Esther* and *Athalie*." *La Tragédie racinienne*. Calais 89-97.
Coudert, Marie-Louise. "Phèdre, femme." *Europe* 453 (1967): 115-20.
Couprie, Alain. *Racine*. Paris: Nathan, 1995.
———. *Lire la tragédie*. Paris: Nathan, 1998.
Cournot, Michel. "*Esther* de Racine, sans homme et avec sa musique d'origine." *Le Monde* 6 June 2003, p. 30.
Couton, Georges. "*Britannicus*, Tragédie des cabales." *Mélanges d'histoire littéraire XVIᵉ-XVIIᵉ siècles offerts à Raimond Lebègue*. Paris: Nizet, 1969: 269-77.
Croquette, Bernard. "Racine et l'eblouissment cornélien." *Littératures classiques* 26 (1996): 115-21.
Cuche, François-Xavier. "Le retour de l'absent." Declercq and Rosellini 167-87.
Cuénin, Micheline. "Traitement romanesque et traitement dramatique sur le sujet de *Bajazet*." Ronzeaud, *Racine* 81-98.
Dahl, Mary. *Political Violence in Drama*. Ann Arbor: UMI Research Press, 1987.
Dandrey, Patrick. *Phèdre de Jean Racine*. Paris: Champion, 1999.
Danger, Pierre. "La culpabilité dans l'univers de la tragédie et du drame." *La Licorne* 20 (1991): 83-92.

Declercq, Gilles. "Représenter la passion: la sobriété racinienne." *Littératures classiques* 11 (1989): 69-93.

———. *L'Art d'argumenter. Structures rhétoriques et littéraires.* Paris: Éditions universitaires, 1993.

———. "Une voix doxale: la *vox populi* dans les tragédies de Racine." *17ᵉ siècle* 182 (1994): 105-20.

———. "A l'école de Quintillien. L'hypotypose dans les tragédies de Racine." *Op. cit.* 5 (1995): 73-88.

———. "'Alchimie de la douleur': l'élégiaque dans *Bérénice* ou la tragédie *éthique*." *Littératures classiques* 26 (1996): 139-65.

———. "Racine." Zuber and Fumaroli 125-32.

———. "Poéticité *versus* rhétoricité; pathos et logos dans les tragédies de Racine." Tobin, *Classicisme* 19-53.

Declercq, Gilles, and Michèle Rosellini, eds. *Jean Racine 1699-1999. Actes du colloque du tricentenaire (25-30 mai 1999).* Paris: PUF, 2003.

Defaux, Gérard. "Culpabilité et Expiation dans l'*Andromaque* de Racine." *Romanic Review* 68 (1977): 22-31.

———. "Violence et Passion dans l'*Iphigénie* de Racine." *Papers on French Seventeenth-Century Literature* 11 (1984): 685-715.

———. "Titus or le Héros tremblant." *French Forum* 10 (1985): 271-94.

———. "The Case of *Bérénice*: Racine, Corneille and Mimetic Desire." *Yale French Studies* 76 (1989): 211-39.

Defrenne, Madeleine. "Formes scéniques et création des personnages dans le *Mithridate* de Racine." Hill, *Racine* 107-35.

———. "Récits et architecture dramatique dans *Bajazet* de Racine." *Travaux de linguistique et de littérature* 19 (1981): 53-70.

———. "La substance actorielle dans le monologue central du *Mithridate* de Racine." Döring, Lyroudias, and Zaiser 93-106.

Delacomptée, Jean-Marie. *Racine en majesté.* Paris: Flammarion, 1999.

———. "The Majesty and Pleasure of Racine today." Caldicott and Conroy 177-87.

Delbouille, Paul. "Les tragedies de Racine, reflets de l'inconscient ou chronique du siècle?" *French Studies* 15 (1961): 103-21.

Delcroix, Maurice. *Le sacré dans les tragédies profanes de Racine.* Paris: Nizet, 1970.

———. "Regards sur la critique racinienne." *CAIEF* 31 (1979): 89-103.

———. "Le Songe d'*Athalie*." Ronzeaud, *La Romaine* 27-49.

———. "Racine et la fonction fabulatrice: le cas de Phèdre." Barnett, *Re-lectures* 31-48.

Delehanty, Ann. "God's Hand in History: Racine's *Athalie* as the End of Salvation Historiography." *Papers on French Seventeenth-Century Literature* 28 (2001): 155-66.

Delft, Louis van. "Pleasure in Racine." Caldicott and Conroy 155-76.

Delmas, Christian. "*Bérénice* comme rituel." Hill, *Racine* 191-203.

———. "L'unité du genre tragique au XVIIᵉ siècle." *Littératures classiques* 16 (1992): 103-23.

———. *La Tragédie de l'âge classique (1553-1770).* Paris: Seuil, 1994.

———. *Mythologie et mythe dans le théâtre français (1650-1676).* Geneva: Droz, 1985.

———. "Stratégie de l'invention chez Racine." Népote-Desmarres, *Mythe et histoire* 115-26.

———. "Histoire et mythe dans *Bérénice*." Népote-Desmarres, *Mythe et histoire* 127-43.

———. "'Néron, soleil noir.'" Népote-Desmarres, *Mythe et histoire* 145-52.

Delmas, Laurent. "Requiem pour Racine." *Les Inrockuptibles,* 5-11 September 2000.
Descotes, Dominique, Antony McKenna, and Laurent Thirouin. *Le rayonnement de Port-Royal. Mélanges en l'honneur de Philippe Sellier.* Paris: Champion, 2001.
Descotes, Maurice. *Les grands rôles du théâtre de Jean Racine.* Paris: PUF, 1957.
―――. "Le dosage du tragique dans les dénouements de Racine." *RHLF* 25 (1973): 229-38.
―――. "Menaces sur l'État: le thème des frères ennemis dans l'œuvre de Racine." *Op. cit.* 5 (1995): 89-94.
Desnain, Véronique. "At the Altar: Marriage and/or Sacrifice in Racine." *Seventeenth-Century French Studies* 18 (1996): 159-66.
―――. "'Fille de Jézabel': Female Genealogies in Racine." Tomlinson 191-203.
Donaghue, Denis. *The Pure Good of Theory.* Oxford: Blackwell, 1992.
Donville, Louise Godard de, ed. *La mythologie au XVII<sup>e</sup> siècle. Actes du 11<sup>e</sup> Colloque du CMR 17.* Marseille: Centre Méridional de Rencontres sur le XVII<sup>e</sup> siècle, 1981.
Döring, Ulrich, Antiopy Lyroudias, and Rainer Zaiser, eds. *Ouverture et Dialogue. Mélanges offerts à Wolfgang Leiner.* Tübingen: Narr, 1988.
Dort, Bernard. "Huis-clos racinien." *Cahiers de la Compagnie Madeleine Renaud–Jean-Claude Barrault* 8 (1955): 7-16.
Dosmond, Simone. "*Phèdre*: tragédie païenne ou tragédie chrétienne?" *Information littéraire* 51.2 (1999): 27-36.
Dotoli, Giovanni. *Perspectives de la recherche sur le XVII<sup>e</sup> siècle français aujourd'hui.* Fasano: Schena, 1994.
Doubrovsky, Serge. "L'arrivée de Junie dans *Britannicus*: la tragédie d'une scène à l'autre." *Papers on French Seventeenth-Century Literature* 10 (1978-79): 223-66.
Dubu, Jean. *Racine aux miroirs.* Paris: SEDES, 1992.
―――. "*Mithridate* pourquoi?" *RHLF* 99 (1999): 17-40.
―――. "Racine artiste." *Quaderni di filologia e lingue romanze* 15 (2000): 265-87.
Duchêne, Roger, and Pierre Ronzeaud, eds. *Ordre et contestation au temps des classiques.* Tübingen: Papers on French Seventeenth-Century Literature, 1992.
Dumora, Florence. "Le songe d'Athalie ou le retour du même." *Information Littéraire* 55.4 (2003): 18-25.
Dumur, Guy. "Pourquoi Racine?" *Théâtre populaire,* 20 (1956): 49-60.
Dupeyron, Georges. "De Racine à Racine." *Europe* 453 (1967): 66-74.
Durry, Marie-Jeanne. "Bérénice." *Revue Bimensuelle des Cours et Conférences* 30 Apr. 1940: 81-90.
Ekstein, Nina. *Dramatic Narrative: Racine's "Récits."* New York: Peter Lang, 1986.
―――. "The Destabilization of the Future in Racine's *Iphigénie*." *French Review* 66 (1993): 919-31.
―――. "The Weight of the Future in Racine's Theater." *Alteratives.* Ed. Warren Motte and Gerald Prince. Lexington: French Forum Monographs, 1993. 59-69.
Elliot, Revel. *Mythe et légende dans le théâtre de Racine.* Paris: Minard, 1969.
Elthes, Agnès. "La composition du temps racinien." *Acta Litteraria Academiae Scientiarum Hungaricae* 33 (1991): 23-35.
Emelina, Jean. *Comédie et tragédie.* Nice: Publications de la Faculté des Lettres, Arts et Sciences Humaines, 1998.
―――. "Les tragédies de Racine et le mal." *Œuvres et Critiques* 24 (1999): 95-114.
―――. *Racine infiniment.* Paris: SEDES, 1999.
―――. "Peut-on imaginer un classicisme heureux?" *RHLF* 100 (2000): 1481-1501.
―――. "Le bonheur dans les tragédies profanes de Racine." Tobin, *Classicisme* 243-67.
―――. Rev. of *Avez-vous lu Racine?,* by Jean Rohou. *XVII<sup>e</sup> siècle* 211 (2001): 353-54.

Emelina, Jean. "Les 'Classiques' sont-ils heureux ou malheureux?" *RHLF* 102 (2002): 633-36.

———. "D'*Esther* à *Athalie*, théâtre et religion, profane et sacré." Conesa and Neveu 190-229.

Escola, Marc. *Le tragique*. Paris: Flammarion, 2002.

Evans, William. "Does Titus really love Bérénice?" *Romance Notes* 14 (1974): 454-58.

Faudemay, Alain. *Le Clair et l'obscur à l'âge classique*. Geneva: Slatkine, 2001.

Ford, Boris, ed. *The Age of Shakespeare*. Penguin: Harmondsworth, 1966.

Ford, Philip, and Gillian Jondorf. *The Art of Reading. Essays in memory of Dorothy Gabe Coleman*. Cambridge: Cambridge French Colloquia, 1998.

Forestier, Georges. *Introduction à l'analyse des textes classiques. Éléments de rhétorique et de poétique du XVIIe siècle*. Paris: Nathan, 1993.

———. *Essai de génétique théâtrale. Corneille à l'œuvre*. Paris: Kincksieck, 1996.

———. "Jean Racine. Approche bibliographique." *Littératures classiques* 26 (1996): 217-34.

———. "Éditer Racine aujourd'hui; choix, enjeux, signification." Tobin, *Classicisme* 55-71.

———. *Passions tragiques et règles classiques. Essai sur la tragédie française*. Paris: PUF, 2003.

———. "Le Véritable saint Racine, d'après les *Mémoires* de son fils." Declercq and Rosellini 749-66.

Forman, Edward. "Lyrisme et tragique dans l'*Athalie* de Racine." Jomaron 307-13.

———. "Spirit, Will, and Autonomy in Racine's Later Tragedies." *L'Esprit en France au XVIIe siècle*. Lagarde, *L'Esprit* 273-81.

Fonsny, Joseph. "La leçon de *Bérénice*." *Cahiers raciniens* 23 (1968): 21-30.

Fournier, Nathalie, "*Pouvoir* et *devoir* dans les tragédies de Racine." *Lettres françaises* 84 (1984): 94-116.

Fraisse, L. "La littérature du XVIIe siècle chez les fondateurs de l'histoire littéraire." *XVIIe siècle*, 55 (janvier-mars 2003): 3-26.

France, Peter. *Racine's Rhetoric*. Oxford: Clarendon, 1965.

———. "Myth and Modernity: Racine's *Phèdre*." *Myth and Legend in French Literature. Essays in Honour of A. J. Steele*. Ed. Keith Aspley, David. Bellos, and Peter Sharrat. London: Modern Humanities Research Association, 1982. 227-42.

———. "War and commerce in Racinian tragedy." *Seventeenth-Century French Studies* 22 (2000): 141-51.

Freeman, Bryant, and Alan Batson, *Concordance du théâtre et des poésies de Jean Racine*. 2 vols. Ithica: Cornell UP, 1968.

Frye, Northrop. *Anatomy of Criticism*. Princeton: Princeton UP, 1957.

———. *Fools of Time. Studies in Shakespearean Tragedy*. Toronto: University of Toronto Press, 1967.

Frye, Prosser Hall. *Romance and Tragedy*. Lincoln: University of Nebraska Press, 1961.

Fumaroli, Marc. "Melpomène au miroir: la Tragédie comme héroïne dans *Médée* et dans *Phèdre*." *Saggi e ricerche di letteratura francese* 19 (1980): 175-205.

———. "Entre Athènes et Cnossos: les dieux païens dans *Phèdre*." *RHLF* 93 (1993): 30-61, 172-90.

———. "Les abeilles et les araignées." Lecoq 7-220.

Gans, Eric. *Le Paradoxe de* Phèdre. Paris: Nizet, 1975.

———. "Racine et la Fin de la Tragédie." Barnett, *Re-lectures*. 49-67.

Garapon, Jean. "Le personnage de Monime, 'Femme Forte' et héroïne du sentiment." Landry and Leplatre 131-40.

Garrette, Robert. *La phrase de Racine. Étude stylistique et stylométrique.* Toulouse: Presses Universitaires du Mirail, 1995.
Gauthier, Patricia. "Parole et dramaturgie dans l'*Athalie* de Racine." Landry and Leplatre 231-38.
Gellrich, Michelle. *Tragedy and Theory. The Problem of Conflict since Aristotle.* Princeton: Princeton UP, 1988.
Gérard, Albert. *The Phaedra Syndrome. Of Shame and Guilt in Drama.* Amsterdam: Rodopi, 1993.
Gillibert, Jean. "Une police poétique." *Cahiers de la Compagnie Madeleine Renaud–Jean-Claude Barrault* 8 (1955): 46-50.
Ginestier, Paul. *Valeurs actuelles du théâtre classique.* Paris: Bordas, 1975.
———. "La Problématique d'*Athalie*." *Newsletter of the Society for Seventeenth-Century French Studies* 5 (1983): 96-105.
Girard, René. *La Route antique des hommes pervers.* Paris: Grasset, 1985.
Giraud, Yves. "Lire Racine, vraiment?" *RHLF* 101 (2001): 303-11.
Giraudoux, Jean. *Racine.* Paris: Grasset, 1930.
Giuliani, Pierre. "Le Sang d'Hippolyte." Landry and Leplatre 167-75.
Gliksohn, Jean-Michel. *Iphigénie, de la Grèce antique à l'Europe des Lumières.* Paris: PUF, 1985.
Goldmann, Lucien. *Le Dieu caché: étude sur la vision tragique dans* Les Pensées *de Pascal et dans le théâtre de Racine.* Paris: Gallimard, 1955.
———. *Racine. Une Interprétation marxiste d'un grand classique.* Paris: L'Arche, 1956.
———. "*Bérénice* ou le tragique racinien." *Théâtre populaire* 1 Sep. 1956: 31-36.
———. "*Andromaque* dans l'œuvre de Racine." *Cahiers de la Compagnie Madeleine Renaud–Jean-Claude Barrault* 40 (1962): 107-19.
———. "Structure de la tragédie racinienne." Jacquot 251-64.
Goldzink, Jean. "Que sont nos amours devenues?" *Les Cahiers* 17 (1995): 18-29.
———. "Le torrent et la rivière." Declercq and Rosellini 719-28.
Goodkin, Richard. "The Death(s) of Mithridate(s): Racine and the Double Play of History." *PMLA* 101 (1986): 203-17.
———. "Killing Order(s): Iphigenia and the Detection of Tragic Intertextuality." *Yale French Studies* 76 (1989): 81-107.
———. "The Performed Letter, or How Words Do Things in Racine." *Papers in French Seventeenth-Century Literature* 32 (1990): 85-102.
———. *Birth Marks. The Tragedy of Primogeniture in Pierre Corneille, Thomas Corneille, and Jean Racine.* Philadelphia: U. of Pennsylvania Press, 2000.
Gossip, Christopher. "Le rôle et les antécédents de l'Antiochus de Racine." *Cahiers raciniens* 21 (1967): 45-68.
———. *An Introduction to French Classical Tragedy.* London: Macmillan, 1981.
Gouhier, Henri. *Le Théâtre et l'existence.* Paris: Vrin, 1952.
Goulemot, Jean-Marie. *Discours, révolutions et histoire.* Paris: Union Générale d'Éditions, 1975.
Gravel, Pierre, ed. *Tragique et tragédie.* Montreal: Presses de l'Université de Montreal, 1979.
Grégoire, Vincent. "La Femme et la Loi dans la perspective des pièces bibliques raciniennes représentés à Saint-Cyr." *17$^e$ siècle* 45 (1993): 323-36.
Gros de Gasquet, Julia. "Les Enjeux de la ponctuation du vers racinien: étude comparée de deux tirades de *Bajazet*." Louvat and Moncond'huy 219-34.
Gross, Mark. "*Bajazet* and Intertextuality." *Yale French Studies* 76 (1989): 146-61.
Gruffat, Sabine. "*Bajazet* ou les perversités de la médiation." Landry and Leplatre 121-30.

Guelloz, Suzanne, ed. *Racine et Rome: Britannicus, Bérénice, Mithridate.* Orléans: Paradigme, 1995.

Guénoun, Solange. *Archaïque Racine.* New York: Peter Lang, 1993.

———. "L'invention de Monime: une leçon de monisme en monarchie dans *Mithridate* de Racine." Carlin 113-23.

Gutwirth, Marcel. "La problématique de l'innocence dans le théâtre de Racine." *Revue des Sciences Humaines* 106 (1962): 183-202.

———. *Jean Racine, un Itinéraire poétique.* Montreal: Presses Universitaires de Montréal, 1970.

———. "*Britannicus*, tragédie de qui?" Venesoen, *Racine* 53-69.

———. "Jéhu, le fier Jéhu: la métaphorisation du tragique." Barnett, *Re-lectures* 69-80.

Haley, Sr. Marie Philip. "Peripeteia and Recognition in Racine." *PMLA* 15 (1940): 426-39.

Hall, David. *Eros and Irony.* Albany: State University of New York Press, 1982.

Hammond, Nicolas. "Educating Joas: the Power of Memory in *Athalie.*" *Seventeenth-Century French Studies* 22 (2000): 107-14.

Harth, Erica. "The Tragic Moment in *Athalie.*" *Modern Language Quarterly* 33 (1972): 382-95.

Hausmann, Frank-Rutger, Christoph Miething, and Margarete Zimmermann, eds. *"Diversité c'est ma devise." Studien zur französischen Literatur des 17. Jahrhunderts.* Tübingen: Narr, 1994.

Hawcroft, Michael. *Word as Action: Racine, Rhetoric and Theatrical Language.* Oxford: Clarendon, 1992.

———. "Reading Racine: punctuation and capitalization in the first editions of his plays." *Seventeenth-Century French Studies* 22 (2000): 35-50.

———. "L'apostrophe racinienne." Declercq and Rosellini 397-414.

Heaney, Seamus. *The Government of the Tongue.* London: Faber, 1988.

Heath, Michael. *The Poetics of Greek Tragedy.* Stanford: Stanford UP, 1987.

Henein, Eglal. "De Jocaste à Jézabel: la politique maternelle du compromis chez Racine." Leiner 91-107.

Henry, Martin. *On Not Understanding God.* Maynooth: Columba, 1997.

Hepp, Noémi. "Le personnage de Titus dans *Bérénice.*" *Travaux de linguistique et de littérature* 18 (1980): 85-96.

———. "Autour de *Bérénice, Bajazet, Athalie.* Harmoniques raciniennes." *Information littéraire* 38.2 (1986): 61-66.

———. "*Britannicus, Bérénice, Mithridate*: trois images de Rome." *Op. cit.* 5 (1995): 95-101.

Hepp, Noémi, and Georges Livet. *Héroïsme et création littéraire sous les règnes de Henri IV et de Louis XIV.* Paris: Klincksieck, 1974.

Heyndels, Ingrid. *Le conflit racinien, esquisse d'un système tragique.* Brussels: Éditions de l'Université de Bruxelles, 1985.

Hill, Christine, ed. *Racine. Théâtre et Poésie.* Leeds: Frances Cairns Publications, 1991.

Hill, Robert. "Racine and Pentecost: Christian typology in *Athalie.*" *Papers on French Seventeenth-Century Literature* 17 (1990): 189-210.

———. "*Athalie.* Typology, Rhetoric, and the Messianic Promise." C. Williams 47-63.

Hobson, Marion. *The Object of Art* Cambridge: Cambridge UP, 1982.

Hoogaert, Corinne, ed. *Rhétoriques de la tragédie.* Paris: PUF, 2003.

Howarth, W. "The Nature of Tragedy in *Iphigénie*: a Comparative Approach." Barnett, *Labyrinthe* 119-31.

Howarth, William, Ian McFarlane and Margaret McGowan, eds. *Form and Mean-*

*ing: Aesthetic Coherence in Seventeenth-Century French Drama. Studies presented to Harry Barnwell*. Amersham: Avebury, 1982.
Howe, Alan, and Richard Waller, eds. *En marge du classicisme: essays on the French theatre from the Renaissance to the Enlightenment*. Liverpool: Liverpool UP, 1987.
Hubert, Judd. *Essai d'exégèse racinienne: les secrets témoins*. Paris: Nizet, 1956.
Jacquot, Jean, ed. *Le Théâtre tragique*. Paris: Éditions du CNRS, 1965.
Jacquot, Jean, and Alain. Veinstein, eds. *Entretiens d'Arras, 15-18 1956. La Mise en scène des œuvres du passé*. Paris: Éditions du CRNS, 1957.
James, Edward, and Gillian Jondorf. *Racine: Phèdre*. Cambridge: Cambridge UP, 1994.
James, Susan. *Passion and Action. The Emotions in Seventeenth-Century Philosophy*. Oxford: Oxford UP, 1994.
Jaouën, Françoise. "*Britannicus* ou l'éloge de la cruauté." *Op. cit.* 5 (1995): 103-10.
———. "*Esther/Athalie*: Histoire sacrée, Histoire exemplaire." *Seventeenth-Century French Studies* 21 (1999): 123-31.
Jasinski, René. *Vers le vrai Racine*. 2 vols. Paris: A. Colin, 1958.
Jeffrey, David Lyle, ed. *A Dictionary of Biblical Tradition in English Literature*. Grand Rapids, MI: Eerdmans, 1992.
Jenkins, Keith. *Rethinking History*. London: Routledge, 1991.
Jomaron, Jaqueline de, ed. *Dramaturgies. Langages dramatiques. Mélanges pour Jacques Scherer*. Paris: Nizet, 1986.
Joye, Jean-Claude. *Méditations raciniennes*. Bern: Lang, 1996.
Kaufman, Francine. "L'Echo de l'ancien testament dans les tragédies de Racine." *17ᵉ siècle* 88 (1970): 62-78.
Keller, Luzius. "La Figuration du temps tragique chez Racine." *Versants* 4 (1983): 47-57.
Kerbrat, Marie-Claire. "Le pouvoir, illusion tragique. *Britannicus*." Kerbrat, Le Gall, and Leliepvre-Botton 81-156.
Kerbrat, Marie-Claire, Danielle Le Gall, and Sylvie Leliepvre-Botton, eds. *Figures du pouvoir*. Paris: PUF, 1994.
Kintzler, Catherine. "Temps expérimental du théâtre, temps empirique de l'opéra: la question du spectacle." *Littératures classiques* 43 (2001): 117-25.
Kirschner, Mary. "Poetic Characterization in *Mithridate*: Xipharès and Pharnace." *Cahiers du dix-septième* 3 (1989): 17-27.
Kitto, Harold. *Sophocles*. London: Oxford UP, 1958.
Knapp, Bettina. *Racine. Mythos and Renewal in Modern Theatre*. University of Alabama Press, 1971.
Knight, Roy. *Racine et la Grèce*. Paris: Boivin, 1950.
———. "Les dieux païens dans la tragédie française." *RHLF* 64 (1964): 414-26.
———, ed. *Racine. Modern Judgements*. London: Macmillan, 1969.
———. "Myth in Racine: a Myth?" *Esprit Créateur* 16 (1976): 95-104.
———. "Meditations on *Athalie*." Howarth, McFarlane, and M. McGowan 187-99.
Knights, L. C. "Shakespeare: *King Lear* and the great Tragedies." Ford 228-56.
Knowlson, James. "General Editor's Note." Beckett, *Endgame* ix-x.
Knutson, Harold. "Le dénouement heureux dans la tragédie française du 17ᵉ siècle." *Zeitschrift für französische Sprache und Literatur* 77 (1967): 339-46.
Koch, Erec. "Deferred acts: *Bajazet*, utimeliness and tragic orthodoxy." *Seventeenth-Century French Studies* 21 (1999): 101-11.
———, ed. *Classical Unities: Place, Time, Action*. Tübingen: Narr, 2002.
Kolakowski, Leszek. *God Owes Us Nothing*. Chicago: U. of Chicago Press, 1995.
Krieger, Murray. "Tragedy and the Tragic Vision." Michel and Sewall 130-46.

Kuizenga, Donna. "*Mithridate*: A Reconsideration." *French Review* 52 (1978-79): 280-85.
Lagarde, François, ed. *L'Esprit en France au XVII<sup>e</sup> siècle*. Biblio 17 Tübingen: Papers on French Seventeenth-Century Literature, 1997.
———. "La valeur et l'effet de nature: Réception de Racine après la Révolution." *Papers on French Seventeenth-Century Literature* 29 (2002): 117-34.
Landry, Jean-Pierre. "Phèdre et Marie-Madeleine: un itinéraire de la conversion." *Prémices et Floraison de l'Age classique. Mélanges en l'honneur de Jean Jehasse*. Ed. Bernard Yon. Saint-Étienne: Publications de l'Université de Saint-Étienne, 1995. 407-17.
———. "*Bérénice*: travail de deuil et rituel de sacrifice." *Travaux de Littérature* 10 (1997): 135-47.
———. "*Andromaque* ou le devoir de mémoire." Landry and Leplatre 67-78.
Landry, Jean-Pierre and Olivier Leplatre, eds. *Présence de Racine*. Lyon: Université Jean Moulin, 2000.
Lanson, Gustave. *Histoire de la littérature française*. 18<sup>th</sup> ed. Paris: Hachette, 1940.
———. *Esquisse d'une histoire de la tragédie française*. Paris: Champion, 1945.
Lapp, John. *Aspects of Racinian tragedy*. Toronto: Toronto UP, 1955.
Larthomas, Pierre. *Le Langage dramatique*. Paris: Colin, 1972.
Lassalle, Thérèse. "*Bérénice*: 'Tant de mers' ou une Eternité sans étreinte." Landry and Leplatre 109-19.
Le Bozec, Yves. "*Esther* et *Athalie*: étude de la langue." Conesa and Neveu 232-52.
Lecoq, Anne-Marie, ed. *La Querelle des Anciens et des Modernes*. Paris: Gallimard, 2001.
Leiner, Wolfgang, ed. *Onze nouvelles études sur l'image de la femme dans la literature française du XVII<sup>e</sup> siècle*. Tübingen: Narr, 1988.
Lemaître, Jules. *Jean Racine*. Paris: Calaman-Levy, 1908.
Lépine, Jacques-Jude. "La Barbarie à visage divin: mythe et rituel dans *Athalie*." *French Review* 64 (1990): 19-31.
Leplatre, Olivier. "*Britannicus* ou l'aporie du regard." Landry and Leplatre 79-94.
Levitan, William. "Seneca in Racine." *Yale French Studies* 76 (1989): 185-210.
Lewis, Philip. "Sacrifice and Suicide: Some Afterthoughts on the Career of Jean Racine." Zebouni 53-74.
Lipietz, Alain. *Phèdre: identification d'un crime*. Paris: A.-M. Métailié, 1992.
Lock, William. "The use of Peripeteia in Aristotle's *Poetics*." *Classical Review* 9 (1895): 251-53.
Longino, Michèle. *Orientalism in French Classical Drama*. Cambridge: Cambridge UP, 2002.
Loukovitch, Kosta. *L'Évolution de la tragédie religieuse classique en France*. Paris: Droz, 1933.
Louvat, Bénédicte. *La Poétique de la tragédie classique*. Paris: SEDES, 1997.
———. "Le vocabulaire à l'épreuve de la langue: l'exemple d'*Andromaque*." Louvat and Moncond'huy 323-42.
Louvat, Bénédicte, and Dominique Moncond'huy, eds. *Racine poète*. Poitiers: La Licorne, 1999.
Lyons, John. *Kingdom of Disorder. The Theory of Tragedy in Classical France*. West Lafayette: Purdue University Press, 1999.
———. "What do we mean when we say 'classique'?" Tobin, *Classicisme* 497-505.
———. 'Racine et la dramaturgie du temps." Declercq and Rosellini 127-37.
MacDowell, Douglas. "*Hybris* in Athens." *Greece and Rome* 23 (1976): 14-31.
Magné, Bernard. "L'ironie dans l'*Iphigénie* de Racine." *Papers on French Seventeenth-Century Literature* 9 (1982): 237-52.

Malachy, Thérèse. "*L'Athalie* de Racine: au croisment des traditions." *XVII<sup>e</sup> siècle* 49 (1997): 591-96.
Mambrino, Jean. "*Athalie* de Racine et *Dom Juan* de Molière, mise en scène de Roger Planchon." *Études* 353 (juillet 1977): 152.
———. "*Bérénice* à la Comédie-Française." *Études* 362 (1985): 498-99.
Markus, Roger, ed. *Augustine. A Collection of Critical Essays*. New York: Doubleday, 1972.
———. *The End of Ancient Christianity*. Cambridge: Cambridge UP, 1990.
Maskell, David. *Racine. A theatrical reading*. Oxford: Clarendon, 1991.
Maulnier, Thierry. *Racine*. 2<sup>nd</sup> ed. Paris: Gallimard, 1954.
———. *Lecture de* Phèdre. Paris: Gallimard, 1967.
Maurer, Karl. "*Iphigénie* et *La Jeune Parque*: musicalité et prise de conscience tragique." *Papers on French Seventeenth-Century Literature* 29 (2002): 323-32.
Mauriac, Francois. *La Vie de Jean Racine*. Paris: Plon, 1928.
Mauron, Charles. *L'Inconscient dans l'œuvre et la vie de Racine*. Gap: Ophyrs, 1957.
Maxwell, J. C. "Shakespeare: the Middle Plays." Ford 201-27.
May, Georges. *Tragédie cornélienne, tragédie racinienne: étude sur les sources de l'intérêt dramatique*. Urbana: University of Illinois Press, 1948.
Mazouer, Charles. "Les tragédies bibliques sont-elles tragiques?" *Littératures classiques* 16 (1992): 125-40.
Mercanton, Jacques. *Racine*. Bruges: Desclée de Brouwer, 1966.
Méron, Evelyne. "De l'Hippolyte d'Euripide à la Phèdre de Racine. Deux conceptions du tragique." *17<sup>e</sup> siècle* 100 (1973): 35-54.
Mesguich, Daniel. "A propos de Racine." *Revue d'histoire du théâtre* 4 (1999): 322-28.
Mesnard, Jean. "Racine, Nicole et Lancelot." Declercq and Rosellini 291-372.
Michaut, Gustave. *La* Bérénice *de Racine*. Paris: Société française d'imprimerie et de librarie, 1907.
Michel, Laurence, and Richard. B. Sewall, *Tragedy: Modern Essays in Criticism*. Westport: Greenwood Press, 1963.
Miles, John Edward. "*Athalie*: A Study in the Eternal Triangle." *Sub-Stance* 3 (1972): 85-99.
Miller, Arthur. *The Theatre Essays*. Harmondsworth: Penguin, 1978.
———. *Death of a Salesman*. London: Heineman, 1994.
Miquel, Jean-Pierre. "A propos d'une mise en scène de *Britannicus*." *CAIEF* 31 (1979): 149-54.
Molinié, Georges. "Stylistique ou style racinien?" Louvat and Moncond'huy 271-75.
Moncond'huy, Dominique. "*Mithridate* ou la conquête du tombeau." Guelloz 187-97.
Mongrédien, Georges. *Athalie*. Paris: Edgar Malfère, 1929.
Montherlant, Henri. de, "Racine langouste." *Cahiers de la Compagnie Madeleine Renaud–Jean-Claude Barrault* 8 (1955): 3-6.
Moore, Will. "Le *Bajazet* de Racine: étude de genèse." *Revue des Sciences Humaines* 54 (1949): 69-82.
Moreau, Pierre. *Racine, l'homme et l'œuvre*. Paris: Boivin, 1943.
Morel, Jacques. "A propos de *Bérénice*: le thème du mariage des Romains et des Reines dans la tragédie française du XVII<sup>e</sup> siècle." *Travaux de Linguistique et de Littérature* 13 (1975): 229-38.
———. *Agréables Mensonges*. Paris: Klinksieck, 1991.
———. *Racine en toutes lettres*. Paris: Bordas, 1992.
Mortgat-Longuet, Emmanuelle. "Aux origines du parallèle Corneille-Racine: une question de temps." Declercq and Rosellini 703-17.

Mourgues, Odette de. *Racine or, The Triumph of Relevance.* Cambridge: Cambridge UP, 1967.
Muratore, Mary Jo. "Racinian stasis." Barnett, *Re-lectures* 113-25.
Murray, Gilbert. *The Classical Tradition in Poetry.* London: Oxford UP, 1927.
Myers, Henry Alonzo. *Tragedy.* Ithica: Cornell UP, 1956.
Nancy, Claire. "*Iphigénie*, d'Euripide à Racine." *Poétique* 129 (2002): 33-50.
Nelson, Robert. "Night unto Day unto Night: Racinian Tragedy." Van Baelen and Rubin 95-112.
Népote-Desmarres, Fanny. "*Esther* et *Athalie:* au terme de la vision racinienne du pouvoir." Hausmann, Miething, and Zimmermann 361-73.
———, ed. *Mythe et histoire dans le théâtre classique. Hommage à Christian Delmas.* Paris: Champion, 2002.
Néraudau, Jean-Pierre. "Mais où sont ces Romains que fait parler Racine?" *Littératures classiques,* 26 (1996): 75-90.
Neveu, Bruno. "Grace before desserts." Rev. of *God Owes Us Nothing,* by Leszek Kolakowski. *TLS* 26 Jan. 1996: 29.
Niderst, Alain. *Les Tragédies de Racine. Diversité et unité.* Paris: Nizet, 1975.
———. *Racine et la tragédie classique.* Paris: PUF, 1986.
———. "Analyse de la Préface de *Bérénice.*" Döring, Lyroudias, and Zaiser 319-24.
———. "*Mithridate* opéra?" Carlin 125-36.
Noni, Claire. "*Phèdre*, tragédie du silence." Landry and Leplatre 177-84.
Norman, Buford. "Racine, 1674, and the 'Querelle d'Alceste'." Koch, *Classical Unities* 251-62.
Nurse, Peter. "Towards a definition of *le tragique racinien.*" *Symposium* 21 (1967): 197-228.
———. "Racine and his Gods." *MLR* 72 (1977): 34-45.
O'Donohoe, B. P. "Triumphal Hymn and Fierce Tragic Drama: The Thematic Unity of Racine's *Athalie.*" *Australian Journal of French Studies* 14 (1979): 401-16.
Ogel, Vera. "What is tragic in Racine?" *MLR* 45 (1950): 312-18.
Ogura, Hirotaka. *La Rhétorique du "Naturel:" Limites et Transgressions. Etude sur le langage dramatique des pièces mythologiques et bibliques de Racine.* Villeneuve d'Ascq: Presses Universitaires du Septentrion, 1999.
Orcibal, Jean. *La Genèse d'*Athalie *et d'*Esther. Paris: Vrin, 1950.
O'Regan, Michael. *The Mannerist Aesthetic: A Study of Racine's* Mithridate. Bristol: University of Bristol Press, 1980.
Orwell, George. *Homage to Catalonia.* London: Secker and Warburg, 1938.
Paraf, Pierre. "Racine et Israël." *Europe* 45 (1967): 91-96.
Parent, Monique. "Titus aime-t-il encore Bérénice? Trois études des formes verbales comme fait d'enonciation dans *Bérénice*, acte II, scène 2." *Le Génie de la forme. Mélanges offerts à Jean Mourot.* Nancy: Presses Universitaires de Nancy, 1982. 197-207.
Parish, Richard. *Racine: the limits of tragedy.* Tübingen: Papers on French Seventeenth-Century Literature, 1993.
Pasquier, Pierre. "L'Ombre du temps: réflexion sur le statut du temps dramatique dans le discours esthétique du XVIIe siècle." *Littératures classiques* 43 (2001): 89-116.
Pavel, Thomas. "Parole sacrée et action politique: *Athalie* de Racine." *Liberté* 15 (1973): 133-40.
Péguy, Charles. *Victor-Marie, comte Hugo.* Paris: Gallimard, 1934.
Pelous, Jean-Michel. "Métaphores et figures de l'amour dans la *Phèdre* de Racine." *Travaux de Linguistique et de Littérature* 19 (1981): 71-81.
Périvier, Jacques-Henri. "Le problème du mal dans l'*Iphigénie* de Racine." *French Forum* 14 (1989): 147-71.

Pfohl, Russell. *Racine's* Iphigénie: *Literary Rehearsal and Tragic Recognition*. Geneva: Droz, 1974.
Phillippo, Susanna. *Silent Witness. Racine's Non-Verbal Annotations of Euripides*. Oxford: Legenda, 2003.
Phillips, Henry. *The Theatre and its Critics in Seventeenth-Century France*. Oxford: Oxford UP, 1980.
———. *Racine:* Mithridate. London: Grant and Cutler, 1990.
———. *Racine: Language and Theatre*. Durham: University of Durham Press, 1994.
———. "The Divine Sentence." Ford and Jondorf 105-13.
———. "'L'Art de bien mourir': Last Moments in Racinian Tragedy." *Seventeenth-Century French Studies* 22 (2000): 153-65.
———. "Racine et le temps du futur, temps tragique." Declercq and Rosellini 147-65.
Picard, Raymond. *La Carrière de Jean Racine*. 2nd ed. Paris: Gallimard, 1961.
———. *Nouvelle critique, nouvelle imposture*. Paris: Pauvert, 1965.
———. *Racine polémiste*. Paris: Pauvert, 1967.
———. *Nouveau corpus racinianum*. Paris: Éditions du CNRS, 1976.
———. *De Racine au Parthénon*. Paris: Gallimard, 1977.
Pineau, Joseph. "Sur la culpabilité de la Phèdre de Racine: augustinisme et poésie." *La Licorne* 20 (1991): 41-50.
Pittaluga, Maria. *Aspects du vocabulaire de Jean Racine*. Fasano: Schena, 1991.
Pocock, Gordon. *Corneille et Racine: Problems of Tragic Form*. Cambridge: Cambridge UP, 1973.
Poirot-Delpech, Bertrand. "*Bajazet* à la Comédie-Française." *Le Monde* 24 November 1966: 14.
Pommier, Jean. *Aspects de Racine*. Paris: Nizet, 1954.
———. "Un nouveau Racine." *RHLF* 60 (1960): 500-30.
Pommier, René. *Le* Sur Racine *de Roland Barthes*. Paris: SEDES, 1988.
———. *Étude sur* Britannicus. Paris: SEDES, 1995.
Pons, Roger. "L'Angoisse de la damnation: *Phèdre*, IV, 6." *Information littéraire* 13 (1961): 167-73.
Pot, Olivier. "Racine: théâtre de la culpabilité ou culpabilité du théâtre." *Travaux de Littérature* 8 (1995): 125-49.
Poulet, Georges. *Études sur le temps humain*. Paris: Plon, 1950.
Prophète, Jean. *Les Para-personnages dans les tragédies de Racine*. Paris: Nizet, 1981.
Prost, Brigitte. *Racine*. Phèdre. Paris: Bréal, 1998.
Racevskis, Roland. "The Time of Tragedy: *Andromaque, Britannicus, Bérénice*." Tobin, *Classicisme* 113-23.
Ranger, Jean-Claude. "Mémoire et pouvoir chez Racine." *Seventeenth-Century French Studies* 22 (2000): 95-106.
Ratermanis, Janis. *Essai sur les formes verbales dans les tragedies de Jean Racine*. Paris: Nizet, 1972.
Regnault, François. "Le nœud dans le vers." *Comédie-Française* 133-34 (1984): 16-19.
———. *La Doctrine inouïe. Dix leçons sur le theatre classique français*. Paris: Hatier, 1996.
Reilly, Mary. "Racine and Orwell: Classical Newspeak." *Seventeenth-Century French Studies* 22 (2000): 63-75.
Reinhardt, Karl. *Sophocles*. Trans. Hazel Harvey and David Harvey. Oxford: Blackwell, 1978.
Reiss, Françoise. "Racine en proie à la critique moderne." *Cahiers raciniens* 29 (1971): 13-62.

Reiss, Timothy. *Tragedy and Truth*. New Haven: Yale UP, 1980.
Revaz, Gilles. "Le cas Racine: les excès de la Nouvelle Critique." *Études de Lettres* 4 (1995): 163-76.
Ricks, Christopher. *Essays in Appreciation*. Oxford: Clarendon, 1996.
Ricœur, Paul. "Culpabilité tragique et culpabilité biblique." *Revue d'Histoire et de Philosophie Religieuses* 33 (1953): 285-307.
———. *Temps et Récit*. 3 vols. Paris: Seuil, 1983.
Ridgway, Ronald S. "*Athalie* vue par Voltaire." *Jeunesse de Racine*. La Ferté-Milon: Association Jeunesse de Racine: 1969. 108-17.
Riffaud, Alain. "Fortune du mot *tragique*." *Papers on French Seventeenth-Century Literature* 21 (1994): 533-52.
Robert, Pierre. *La Poétique de Racine: etude sur le système dramatique de Racine et la constitution de la tragédie française*. 2nd ed. Paris: Hachette, 1891.
Rohou, Jean. "Le Bonheur, la Joie, le Plaisir dans les Tragédies de Racine." *Cahiers raciniens* 24 (1968): 11-76; 25 (1969): 11-81.
———. "Racine: une seule œuvre en onze étapes." *Revue des Sciences Humaines* 81, 215 (1989): 31-51.
———. *L'Évolution du tragique racinien*. Paris: SEDES, 1991.
———. *Jean Racine. Entre sa carrière, son œuvre et son Dieu*. Paris: Fayard, 1992.
———. *Jean Racine: Bilan critique*. Paris: Nathan, 1994.
———. *Le Classicisme*. Paris: Hachette, 1996.
———. "De *Pertharite* à *Andromaque*: les enseignements d'une comparaison historique." *Papers on French Seventeenth-Century Literature* 27 (2000): 57-84.
———. "L'anthropologie pessimiste des 'classiques': tentative de distinction et d'explication." *RHLF* 101 (2001): 1523-50.
———. *Jean Racine. Andromaque*. Paris: PUF, 2000.
———. *Avez-vous lu Racine? Mise au point polémique*. Paris: L'Harmattan, 2000.
———. "Racine à Port-Royal: hypothèses sur la formation d'un auteur." Descotes, McKenna, Thirouin 401-14.
———. *Le XVIIe siècle: une révolution de la condition humaine*. Paris: Seuil, 2002.
———. "La périodisation: une reconstruction révélatrice et explicatrice." *RHLF* 102 (2002): 707-32.
———. *Jean Racine. Athalie*. Paris: PUF, 2003.
———. "Pour une étude humainement profitable d'*Athalie*." *Information Littéraire* 55.3 (2003): 10-16; 55.4 (2003): 11-17.
Romanowski, Sylvie. "The Circuits of Power and Discourse in Racine's *Bajazet*." *Papers on French Seventeenth-Century Literature* 10 (1983): 849-67.
———. "Sacrifice and Truth in Racine's *Iphigénie*." Romanowski and Bilezikian 143-65.
Romanowski, Sylvie, and Monique Bilezikian, eds. *Homage to Paul Bénichou*. Birmingham: Summa, 1994.
Romilly, Jacqueline de. *Time in Greek Tragedy*. Ithica: Cornell UP, 1969.
———. *Tragédies grecques au fil des ans*. Paris: Les Belles Lettres, 1995.
Ronzeaud, Pierre, ed. *Racine: la Romaine, la Turque, la Juive: regards sur Bérénice, Bajazet, Athalie*. Aix-en-Provence: Publications de l'Université de Provence, 1986.
———. "Racine et la politique: la perplexité de la critique." *Œuvres et Critiques* 24.1 (1999): 136-58.
Rosellini, Michèle. "Histoire d'un mythe de l'histoire littéraire, la poésie racinienne." Louvat and Mondcond'huy 277-95.
Roubine, Jean-Jacques. *Lectures de Racine*. Paris: A. Colin, 1971.
Rouquier, André-Louis. "*Athalie* (accomplissement et mort de la Tragédie)." *Revue du Tarn* 37 (1965): 22-30.

Salazar, Philippe-Joseph. "L'Effet rhétorique, *Bérénice.*" Declercq and Rosellini 571-84.
Salomon, H. P. "Athalie et le Dieu des Juifs." *Cahiers raciniens* 23 (1968): 10-19.
Saurel, Renée. "Laissez-nous vivre!" *Les Temps Modernes* 36 (1981): 2049-64.
Schefer, Jean-Louis. "Les deux objets." *Comédie-Française* 133-34 (1984): 52-53.
Scherer, Jacques. *La dramaturgie classique en France.* 2nd ed. Paris: Nizet, 1950.
———. *Racine:* Bajazet. Paris: Centre de documentation universitaire, 1957.
———. "La liberté du personnage racinien." Jacquot 265-69.
———. "Les personnages de *Bérénice.*" *Mélanges d'histoire littéraire (XVIe, XVIIe siècles) offerts à Raymond Lebègue.* Paris: Nizet, 1969. 279-91.
———. *Racine et/ou la cérémonie.* Paris: PUF, 1982.
Schmitt, Michel. "L'hyperclassique (Racine à l'école)." *Œuvres et Critiques* 24.1 (1999): 281-92.
Schröder, Volker. "La place du roi: guerre et succession dans *Mithridate.*" Carlin 147-58.
———. "Racine et l'éloge de la guerre de Hollande: de la campagne de Louis XIV au 'dessein' de Mithridate." *XVIIe siècle* 50 (1998): 113-36.
———. *La Tragédie du sang d'Auguste. Politique et intertextualité dans* Britannicus. Tübingen: Narr, 1999.
———. "Situation des études raciniennes: histoire et littérature." Declercq and Rosellini 11-24.
Sedgewick, Garnett. *Of Irony: Especially in Drama.* Toronto: University of Toronto Press, 1948.
Sellier, Philippe. "Le Jansénisme des tragédies de Racine: Réalité ou illusion." *CAIEF* 31.1 (1979): 135-48; 264-68.
———. "Une catégorie-clé de l'esthétique classique: le mérveilleux vraisemblable." Donville 43-48.
———. *Port-Royal et la littérature.* 2 vols. Paris: Champion, 1999-2001.
Senart, Philippe. "*Bérénice* à la Comédie-Française." *Revue des Deux Mondes* Jan.-Mar. 1982: 452-56.
Servin, Micheline. "Du bon usage des classiques." *Les Temps Modernes* 45, 125 (1990): 180-90.
Sienaert, E. R. "*Bérénice* de Jean Racine ou la vocation tragique." *French Studies in Southern Africa* 13 (1984): 27-38.
Sioffi, Gilles. "Les tragédies comme représentation de la langue française." Declercq and Rosellini 415-35.
Slater, Maya. "Racine's *Bajazet.* The language of violence and secrecy." *Themes in Drama* 13 (1991): 141-50.
Smith, James. *Melodrama.* London: Methuen, 1973.
Soares, Sandra, and Claude Abraham, "Time in *Bérénice.*" *Romance Notes* 15 (1973): 104-9.
Spencer, Catherine. *La Tragédie du prince: étude du personnage médiateur dans le théâtre tragique de Racine.* Tübingen: Papers on French Seventeenth-Century Literature, 1987.
Spillebout, Gabriel. *Le Vocabulaire biblique dans les tragédies sacrées de Racine.* Geneva: Droz, 1968.
Spitzer, Leo. *Essays on Seventeenth-Century French Literature.* Trans. David Bellos. Cambridge: Cambridge UP, 1983.
Spoerri, Théophile. "Le rythme tragique." *Trivium* 3 (1945): 161-84.
Starobinski, Jean. "Racine et la poétique du regard." *Nouvelle Nouvelle Revue Française* 5 (1957): 246-63.
Starre, Evert van. *Racine et le théâtre de l'ambiguïté: Étude sur Bajazet.* Leiden: Université Pers Leiden, 1966.
Steiner, George. *The Death of Tragedy.* London: Faber, 1961.

Stewart, William. "Le Tragique et le sacré chez Racine." Jacquot 271-85.
———. "Mise en scène d'*Athalie*." Jacquot and Veinstein 241-53.
Stone, H. *Royal DisClosure. Problematics of Representation in French Classical Tragedy*. Birmingham: Summa, 1987.
———. "*Bérénice*: les voiles du pouvoir." Duchêne and Ronzeaud 225-33.
———. "Racine for the next Millennium." *Esprit Créateur* 38.2 (1998): 5-10.
———. "Marking Time: Memorializing History in *Athalie*." *Esprit Créateur* 38.2 (1998): 95-104.
Stone, John. *Sophocles and Racine*. Geneva: Droz, 1964.
Strachey, Lytton. *Landmarks in French Literature*. London: Williams and Norgate, 1912.
Supple, James. *Racine's* Bérénice. London: Grant and Cutler, 1986.
———. "The role of Antiochus in *Bérénice*." *Seventeenth-Century French Studies* 11 (1989): 151-62.
———. "Pommier versus Barthes: Critique et Contrevérités." *Seventeenth-Century French Studies* 13 (1991): 153-61.
Surber, Christian. *Parole, personage et référence dans le théâtre de Jean Racine*. Geneva: Droz, 1992.
Sussman, Ruth. "*Bérénice* and the Tragic Moment." *Esprit Créateur* 15 (1975): 241-51.
Sweetser, Marie-Odile. "Racine rival de Corneille; 'innutrition' et innovations dans *Britannicus*." *Romanic Review* 66 (1975): 13-31.
———. "Néron et Titus vus par Racine." *French Literature Series* 8 (1981): 21-30.
———. "Les femmes dans la vie et l'œuvre de Racine." *Œuvres et Critiques* 24.1 (1999): 193-215.
Tanquerey, F. J. "Le Jansénisme et les tragédies de Racine." *Revue des Cours et Conférences* 37 (1935-36): 457-68.
Tans, J. A. G. "Un thème-clef racinien: la rencontre nocturne." *RHLF* 65 (1965): 577-89.
Taveneaux, René. "Port-Royal, ou l'héroïsme de la sainteté." Hepp and Livet 99-109.
Thirouin, Laurent. *L'Aveuglement salutaire: réquisitoire contre le théâtre dans la France classique*. Paris: Champion, 1997.
———. "Les dévots contre le théâtre, ou de quelques simplifications fâcheuses." *Littératures classiques* 39 (2000): 105-21.
Tillyard, E. M. W. *Shakespeare's Problem Plays*. London, Chatto and Windus, 1950.
Tobin, Ronald. "Myth criticism and the Seventeenth Century." *Esprit Créateur* 16 (1976): 91-94
———. "Le sentiment d'incomplétude chez les personnages de Racine." *CAIEF* 31 (1979): 119-33.
———. "Néron et Junie: Fantasme et Tragédie." *Papers on French Seventeenth-Century Literature* 10 (1983): 681-99.
———. "Molière, Racine, or the Red and the Black." C. Williams 11-32.
———. *Jean Racine Revisited*. Twayne: New York, 1999.
———, ed. *Racine et/ou le classicisme*. Tübingen: Narr, 2001.
———. "Andromaque's choice." *Orbis Litterarum* 58 (2003): 317-34.
Tomlinson, Philip, ed. *French "Classical" Theatre Today. Teaching, Research, Performance*. Amsterdam: Rodopi, 2001.
Truchet, Jacques. *La tragédie classique en France*. Paris: PUF, 1975.
———. "Remarques sur le lieu et le temps dans *Athalie*." *Information littéraire* 37.5 (1985): 195-97.
Tynan, Kenneth. *Tynan on Theatre*. Penguin: Harmondsworth, 1964.

Ubersfeld, Anne. Andromaque *de Jean Racine*. Paris: Éditions sociales, 1961.
———. "Racine auteur tragique." *Europe* 453 (1967): 46-65.
———. *Lire le théâtre*. Paris: Éditions sociales, 1978.
Unamuno, Miguel de. "The Man of Flesh and Bone." Michel and Sewall 1-5.
Urbain, Charles, and Eugène Levesque, ed. *L'Eglise et le théâtre: Bossuet, Maximes et réflexions sur la comédie*. Paris: Grasset, 1930.
Valéry, Paul. *Œuvres*. Éditions de la Pléiade. Vol. 1. Paris: Gallimard, 1957.
Van Baelen, Jacqueline, and David L. Rubin. *La Cohérence intérieure: Études sur la littérature française du dix-septième siècle présentées en hommage à Judd D. Hubert*. Paris: J.-M. Place, 1977.
Venesoen, Constant, ed. *Racine. Mythes et réalité*. Paris: Librairie d'Argens, 1976.
———. "*Athalie* ou le demi-échec de la théologie tragique." Venesoen, *Racine* 25-48.
———. *Le Complexe maternel dans le théâtre de Racine*. Paris: Minard, 1987.
Viala, Alain. *Lectures intégrales. Théâtre*. Paris: Poche, 1986.
———. *Racine. La Stratégie du caméléon*. Paris: Seghers, 1990.
———. "Racine galant, ou l'amour au pied de la lettre." *Les Cahiers* 17 (1995): 39-48.
———. "Périls, conseil et secret d'État dans les tragédies romaines de Racine: Racine et Machiavel." *Littératures classiques* 26 (1996): 91-113.
———. "Tendances actuelles de la représentation de Racine." *Seventeenth-Century French Studies* 22 (2000): 21-33.
Vilar, Jean. "Petites nouvelles." *Théâtre populaire* 20 (1956): 17-30.
Vinaver, Eugène. *Racine et la poésie tragique*. Paris: Nizet, 1951.
———. *Entretiens sur Racine*. Paris: Nizet, 1984.
Vincent, Rose. *L'Enfant de Port-Royal: le roman de Jean Racine*. Paris: Seuil, 1991. 162.
Voltz, Pierre. "*Bérénice, Bajazet, Athalie*: Réflexions dramatiques à partir de la notion d'espace dans la tragédie racinienne." Ronzeaud, *La Romaine* 51-75.
Vossler, Karl. *Jean Racine*. New York: Ungar, 1972.
Vuillemin, Jean-Claude. "Troie/Buthrote; problématique de l'origine dans *Andromaque*." *Australian Journal of French Studies* 27 (1990): 3-16.
Vuillermoz, Marc, ed. *Dictionnaire analytique des œuvres théâtrales françaises du XVIIᵉ siècle*. Paris: Champion, 1998.
Webster, T. B. L. *Greek Art and Literature*. Oxford: Clarendon, 1939.
Weinberg, Bernard. *The Art of Jean Racine*. Chicago: Chicago UP, 1967.
Williams, Charles, ed. *Actes de Columbus*. Paris: Papers on French Seventeenth-Century Literature, 1990.
Williams, Edwin. "*Athalie*: The Tragic Cycle and the Tragedy of Joas." *Romanic Review* 28 (1937): 36-45.
Worth-Stylianou, Valérie. *Confidential Strategies. The Evolving Role of the Confident in French Tragic Drama (1635-77)*. Geneva: Droz, 1999.
Woshinsky, Barbara. "Iphigénie Transcendent." Williams 87-95.
———. *Signs of Certainty. The Linguistic Imperative in French Classical Literature*. Saratoga: Anma Libri, 1991.
Wygant, Amy. *Towards a Cultural Philogy:* Phèdre *et Racine*. Oxford: Legenda, 1999.
Yandell, Cathy. *Carpe Corpus: Time and Gender in Early Modern France*. Newark: University of Delaware Press, 2000.
Yarrow, Philip. *Racine*. Oxford: Blackwell, 1978.
Yashinsky, Jack. "'Pourquoi ce livre saint, ce glaive, ce bandeau?' Commentaires textuels sur *Athalie*." *Lettres Romanes* 38 (1984): 65-75.
Yon, Bernard. "Racine lecteur de l'*Astrée*." *Œuvres et Critiques*, 12 (1987): 77-83.

Yourcenar, Marguerite. *Essais et mémoires*. Bibliothèque de la Pléiade. Paris: Gallimard, 1991.
Zebouni, Selma, ed. *Actes de Baton Rouge*. Tübingen: Romanisches Seminar, 1986.
Zimmermann, Eléonore. *La Liberté et le destin dans le théâtre de Jean Racine*. Saratoga: Anma Libri, 1982.
Zoberman, Pierre. "Représentation de l'homme, représentation du roi." Declercq and Rosellini 211-29.
Zuber, Roger, and Marc Fumaroli, eds. *Dictionnaire de littérature française du XVII$^e$ siècle*. Paris: PUF, 2001.
Zysberg, André. "*Athalie*: Odéon/Planchon. Une pièce sur le Goulag." *Nouvelles Littéraires* 7 Nov. 1980: 42.

THE FOLLOWING WORKS OF REFERENCE ARE ALSO REFERRED TO:

*Le Petit Larousse 2001*.
*Le Petit Robert des noms propres*. Paris: Dictionnaires Le Robert, 2000.

# NORTH CAROLINA STUDIES IN THE ROMANCE LANGUAGES AND LITERATURES

I.S.B.N. Prefix 0-8078-

## Recent Titles

'PUEBLOS ENFERMOS': THE DISCOURSE OF ILLNESS IN THE TURN-OF-THE-CENTURY SPANISH AND LATIN AMERICAN ESSAY, by Michael Aronna. 1999. (No. 262). -9266-1.
RESONANT THEMES. LITERATURE, HISTORY, AND THE ARTS IN NINETEENTH- AND TWENTIETH-CENTURY EUROPE. ESSAYS IN HONOR OF VICTOR BROMBERT, by Stirling Haig. 1999. (No. 263). -9267-X.
RAZA, GÉNERO E HIBRIDEZ EN EL LAZARILLO DE CIEGOS CAMINANTES, por Mariselle Meléndez. 1999. (No. 264). -9268-8.
DEL ESCENARIO A LA PANTALLA: LA ADAPTACIÓN CINEMATOGRÁFICA DEL TEATRO ESPAÑOL, por María Asunción Gómez. 2000. (No. 265). -9269-6.
THE LEPER IN BLUE: COERCIVE PERFORMANCE AND THE CONTEMPORARY LATIN AMERICAN THEATER, by Amalia Gladhart. 2000. (No. 266). -9270-X.
THE CHARM OF CATASTROPHE: A STUDY OF RABELAIS'S QUART LIVRE, by Alice Fiola Berry. 2000. (No. 267). -9271-8.
PUERTO RICAN CULTURAL IDENTITY AND THE WORK OF LUIS RAFAEL SÁNCHEZ, by John Dimitri Perivolaris. 2000. (No. 268). -9272-6.
MANNERISM AND BAROQUE IN SEVENTEENTH-CENTURY FRENCH POETRY: THE EXAMPLE OF TRISTAN L'HERMITE, by James Crenshaw Shepard. 2001. (No. 269). -9273-4.
RECLAIMING THE BODY: MARÍA DE ZAYA'S EARLY MODERN FEMINISM, by Lisa Vollendorf. 2001. (No. 270). -9274-2.
FORGED GENEALOGIES: SAINT-JOHN PERSE'S CONVERSATIONS WITH CULTURE, by Carol Rigolot. 2001. (No. 271). -9275-0.
VISIONES DE ESTEREOSCOPIO (PARADIGMA DE HIBRIDACIÓN EN EL ARTE Y LA NARRATIVA DE LA VANGUARDIA ESPAÑOLA), por María Soledad Fernández Utrera. 2001. (No. 272). -9276-9.
TRANSPOSING ART INTO TEXTS IN FRENCH ROMANTIC LITERATURE, by Henry F. Majewski. 2002. (No. 273). -9277-7.
IMAGES IN MIND: LOVESICKNESS, SPANISH SENTIMENTAL FICTION AND DON QUIJOTE, by Robert Folger. 2002. (No. 274). -9278-5.
INDISCERNIBLE COUNTERPARTS: THE INVENTION OF THE TEXT IN FRENCH CLASSICAL DRAMA, by Christopher Braider. 2002. (No. 275). -9279-3.
SAVAGE SIGHT/CONSTRUCTED NOISE. POETIC ADAPTATIONS OF PAINTERLY TECHNIQUES IN THE FRENCH AND AMERICAN AVANT-GARDES, by David LeHardy Sweet. 2003. (No. 276). -9281-5.
AN EARLY BOURGEOIS LITERATURE IN GOLDEN AGE SPAIN. LAZARILLO DE TORMES, GUZMÁN DE ALFARACHE AND BALTASAR GRACIÁN, by Francisco J. Sánchez. 2003. (No. 277). -9280-7.
METAFACT: ESSAYISTIC SCIENCE IN EIGHTEENTH-CENTURY FRANCE, by Lars O. Erickson. 2004. (No. 278). -9282-3
THE INVENTION OF THE EYEWITNESS. A HISTORY OF TESTIMONY IN FRANCE, by Andrea Frisch. 2004. (No. 279). -9283-1.
SUBJECT TO CHANGE: THE LESSONS OF LATIN AMERICAN WOMEN'S TESTIMONIO FOR TRUTH, FICTION, AND THEORY, by Joanna R. Bartow. 2005. (No. 280). -9284-X
QUESTIONING RACINIAN TRAGEDY, by John Campbell. 2005. (No. 281). -9285-8

---

When ordering please cite the ISBN Prefix plus the last four digits for each title.

Send orders to:   University of North Carolina Press
P.O. Box 2288
Chapel Hill, NC 27515-2288
U.S.A.
www.uncpress.unc.edu
FAX: 919 966-3829

www.ingramcontent.com/pod-product-compliance
Lightning Source LLC
Chambersburg PA
CBHW020643230426
43665CB00008B/294